Elizabeth G. Martin, Constant

Memoirs of Constant

First valet de chambre of the emperor, on the private life of Napoleon, his family and his court - Vol. 1

Elizabeth G. Martin, Constant

Memoirs of Constant
First valet de chambre of the emperor, on the private life of Napoleon, his family and his court - Vol. 1

ISBN/EAN: 9783337351236

Printed in Europe, USA, Canada, Australia, Japan

Cover: Foto ©ninafisch / pixelio.de

More available books at **www.hansebooks.com**

MEMOIRS OF CONSTANT

FIRST VALET DE CHAMBRE OF THE EMPEROR

ON THE

PRIVATE LIFE OF NAPOLEON

HIS FAMILY AND HIS COURT

TRANSLATED BY

ELIZABETH GILBERT MARTIN

WITH A PREFACE TO THE ENGLISH EDITION

BY

IMBERT DE SAINT-AMAND

Vol. I

NEW YORK
CHARLES SCRIBNER'S SONS
1895

COPYRIGHT, 1895, BY
CHARLES SCRIBNER'S SONS

Norwood Press
J. S. Cushing & Co. — Berwick & Smith
Norwood Mass. U.S.A.

PREFACE TO THE ENGLISH EDITION

By Imbert de Saint-Amand

HISTORY is, of all branches of literature, that which has made the most progress. Like science it now rests upon both analysis and synthesis and disdains details no more than generalities. The time is past when historians studied neither the character of their personages nor what one might call the stage decorations amid which the events treated of took place. Psychology and local color have regained their rights. History was formerly a simple monochrome; it is now a splendid fresco. One of the causes of this happy change is the extreme importance that memoirs have come to have. Their authors are just so many ocular and auricular witnesses who defile in turn before their contemporaries or before posterity, and whose depositions, reciprocally rectified, furnish public opinion with the means of rendering its judgments upon men and things. Thanks to memoirs, the remark of Michelet is realized: "History is the resurrection of the dead." It is memoirs that have prompted it to use at the same time the telescope and the magnifying-glass. The passion for detail has nothing puerile about it. The infinitely little play a great rôle in nature and in history, as Pasteur and Taine have demonstrated.

In proportion as the popularity of the novel diminishes, that of memoirs increases. We begin to realize that there are no inventions so impressive as reality. Could a novelist, however great his genius, ever find as extraordinary, as pathetic, and as attractive material as the destinies of Marie-Antoinette and Napoleon? What character imagined by Alexandre Dumas or by Balzac can be compared with the Martyr Queen or with the modern Charlemagne? We witness at this moment in the New World as in the Old the triumph of what might be called Napoleonic literature. Chateaubriand has said in his *Mémoires d'Outre Tombe*: "The world belongs to Bonaparte — that which the spoiler could not finish conquering, his fame usurps. Living, he failed of the world; dead, he possesses it." One may add that in no legend is there more poetry than there is in his history. When the Shah of Persia came to Paris under the presidency of Marshal MacMahon, the first visit of the Asiatic sovereign was to the tomb of the Emperor at the Invalides, and before descending into the crypt he respectfully took off his sword as if he dared not appear armed before the shade of the great man. What country of the universe is there in which the echo of this magic name Napoleon has not vibrated. The giant of battles, the victor of Austerlitz, the vanquished of Waterloo, the captive of Saint-Helena is the principal personage of the epoch, which is itself but a series of phenomenal wonders. No century has produced a man so extraordinary, so great an artist in prestige and glory.

M. George Duruy, son of the celebrated historian, has recently written in the introduction to the *Memoirs of Barras* which he has just published: "The Emperor continues tranquilly to dominate the century, on the threshold of which his colossal figure stands. Such is the statue of Memnon at the entrance of the Egyptian desert. Sacrilegious hands have tried to disfigure the calm visage of granite which the centuries had respected, but so long as men shall exist they will pause pensive at the foot of the giant image and measure their littleness by its grandeur. Thus will posterity stand before the sphinx with enigmatic and sovereign countenance — Napoleon." The events in which the man of destiny took part present themselves to our mind in proportions as epic and as grandiose as if they dated back to the most distant ages, and the heroes of the Empire have already become lyric personages like the legionaries of Cæsar or the Knights of Charlemagne. Since the striking success of the *Memoirs of General Marbot* which, amusing as a novel, are sublime as an epic poem, the popularity of all publications relating to the imperial epoch is continually increasing. Unpublished memoirs like those of General Thiébault, of Marshal Castellane, of Planal de la Faye, are printed. Old memoirs are republished, such as those of General de Ségur, of Bourrienne, of

Baron de Méneval, and of Constant, the valet de chambre of Napoleon I.; and the resurrection of these works which seemed forgotten produces perhaps a greater effect than did their first appearance.

The Memoirs of Constant, the reprint of which has just been very favorably received in France, merit, we believe, the honor of being translated and published in the United States. No man had a nearer view of Napoleon I.; and no one has given more exact details regarding the great man's character. M. Frédéric Masson, in his interesting books, entitled, one, *Napoléon et les Femmes*, and the other, *Napoléon chez lui: La Journée de l'Empereur aux Tuileries*, and M. Lévy in his work, *Napoléon intime*, have borrowed largely from the Memoirs of Constant, and the modest but authentic account of the Emperor's valet de chambre will never be disdained by any historian.

Constant was born December 22, 1778, at Péruelz, a city which became French upon the reunion of Belgium with France and which was then included in the department of Jemmapes. His father, who had been the Prince de Croï's maître d'hôtel, kept at the baths of Saint-Amand, an establishment where persons lodged who came for the waters. The future valet de chambre of Napoleon was brought up by the liberality of the Count de Lure, head of one of the oldest families of Valenciennes, who had him given a good education on an estate situated near Tours. Toward the end of 1799 Constant entered the service of

Eugène de Beauharnais. A month after he was attached to the household of the wife of General Bonaparte, and one day at the end of March, 1800, the First Consul glanced at him during the dinner and, after having examined and scrutinized him from head to foot, said to him: "Young man, should you like to follow me on the campaign?" Constant replied with much emotion that he would like nothing better. From the departure of Napoleon for the campaign of Marengo, whither he followed him, to the departure from Fontainebleau, where he was obliged to leave him, that is, during fourteen consecutive years, he was only absent from him on two occasions, one of three and the other of seven or eight days. Outside of these extremely brief furloughs, the latter of them rendered necessary by his health, he was as inseparable from the Emperor as his shadow.

Constant was perfectly right in saying: "Nothing that relates to great men is to be disdained. Posterity is eager to know the smallest circumstance connected with their kind of life, their characteristic traits, their tastes, their most trivial habits. I remember," he adds, "that I never had so much pleasure at the theatre as the day I saw for the first time the charming play, the *Deux Pages*. Fleury, who played the part of Frederick the Great, rendered the slow walk, the abrupt speech, the brusque movements, and even the near-sightedness of the monarch so perfectly, that from the moment of his entrance the whole house broke out into applause. . . . I feel some pride, I confess, at the thought that these Memoirs may succeed in giving something of the pleasure I have endeavored to depict here, and that in a future, no doubt still distant but nevertheless certain to come about, the artist, who wishes to make the greatest man of this time live and move again before the public, will be compelled, if he desires to be a faithful imitator, to form himself upon the portrait which better than any one I am able to sketch from nature."

The resemblance of the portrait of the Emperor by Constant is, we believe, perfect. The valet de chambre dissembles neither the weaknesses nor the defects of his master, but he admires sincerely the genius of the sovereign and the winning qualities of the man. "It has been maintained," says he, "that no man is a hero to his valet. I beg to be allowed to be of a different opinion. However near at hand one was accustomed to see the Emperor, he was always a hero, and there was also much to be gained by seeing in him *the man*, intimately and minutely. At a distance one could feel only the prestige of his fame and power; approaching nearer one enjoyed still further, with surprise, all the charm of his conversation, all the simplicity of his family life, and, I do not hesitate to add, the habitual benevolence of his character."

The Memoirs of Constant contradict these lines addressed to Napoleon by Lamartine:

> Tu grandis sans plaisir, tu tombas sans murmure,
> Rien d'humain ne battait sous ton épaisse armure,
> Sans haine et sans amour, tu vivais pour passer
> Comme l'aigle régnant dans un ciel solitaire,
> Tu n'avais qu'un regard pour mesurer la terre
> Et des serres pour l'embrasser.[1]

Napoleon was not the impassive man, with heart of bronze, that the poet of the *Méditations* represents. "I can only speak," says Constant, "of the hero *en déshabillé*, and at that time he was always kind and patient, rarely unjust. He took a real interest in you and received with pleasure and good nature the attentions of those he liked. The hardness of the Emperor and his brutality towards women are part of the thousand and one calumnies of which he has been the object. He was not always *galant*, but he was never coarse; he professed the greatest veneration for a woman of exemplary conduct, made much of self-respecting family circles, and disliked cynicism whether in behavior or in language." Let us add that the testimony of Bourrienne and of the Baron de Méneval, who were both secretaries of the great man, agrees thoroughly with that of Constant. Bourrienne says: "Bonaparte was susceptible, kind, accessible to pity; he loved children greatly, and it is rare that a bad man has an

---

[1] You grew great without pleasure, you fell without a murmur — Nothing human beat under your thick armor — Without love and without hate, you lived only to pass — Like the eagle reigning alone in the heavens — You had only a look to measure the earth with — And talons with which to seize it.

inclination for children; in the daily routine of private life he was full of good nature and indulgence for human weakness." The Baron de Méneval thus expressed himself: "In the midst of his family Napoleon appeared truly a father. There was an inexpressible charm about this abnegation of his grandeur. I could not get over my surprise at seeing this simplicity of conduct in a man who, from a distance, seemed so imposing. I expected rudenesses and unevenness of temper. Instead I found Napoleon patient, easy to live with, in nowise exacting, of a gaiety that was not seldom boisterous and jesting, and sometimes of a winning good humor."

We may consider this passage of Constant's Memoirs as their summing up: "I must make the avowal that only after having left the Emperor's service did I comprehend all the immensity of his greatness. Attached to his service almost from the beginning of the Consulate, at a period when I was still very young, he had grown great, so to say, without my perceiving it, and I had especially seen in him, on account of the nature of my service, an excellent master even more than a great man. But what a contrary effect from that which it produces ordinarily did separation have upon me! Even to-day I often wonder at the bold frankness with which I have dared to sustain before the Emperor things I thought true; but his kindness seemed to encourage me to do so, for very often, instead of being vexed at my vivacities, he used to say to me gently, with a benevolent smile, 'Come, come, Monsieur Constant, do not get angry.' Adorable kindness in a man of so lofty a rank! Well, I hardly perceived this, in the interior of his chamber; but since then I have felt all its worth."

Napoleon gains in being studied from the standpoint of intimacy. The mask falls, the man remains, and the hero does not vanish.

The vogue of Constant's Memoirs when they first appeared in 1830 was very great. At that epoch the imperial epic exercised over the French nation such an ascendency that if the Duke de Reichstadt had been restored to liberty by Austria, everything indicates that *the Son of the Man*, as the heir of the victor of Austerlitz was then called, would have been proclaimed emperor. To-day the re-establishment of the Empire is no longer in question in France, but the prestige of Napoleon has never been more striking there. At Paris the Military Exposition of the Avenue des Champs-Elysées has been an enthusiastic success. Like religion, glory has its relics. During the months of May and June, 1895, an enormous crowd visited with pious eagerness the historical museum where so many objects that belonged to the Emperor and his companions in arms were displayed. The organizers of this exhibition belonged to all parties. One of them, a young officer and a son of M. Carnot, said: "I would that the entire army might pass through these halls and steep themselves here in heroism."

The present moment was well chosen for bringing out anew memoirs such as those of Constant, not only in France but in the United States. It may be said that the two names best known in the great American republic are those of Washington and Napoleon. Is there in the United States a garret or a hovel into which these two names have not penetrated? New York, the Paris of the New World, has begun a movement of Napoleonic literature which is spreading in all the cities of the Union, and it will not be long before the imperial epic will be as well known by Americans as by the French themselves.

In the domain of thought a species of electric current has been established between the United States and France. The force that unites the two great sister republics is not only a community of institutions, it is the possession of the same taste for the arts, for letters and history. The finest pictures of the modern French school belong to Americans. The artists most in vogue in France repair to the United States to seek a fresh affirmation of their success. We may say that in all departments French reputations renew their youth, as it were, in the country of Washington. One of the causes of this sympathy is the remembrance, more active than ever, of the American War of Independence, in which the French had a noble share. The citizens of the Union desire to understand all French annals from that epoch to our own time. The military accounts of the Revolution and the Empire interest them all the more in that they also have had their battles, and that they only have to stamp on the ground to cause immense and magnificent armies to issue from it. The combatants of the War of Secession, Northern and Southern alike, showed no less heroism than the French volunteers of 1792. And after the struggle the reconciliation of victors and vanquished was based on a sentiment of mutual esteem and military confraternity. The resonant echo of the imperial epoch in the United States is wholly natural. A genius like Napoleon was certain to be admired by a nation which, after having triumphed in the contests of commerce and industry, has proved that when the occasion arose, it could be a great warlike nation as well.

IMBERT DE SAINT-AMAND.

MEMOIRS OF CONSTANT

INTRODUCTION

THE life of a man obliged to make his own way, and who is neither a mechanic nor a tradesman, does not ordinarily begin until about his twentieth year. Until then he vegetates, uncertain of his future, and neither having nor being able to have any definite end in view. It is only when his powers have attained their full development, and his character and propensities at the same time incline him toward such or such a part, that he can decide upon the choice of a career and a profession; it is only then that he understands himself and sees his surroundings clearly; in fine, it is at this age only that he begins to *live*.

Reasoning in this fashion, my own life, since I attained my twentieth year, has comprised thirty years, which may be divided into two equal parts as to months and days, but which could not differ more widely if one considers the events which passed during these two periods of my existence.

Attached during fifteen years to the person of the Emperor Napoleon, I have seen all the men and all the important things of which he alone was the rallying-point and centre. I have seen still more than that; for I have had under my eyes, in every circumstance of life, the least as well as the most serious, the most private as well as those which belong the most to history and already form part of it; I have had, I say, incessantly in view, the man whose single name fills the most glorious pages in our annals. Fifteen years I have attended him in his journeys and his campaigns, at his court and in the privacy of his family. Whatever step he might decide on, whatever order he might give, it was difficult for the Emperor not to take me, even involuntarily, into his confidence; and it was without my own will that I more than once found myself in possession of secrets which I would frequently have preferred not to know. How many things occurred during those fifteen years! In the Emperor's vicinity you lived in the midst of a whirlwind. It was a succession of swift, bewildering events. You were dazzled, and if you tried to fix your attention for an instant, another flood of incidents came with a rush which carried you off your feet without giving you leisure to consider them.

At present, these times of dizzying activity have been succeeded, for me, by the most absolute repose, in the most isolated of retreats. And again it is an interval of fifteen years which has elapsed since I quitted the Emperor. But what a difference! What is there left to do, nowadays, for those who, like me, ive lived amidst the conquests and marvels of the mpire? If, in the vigor of manhood, our life has ьeen blended with the movement of those years, so short but so thoroughly occupied, it seems to me that our career has been long enough and sufficiently well filled. It is time for us to betake ourselves to repose. We may well withdraw from the world and close our eyes. What is there left for us to see which can compare with what we have already seen? Such spectacles do not occur twice in a man's lifetime. After having passed before his eyes, they suffice to replenish his memory during the rest of the time he has to live; and in his retirement he has nothing better to do than to occupy his leisure with the memory of what he has beheld.

And it is this which I have done. The reader will easily believe that I have no more customary pastime than to recur in fancy to the years I spent in the Emperor's service. As far as possible, I have kept myself acquainted with all that has been written about my former master, his family and his court. What long evenings have slipped by like moments while my wife and my sister-in-law have been reading these aloud to the family! Whenever I encountered in these books, some of which are really nothing but miserable rhapsodies, statements that were inexact, calumnious, or false, I took pleasure in rectifying them, or rather in proving their absurdity. My wife, who lived like me and with me in the midst of these events, also acquainted us with her reflections and explanations; and, with no other object but our own satisfaction, she noted down our common observations.

All who came from time to time to see us in our solitude, and who took pleasure in making me talk of what I had seen, astonished and too often indignant at the falsehoods which ignorance or bad faith have vied with each other in retailing about the Emperor and the Empire, evinced to me their satisfaction with the information I was enabled to give them, and advised me to communicate it to the public. But I had never dwelt upon this thought and was very far from imagining that I might some day be the author of a book myself, when M. Ladvocat arrived at our hermitage, and urged me with all his might to publish my Memoirs, which he proposed to bring out himself.

At the time when I received this visit, which I was not expecting, we were reading in the family the Memoirs of M. de Bourrienne, which had just been published by the firm of Ladvocat, and we had more than once remarked that these Memoirs were exempt from that spirit of depreciation or infatuation we had met with so frequently, and not without disgust, in other books treating of the same subject. M. Ladvocat advised me to complete the biography of the Emperor, which M. de Bourrienne, on account of his high position and customary occupations, had been intent on displaying merely on its political side. After the excellent things he had said of this, it still remained to me, according to his publisher, to relate simply and in a manner suitable to my former position near the Emperor, that which M. de Bourrienne had necessarily been obliged to neglect, and which no one could know better than I.

I willingly confess that I found but little to urge against M. Ladvocat's arguments, and that he ended by convincing me when he made me re-read this passage from the introduction to M. de Bourrienne's Memoirs:

"If all the persons who approached Napoleon, no matter at what time or place, will *frankly* record all they saw and heard, without any sort of prepossession, the future historian will have an abundance of materials. I desire that he who shall undertake this difficult task may find in my notes some hints that may be useful to the perfection of his work."

And I, too, said I to myself after having re-read these lines attentively, I can furnish notes and explanations, point out errors, stigmatize falsehoods, and make public what I know to be the truth; in a word, I can and I *ought* to bear my testimony in the long trial which has been going on since the Emperor's downfall; for I was *a witness*, I saw everything, and I can say: *I was there*. Others also have seen the Emperor and his court at close quarters, and it must often happen to me to repeat what they have said on the subject; because, what they know, I also was in a position to know. But what I, in my turn, know of details, and what I can relate of secret and unknown matters, no one else has been able to know, nor consequently to say before me.[1]

From the departure of the First Consul for the campaign of Marengo, whither I attended him, until the departure from Fontainebleau, where I was obliged to leave the Emperor, I was absent from him only twice; the first time for three times twenty-four hours; the second for seven or eight days. Aside from these brief holidays, the last of which was necessary in order to restore my health, I quitted the Emperor no more than his shadow did.

It has been claimed that *no man is a hero to his valet de chambre.* I ask permission to hold a different opinion. The Emperor, no matter how close at hand he might be seen, was always *a hero*, and there was much to be gained by seeing the *man* in him also, near by and in detail. From a distance one experienced merely the prestige of his glory and his power; on approaching him, one enjoyed in addition,

---

[1] In support of what I have here advanced, I am happy to be able to cite the opinion expressed by M. de Bourrienne, apropos of a sad occurrence which I will relate in its own place: "We are assured that it was in the night preceding Marshal Macdonald's return to Fontainebleau that Napoleon attempted to poison himself; but as I have no certain details concerning this attempt, and as I will not speak of what I am not very sure, I abstain from giving, as certain persons have done, any conjectures, always hazardous, on a grave matter which was strongly repudiated by Napoleon in his conversations at Saint-Helena. The only person who could solve the doubts that exist on the subject is Constant, who, I am assured, never left Napoleon during that night." *Memoirs de M. de Bourrienne*, p. 161 t. x.

and with surprise, all the charm of his conversation, all the simplicity of his family life, and, I am not afraid to say, the habitual benevolence of his character.

The reader, curious to know in advance the spirit in which my Memoirs will be written, will perhaps like to find here an extract from a letter I wrote to my publisher on the 19th of January last:

"M. de Bourrienne is perhaps justified in treating the political man with severity; but that is not my own point of view. I can only speak of the hero *en déshabillé;* and then he was nearly always kind, patient, and seldom unjust. He became much attached, and received the attentions of those whom he liked with pleasure and good nature. He was a man of routine. I desire to speak of the Emperor as an attached servant, and in nowise as a censor. On the other hand, I do not wish to make an apotheosis in several volumes. With regard to him I am somewhat like those fathers who recognize defects in their children, blame them severely, but at the same time very readily find excuses for their faults."

I beg pardon for the familiarity, or, if you like, the impropriety of this comparison, on behalf of the sentiment which inspired it. For the rest, I propose neither to praise nor to blame, but simply to relate what is within my own cognizance, without seeking to bias the judgment of any one.

I cannot finish this introduction without saying a few words about myself, in reply to the calumnies which have pursued even into his retirement a man who ought not to have enemies, if, in order to avert this misfortune, it were enough to have done a little good, and never any evil. I have been reproached with having abandoned my master after his downfall, with not having shared his exile. I will prove that if I did not follow the Emperor, it was not the will to do so which failed me, but rather the possibility. God forbid that I should here depreciate the loyalty of the faithful servants who remained attached to the last to the Emperor's fortunes; but perhaps I may be permitted to say that, however terrible was the downfall for the Emperor himself, the *situation* (to speak here of purely personal considerations only) was still honorable enough for those who remained in His Majesty's service, and who were not detained in France by an imperious necessity. Hence it was not personal interest which led me to separate myself from the Emperor. I will explain the motives of this separation.

The truth will also be made known concerning a pretended abuse of confidence of which, according to other rumors, I was guilty with regard to the Emperor. The simple recital of the misapprehension which gave rise to this fable will suffice, I hope, to clear me from all suspicion of indelicacy. But if additional testimonies are needed, I will invoke those of the personages who lived in the greatest intimacy with the Emperor, and who were likewise in a position to know and appreciate what passed between him and me; finally, I will appeal to fifty years of an irreproachable life, and say:

"In times when I found myself so situated that I could render great services, I rendered many, but I never sold them. I might have derived advantage from the measures I took for persons who, as a result of my solicitations, have acquired an immense fortune; and I have refused even the legitimate profit which, in their gratitude, very lively at that epoch, they thought they ought to offer me by proposing that I should have an interest in their enterprise. I never tried to take advantage of the benevolence with which the Emperor so long deigned to honor me, in order to enrich or secure places for my relatives, and I retired poor, after fifteen years spent in the special service of the richest and most powerful sovereign in Europe."

This said, I will await with confidence the judgment of the reader.

CHAPTER I

Birth of the author — His father, his relatives — His first protectors — Emigration and abandonment — A suspicious character twelve years old — Municipal officers or *imbéciles* — Major Michau — M. Gobert — Carrat — Madame Bonaparte and her daughter — Bouquets and the sentimental scene — Carrat's frugality to others and his generosity to himself — Poltroonery — Frolics of Madame Bonaparte and Hortense — The phantom — The nocturnal douche — The fall — The author enters the service of M. Eugène de Beauharnais.

I SHALL say very little about myself in my Memoirs; for I do not blink the fact that nothing in them can interest the public but details concerning the great man to whose service my destiny attached me during sixteen years, and whom I hardly ever quitted throughout that period. Still, I shall ask permission to say a few words about my childhood, and the circumstances which led me to the post of valet de chambre to the Emperor.

I was born December 2, 1778, at Péruelz, a town which became French at the time of the reunion of Belgium to the Republic, and which then found itself comprised in the department of Jemmapes. Shortly after my birth, my father took a little establishment called the Petit-Château, at the baths of Saint-Amand, where persons lodged who came to take the waters. He was assisted in this enterprise by Prince de Croï, in whose house he had been steward. Our affairs prospered beyond my father's expectations, for we received a great number of illustrious invalids. When I had just reached my eleventh year, Count de Lure, head of one of the first families of Valenciennes, was one of the residents of the Petit-Château; and as this excellent man had taken a great liking to me, he asked my parents to allow him to bring me up with his sons, who were near my own age. At this time it was the intention of my family to educate me for holy orders, in order to please one of my uncles, who was dean of Lessine. He was a man of great learning and austere virtue. Thinking that Count de Lure's proposition could make no change in his future projects, my father accepted it, believing that a few years spent in so distinguished a family would give me a taste for learning and prepare me for the more serious studies I would have to make in order to embrace the ecclesiastical career. I set off therefore with Count de Lure, extremely sorry to leave my parents, but at the same time very glad, as is usual at my then age, to see a new place. Count de Lure took me to one of his estates near Tours, where I was received with the most benevolent friendship by the Countess and her children and was treated on a footing of perfect equality with them, and given daily lessons by their tutor.

Alas! I unfortunately did not profit long enough

by the kindness of the Count de Lure and the lessons I received in his house. Hardly a year had elapsed since our installation at the château when we heard of the King's arrest at Varennes. The family in which I found myself experienced profound despair on account of it, and, child as I was, I remember that I keenly regretted this news, without being able to tell myself why, but doubtless because it is natural to share the sentiments of those with whom we live, when they treat us as kindly as the Count and Countess de Lure had treated me. Nevertheless I was still in the happy thoughtlessness of childhood when I was awakened one morning by a great noise. Presently I found myself surrounded by a considerable number of strangers, not one of whom was known to me, and who asked me a host of questions which it was quite impossible for me to answer. I learned then only that the Count and Countess de Lure had emigrated. I was taken to the municipality, where the questions began again in fine style, but as uselessly as ever, seeing that I could only respond by the abundant tears I shed at seeing myself abandoned in this fashion, and far away from my family. I was too young then to reflect on the Count's conduct; but I have thought since that my abandonment itself was an act of delicacy on his part, as he was unwilling to make me emigrate without my parents' consent. I have always had the conviction that before his departure, Count de Lure had recommended me to some persons who had not dared to claim me lest they should compromise themselves, which, as every one knows, was then extremely dangerous.

Here I was then, at the age of twelve, without guide, support, or shelter, without advice or money, more than a hundred leagues from my native place, and already accustomed to the amenities of life in a good family. Who would believe it? In this condition of things I was regarded as a suspicious character, and the authorities of the place required me to present myself monthly to the municipality for the greater security of the Republic. I remember perfectly, moreover, that whenever it pleased the Emperor to have me relate these tribulations of my childhood, he never failed to repeat several times: *The imbéciles!* in speaking of my worthy municipal officers. However, the authorities of Tours, concluding at last that a twelve-year-old child was incapable of overthrowing the Republic, gave me a passport with the express injunction to leave the city within twenty-four hours; which I did very willingly, yet not without a profound uneasiness at finding myself afoot and alone on the road and with a long journey to make. By dint of many privations and much trouble, I finally arrived in the vicinity of Saint-Amand, which I found in the hands of the Austrians. The French surrounded the town, but it was impossible for me to enter it. In despair, I sat down on the side of a ditch and was weeping bitterly there when I was noticed by Major

Michau,[1] who afterwards became colonel and aide-de-camp to General Loison. Major Michau came up and questioned me with much interest. He made me tell him all my sad adventures and seemed touched by them, but showed me how impossible it was for him to have me taken to my family. Having just received a furlough, which he was going to spend with his own family at Chinon, he proposed that I should accompany him thither, and I accepted wit' lively gratitude. I could never express the kindne and care shown me by the family of M. Micha during the three or four months I spent among them; at the end of that time, M. Michau took me to Paris with him, where I soon found a place in the house of one M. Gobert, a rich merchant, who treated me with the greatest kindness all the time that I remained there.

I saw M. Gobert recently, and he reminded me, that, when we travelled together, he was careful to leave one of the seats in his carriage at my disposal, on which I lay down to sleep. I mention this circumstance with pleasure, since, although otherwise of small consequence, it shows M. Gobert's kindness toward me.

Some years afterward, I made the acquaintance of Carrat, who was in Madame Bonaparte's service while the General was still on his Egyptian expedi-

---

[1] I was afterwards so happy as to obtain for him, from the Emperor, a place he desired on his retirement, after losing the use of his right arm.

tion. But before saying how I came to enter the establishment, I think it will be apropos to begin by relating how Carrat himself became one of Madame Bonaparte's dependents, and at the same time some anecdotes concerning him which are calculated to throw light on the earlier diversions of the residents of Malmaison.

Carrat was at Plombières when Madame Bonaparte went there to take the waters. He carried bouquets her every day, and paid her little compliments so odd and even droll, that Josephine was much diverted; so were the ladies who accompanied her, among whom were Mesdames de Cambis and de Crigny,[1] and especially her daughter Hortense, who was in fits of laughter at these pleasantries. The fact is that he was extremely amusing on account of a certain foolishness and a sort of originality which did not prevent his being witty. His drolleries having pleased Madame Bonaparte, he completed them by a sentimental scene at the time when that excellent woman was about leaving the watering-place. Carrat wept, expressed as well as he knew how the keen regret he would feel at not seeing Madame Bonaparte daily, as he had contracted a habit of doing, and Madame Bonaparte was so good-natured that she did not hesitate to carry him back with her to Paris. She had him taught the trade, and then attached him to her service in the capacity

---

[1] Madame de Crigny was afterwards Madame Denon.

of hair-dresser and lackey. Such, at least, were the functions he fulfilled when I made Carrat's acquaintance. He used an extraordinary freedom of speech with her, so much so that at times he even scolded her. When Madame Bonaparte, who was extremely generous and always good-natured to everybody, made presents to her women or chatted with them familiarly, Carrat reproached her on account of it: "Why do you give that?" he would say, and then add: "That is the way you are, Madame, you begin joking with your domestics! very well, some fine day they will fail to respect you." But if he tried to put obstacles in the way of his mistress's generosity when it extended to others, he was at no pains to restrain it where he was concerned himself, and when anything took his fancy he would say bluntly: "Don't you want to give me that?"

Bravery is not always the inseparable companion of wit, as Carrat proved more than once. He was endowed with one of those artless and insurmountable dispositions to poltroonery which in comedies never fail to excite the laughter of the spectators, and it was a great amusement for Madame Bonaparte also to play tricks on him which displayed his singular caution.

The reader must know, in the first place, that one of Madame Bonaparte's greatest pleasures at Malmaison was to walk on the high road bordering the walls of the park. She always preferred this promenade, where there were almost continual clouds of dust, to the delightful alleys inside the park. One day, being accompanied by her daughter Hortense, Madame Bonaparte told Carrat to follow them in their walk. He was in a state of great rapture at this distinction, when suddenly there arose from one of the ditches a large figure draped in a white sheet, in a word, a real spectre, such as I have seen described in translations of some old English romances. It is needless to say that the phantom was simply a person expressly placed there by these ladies to frighten Carrat, and the comedy certainly had a marvellous success. Carrat, in fact, no sooner caught sight of the spectre than he came up to Madame Bonaparte in alarm, and said to her, all in a tremble: "Madame, Madame, look at that phantom! . . . 'tis the ghost of that lady who died lately at Plombières!" "Keep quiet, Carrat, you are a poltroon!"—"Ah! it is certainly her ghost that is coming back!" As Carrat was talking in this way, the man in the white sheet, carrying out his part, came toward him, shaking his long veil, and poor Carrat, seized with terror, fell over backward and became so ill that every effort was required to restore him to consciousness.

Another day, while the General was still in Egypt, and hence before I became a member of her household, Madame Bonaparte wished to give one of her ladies a notion of Carrat's fear. A general plot was got up between the ladies of Malmaison, in which Mademoiselle Hortense played the part of chief conspirator. I have heard the story told so often by Madame Bonaparte that I can give some rather comical details about it. Carrat slept in a room adjoining a small cabinet. A hole was pierced in the partition between them, through which a string was passed, at the end of which was hung a jug full of water. This cooling vase was suspended exactly over the head of the patient. Nor was this all; for they had taken the precaution of having the screws removed which kept Carrat's folding bed in place, and as the latter was in the habit of going to bed without a light, he saw neither the preparations for his premeditated fall, nor the vase containing the water destined for his novel baptism. All the conspirators had been waiting for some minutes in the cabinet when he threw himself, heavily enough, on his bed, which instantly sank under him, the watering-pot, meanwhile, responding to a jerk on the string, and producing the effect intended. Simultaneously the victim of a fall and a nocturnal inundation, Carrat protested loudly against this combined attack! "This is horrible!" he shouted with all his might, the malicious Hortense, meanwhile, in order to increase his tribulations, saying to her mother, to Madame de Crigny, Madame de Charvet, and several other ladies of the household: "Ah! mamma, the frogs and toads that are in the water have just fallen on his face." These words, added to the profound darkness, merely served to augment Carrat's terror, and becoming seriously angry, he cried out: "It is a horrible thing, Madame, it is an atrocity to play such tricks on your domestics." I would not venture to asseverate that Carrat's complaints were entirely out of place, but they merely served to excite the gaiety of the ladies, who had taken him for the butt of their pleasantries.

However that may be, such were the character and the position of Carrat when, after I had been some time acquainted with him, and General Bonaparte had returned from his Egyptian expedition, he told me that M. Eugène de Beauharnais had applied to him for a confidential valet, his own having been detained at Cairo by a rather serious malady at the moment of departure. This man was called Lefebvre, and was an old servant entirely devoted to his master, as all persons must have been who were acquainted with Prince Eugène; for I do not believe there ever existed a better man, more polite, more full of consideration and even attentions for the persons in his service. Carrat having told me therefore that M. Eugène de Beauharnais wanted a young man to replace Lefebvre, and proposed that I should take his position, I had the happiness of being presented to and suiting him. He was even kind enough to say to me, on the very first day, that my physiognomy pleased him greatly, and that he would like me to come to him at once. On my part, I was enchanted with this situation, which, I don't know why, presented itself to my imagination under the gayest colors. I went without loss of time to find my modest luggage, and there I was, valet de chambre *ad interim* of M. de Beauharnais, never thinking that I would one day be admitted to the special service of General Bonaparte, and still less that I would become the chief valet de chambre of *an emperor.*

CHAPTER II

Prince Eugène apprenticed to a carpenter — Bonaparte and the sword of Marquis de Beauharnais — First interview between Napoleon and Josephine — Appearance and qualities of Eugène — Frankness — Kindness — Love of pleasure — Breakfasts of young officers and artists — Hoaxes and hoaxed — Thiémet and Dugazon — The stutterers and the cold douche — The old valet reinstated — Constant passes into the service of Madame Bonaparte — Attractions of his new situation — Souvenirs of the 18th Brumaire — Political breakfasts — The directors in caricature — Barras in the Greek style — Abbé Sieyès on horseback — The rendezvous — Murat's mistake — President Gohier, General Jubé, and the great manœuvre — General Marmont and the riding-school horses — Malmaison — Josephine's salon — M. de Talleyrand — General Bonaparte's family — M. Volney — M. Denon — M. Lemercier — M. de Laigle — General Beurnonville — Excursion on horseback — Hortense's fall — Happy married life — Prisoner's base — Bonaparte a bad runner — Net income of Malmaison — Embellishments — Theatres and society actors: MM. Eugène, Jérôme, Bourrienne, Lauriston, etc.; Mademoiselle Hortense, Madame Murat, the two Demoiselles Auguié — Napoleon a simple spectator.

IT was the 16th of October, 1799, when Eugène de Beauharnais arrived in Paris on his return from the Egyptian expedition, and it was immediately after his arrival that I had the happiness of entering his service. M. Eugène was then twenty-one years of age, and I will not defer the recital of some details that I believe to be little known concerning his life before his mother's marriage with General Bonaparte.

The reader is aware that his father was one of the victims of the Revolution. After the Marquis de Beauharnais perished on the scaffold, his widow, whose property had been confiscated, finding herself reduced to a condition bordering on poverty, and fearing lest her son, although still very young, might also be prosecuted on account of his noble birth, placed him in a carpenter's shop on the rue de l'Echelle. A lady of my acquaintance, who lived on that street, has often seen him pass by carrying a board on his shoulder. It was a good ways from there to the command of the regiment of consular *guides*, and above all to the vice-royalty of Italy. I learned, by hearing Eugène himself relate it, the singular circumstance by which he occasioned the first interview of his mother with his stepfather.

Eugène, being at the time only fourteen or fifteen years old, having been informed that General Bonaparte had become possessor of the sword of the Marquis de Beauharnais, ventured to call on him, a proceeding that obtained complete success. The General received him graciously, and Eugène said he came to ask whether he would not be so kind as to return to him his father's sword. His face, his manner, his frank request, were all pleasing to Bonaparte, who instantly restored the sword he asked for. Hardly had he taken it in his hands than he covered it with tears and kisses, and that with so natural an air that Bonaparte was enchanted. On learning how the General had received her son, Madame de Beauharnais thought it her duty to call and thank him. Josephine having greatly pleased Bonaparte at this first interview, he returned her visit. They frequently saw each other, and everybody knows how, by one thing after another, she became the first Empress of the French; and I can affirm, in conformity with many proofs which I afterwards obtained of the fact, that Bonaparte never ceased to love Eugène as much as he could have loved his own son.

Eugène's qualities were both amiable and solid. His features were not handsome, and yet his countenance prepossessed one in his favor. His figure was well-shaped, and yet his appearance was not distinguished, on account of a habit of slouching in his gait. He was about five feet and three or four inches tall. He was kind, gay, amiable, full of spirit, lively, and generous; and one may say that his open, candid physiognomy was truly the mirror of his soul. How many services did he not render during the course of his life, and that, too, at the period when he was obliged to impose privations on himself in order to do so!

We shall see presently why I passed only one month with Eugène; but I remember that during this brief period, while scrupulously fulfilling his duties toward his mother and his stepfather, he was very much addicted to the pleasures so natural to his age and in his position. One of the things which pleased him most was to give breakfasts to his friends; hence he gave them very often; and that, for my part, amused me greatly, on account of the comical scenes of which I was a spectator. In addition to the young military men belonging to Bonaparte's staff, who were his most punctual guests, he had among other habitual visitors Thiémet, the ventriloquist, Dazincourt and Michau of the Théâtre Français, and several other persons whose names just now escape me. As may be easily believed, these reunions were extremely gay; the young officers especially, who had returned like Eugène from Egypt, sought for nothing but how to compensate themselves for the recent privations they had had to endure. At this epoch hoaxes were all the fashion in Paris; their practitioners were brought to reunions, and Thiémet held a very distinguished rank among them. I recollect that one day at a breakfast of Eugène's, Thiémet called several of those present by their names, by imitating the voices of their servants, as if these voices came from outside; while he remained quietly in his place, and seemed never to move his lips except for the purpose of eating and drinking, two functions which he fulfilled very well. Each of the officers called in this way, went downstairs and found nobody. Then Thiémet, assuming a feigned politeness, went down with them under pretence of assisting in their search, and prolonged their embarrassment by making them continue to hear voices they knew. Most of them laughed heartily at a pleasantry of which they were the victims; but there was one who, being rather duller than his comrades, took the thing seriously and was going to be angry, when Eugène avowed that he had headed the conspiracy.

I recall another amusing scene the two heroes of which were this same Thiémet of whom I have just spoken, and Dugazon. Several foreigners were assembled in Eugène's apartment, the rôles were distributed and learned in advance, and the two victims designated. When they were all seated at table, Dugazon, pretending to be a stutterer, addressed some remark to Thiémet, who, having a similar rôle, replied by stuttering also. Then each of the two pretended to believe that the other was mocking at him, and there ensued a quarrel of stutterers who, the angrier they grew, the harder they found it to express themselves. Thiémet, who besides playing the stutterer had also assumed the character of a deaf man, turned to his neighbor, his ear-trumpet at his ear, and asked: "Wh-wh-what i-i-is he s-s-saying?" "Nothing," responded the officious neighbor, who wanted to prevent a quarrel and take his stutterer's side. "Y-y-yes he i-i-s m-m-mock-mock-ing at me." Then the quarrel grew more lively; they were about to come to blows, and each of the two stutterers had seized a carafe to throw at his antagonist's head, when a copious immersion from the water contained in the carafes made their officious neighbors comprehend the danger of attempts at conciliation. The two stutterers, however, continued shouting like deaf men until the last drop of water was spilled; and I remember that Eugène, who was the author of this plot, was in fits of laughter all the time it lasted. People dried themselves, and all was presently arranged, glasses in hand. Eugène, whenever he got up a joke of this kind, never failed to relate it to his mother, and sometimes even to his stepfather, who were greatly amused by it, Josephine especially.

I had been leading a rather joyous life for a month with Eugène, when Lefebvre, the valet whom he had left ill at Cairo, came back cured, and asked to have his place again. Eugène, whom I suited better, on account of my youth and activity, proposed that he should enter his mother's household, calling his attention to the fact that he would be much more tranquil there. But Lefebvre, who was extremely attached to his master, went to find Madame Bonaparte and displayed all his chagrin at Eugène's resolution. Josephine promised to take his part; she consoled him, assured him that she would talk to her son, said she would see that he returned to his former post, and that it would be I that she would take into her service. Josephine did, in fact, speak to her son, as she had promised Lefebvre to do; and, one morning, Eugène announced to me, in the kindest terms, my change of domicile. "Constant," said he, "I am very sorry for the circumstance which obliges us to part; but, as you know, Lefebvre followed me to Egypt; he is an old servant; I cannot avoid taking him back. Moreover, you are not going to become a stranger to me; you are going to my mother's house, where you will be very well off; and there we shall often see each other. Go there from me, this very morning; I have spoken to her about you; it is an understood thing; she expects you."

As may be believed, I lost no time in presenting myself at Madame Bonaparte's house. Knowing that she was at Malmaison, I went there at once, and was received by Madame Bonaparte with a kindness that filled me with gratitude, not knowing that she showed this kindness to everybody, and that it was as inseparable from her character as grace was from her person. I had very little to do; my time was almost entirely at my own disposal, and I profited by it to make frequent excursions to Paris. Hence the life I led was very pleasant for a young man, who could not yet suspect that, some time afterwards, it would become as constrained as it was then free.

Before quitting a service which I had found so agreeable, I will relate some facts belonging to that period which my position near the stepson of General Bonaparte allowed me to become acquainted with.

M. de Bourrienne has perfectly recounted the events of the 18th Brumaire in his Memoirs. The account he has given of that famous day is as exact as it is interesting, and all who are curious to know the secret causes which bring about political changes will find them faithfully exposed in the narrative of the Minister of State. I am very far from pretending to excite an interest of this nature; but the reading of M. de Bourrienne's work has set me also on the track of my souvenirs. There are circumstances he may not have known, or may even have omitted voluntarily as being of small importance; and what he has let fall upon the road I esteem myself fortunate to be able to gather up.

I was still with M. Eugène de Beauharnais when General Bonaparte overthrew the Directory; but I was just as much in the way of learning all that passed as if I had been in the service of Madame Bonaparte or of the General himself; for my master, although very young, had the full confidence of his stepfather, and above all that of his mother, who consulted him on every occasion.

Several days before the 18th Brumaire, M. Eugène ordered me to busy myself with the preparations for a breakfast he was to give on that very day to his friends. The number of the guests, who were all military men, was much larger than usual. The repast was made very lively by an officer who undertook to caricature the manners and deportment of the directors and some of their trusty adherents. To personate Director Barras, he draped himself *à la grecque* with the tablecloth, took off his black cravat, turned down his shirt collar, and advanced with many airs and graces, resting his left arm on the shoulder of the youngest of his comrades and pretending to chuck him under the chin with his right hand. There was not a soul present who did not comprehend the meaning of this sort of charade, and it was greeted with shouts of laughter that seemed as if they would never end.

Afterwards he personated the Abbé Sieyès, by passing an enormous rabbi [1] of paper through his necktie, elongating indefinitely a pallid visage, and then prancing several times around the room astride on his chair, ending at last in a grand somersault, as if his horse had thrown him. To comprehend the meaning of this pantomime, it must be known that the Abbé Sieyès had been taking riding lessons for some time in the Luxembourg garden, to the great amusement of the promenaders, who assembled in crowds to enjoy the stiff and awkward appearance of the new horseman.

When breakfast was over, M. Eugène repaired to General Bonaparte, whose aide-de-camp he was, and his friends rejoined their several corps. I followed them out; for certain remarks that had just been made in the rooms of my young master made me suspect that something serious and interesting was about to happen. M. Eugène had agreed to meet his comrades at the Pont-Tournant; I went there, and found a considerable assemblage of mounted officers in uniform, all in readiness to follow General Bonaparte to Saint-Cloud.

---

[1] The name given to the bands worn by priests as a part of their ordinary costume. They go around the neck and over the breast, descending to different lengths at the wearer's pleasure.— *Translator's note.*

The commanders of all arms had been requested by General Bonaparte to give breakfasts to their official corps, and they had done the same thing as my young master. And yet not all the officers, not even the generals, were in the secret; and General Murat himself, who rushed into the hall of the Cinq-Cents, at the head of his grenadiers, thought the only matter in dispute was a dispensation as to age which General Bonaparte was about to ask, in order to obtain a place as Director.

I have learned, from a sure source, that at the moment when General Jubé, who was devoted to General Bonaparte, was assembling in the court of the Luxembourg the Directory's guard, of which he was the commander, the worthy M. Gohier, president of the Directory, put his head out of the window and shouted to Jubé: "Citizen-general, what are you doing there?"—"Citizen-president, you see well enough what I am doing; I am assembling the guard."—"No doubt I see that very well, Citizen-general; but what are you assembling them for?" "Citizen-president, I am going to make an inspection of them, and to command a great manœuvre. Forward, march!" And the Citizen-general started at the head of his troops to go and rejoin General Bonaparte at Saint-Cloud, while the latter was expected at the house of the Citizen-president, who waited for him in vain at the breakfast to which he had invited him.

General Marmont also had breakfasted the officers

of the arm he commanded (I think it was the artillery). At the end of the repast he had made a few remarks, persuading them not to separate their cause from that of the conqueror of Italy, and to accompany him to Saint-Cloud. "But how do you want us to follow him?" exclaimed one of the guests; "we have no horses." "If that is all that hinders you," said the General, "you will find some in the court of this hotel. I have kept all those of the national riding-school. Let us go down and mount." All the officers present accepted this invitation, excepting General Allix, who declared that he would not be mixed up in any squabble.

I was at Saint-Cloud on the 18th and 19th Brumaire. I saw General Bonaparte harangue the soldiers and read them the decree appointing him commander-in-chief of all the troops in Paris and throughout the whole extent of the seventeenth military division. I saw him in the first place come out very much agitated from the council of the Anciens, and afterwards from the assembly of the Cinq-Cents. I saw M. Lucien led out of the hall where this assembly was sitting by some grenadiers sent to protect him from the violence of his colleagues. Pale and furious, he sprang upon a horse and galloped straight to the troops to harangue them. At the moment when he turned his sword toward the breast of the General his brother, saying that he would be the first to immolate him if he dared to make an assault on liberty, cries of *Long live Bonaparte! Down with the lawyers!* broke out on all sides, and the soldiers, led by General Murat, rushed into the hall of the Cinq-Cents. Everybody knows what happened there, and I will not enter into details which have been recounted so many times.

The General, on becoming First Consul, installed himself at the Luxembourg. At this time he also inhabited Malmaison; but he was often on the road, and so was Josephine; for their journeys to Paris, when they occupied this residence, were very frequent, not simply for government affairs, which often necessitated the presence of the First Consul, but also to go to the play, which General Bonaparte was very fond of, always giving the preference to the Théâtre Français and the Italian opera. This is a passing observation merely, as I intend to reserve until later on the facts I have collected concerning the tastes and familiar habits of the Emperor.

Malmaison, at the time of which I am speaking, was a place of delights where no one was ever seen to arrive without an expression of satisfaction; and everywhere I went, I also heard blessings invoked on the First Consul and Madame Bonaparte. In Madame Bonaparte's salon there was not as yet the shadow of that rigid etiquette which it was afterward necessary to observe at Saint-Cloud, the Tuileries, and all the palaces where the Emperor might find himself. Society there displayed a simple elegance alike removed from republican grossness and the luxury of the Empire. M. de Talleyrand was at this period one of the most assiduous visitors at Malmaison. He sometimes dined there, but it was more usual for him to come in the evening, between eight and nine o'clock, and return at one or two, and occasionally at three in the morning. Everybody was admitted at the house of Madame Bonaparte on a footing of equality which pleased her much. Murat, Duroc, Berthier, and all the persons who have since figured as great dignitaries, and sometimes with crowns, in the annals of the Empire, came there familiarly. General Bonaparte's family was likewise very attentive, but we knew very well amongst ourselves that they did not like Madame Bonaparte; I acquired proofs of this afterward. Mademoiselle Hortense never quitted her mother, and they loved each other very much. Besides the men distinguished by their functions in the government and the army, there came also some who were not less so by their personal merit, and who had been so by their birth before the Revolution. It was a veritable magic lantern in which we could see the personages defiling before our eyes, and this spectacle, without recalling the gaiety of Eugène's breakfasts, was far from devoid of attractions. Among the persons whom we saw most frequently, I must mention: M. de Volney, M. Denon, M. Lemercier, Prince de Poix, MM. de Laigle, M. Charles, M. Baudin, General Beurnonville, M. Isabey, and a large number of other men celebrated in science, literature, and art; in fine, the majority of those who formed the society of Madame de Montesson.

Madame Bonaparte and Mademoiselle often went out into the country on horseback; the most constant equerries on these excursions were usually Prince de Poix and MM. de Laigle. One day, as one of these cavalcades was re-entering the court of Malmaison, Mademoiselle Hortense's horse became frightened and ran away. Mademoiselle Hortense, who sat a horse perfectly, and who was very agile, attempted to spring off on the grass beside the road, but the fastening which kept the bottom of her riding habit under her foot prevented her extricating herself quickly enough, so that she was upset and dragged along by her horse for several feet. Happily, the gentlemen who accompanied her, having seen her fall, had sprung off their horses and arrived in time to pick her up. By an extraordinary piece of good luck, she had received no contusion, and was the first to laugh at her mishap.

During the earliest period of my sojourn at Malmaison, the First Consul always occupied the same bed with his wife, like an honest citizen of Paris, and I never heard of a single gallant intrigue that took place in the château. This society, the majority of whose members were young, and who were often very numerous, frequently gave themselves up to exercises which reminded one of college recreations; indeed, one of the great diversions of the inhabitants of Malmaison was to play prisoner's base. It was after dinner, usually, that Bonaparte, MM. de Lauriston, Didelot, de Lucay, de Bourrienne, Eugène, Rapp, Isabey, Madame Bonaparte, and Mademoiselle Hortense divided themselves into two camps, where the prisoners made and exchanged reminded the First Consul of the great game to which he gave the preference.

The most agile runners in these games of prisoner's base were M. Eugène, M. Isabey, and Mademoiselle Hortense; as to General Bonaparte, he often fell down, but he picked himself up again with shouts of laughter.

General Bonaparte and his family seemed to enjoy an unusual happiness, especially while they were at Malmaison. This habitation, in spite of the pleasures enjoyed there, was far from resembling what it has been since. The property comprised a château which General Bonaparte found in a rather bad condition on his return from Egypt, a park which was already very pretty, and a farm the yearly income from which certainly did not exceed twelve thousand francs. Josephine herself superintended all the works executed there, and never has any woman been endowed with so much taste.

From the commencement they acted plays at Malmaison. This was a kind of recreation which the First Consul liked greatly, but he never took any part except that of spectator. All who formed part of the household were present at the representations, and I will not conceal the pleasure we enjoyed, more perhaps than any of the others, in seeing the persons in whose service we were thus travestied on the stage. The Malmaison troupe, if I may be permitted thus to designate actors of so exalted a social position, was composed principally of MM. Eugène, Jérôme, Lauriston, de Bourrienne, Isabey, de Leroy, Didelot; Mademoiselle Hortense, Madame Caroline Murat, and the Demoiselles Auguié, one of whom afterwards married Marshal Ney, and the other M. de Broc. All four were very young and charming, and few Parisian theatres could have brought together such pretty actresses. Moreover, they were very graceful on the stage, and played their parts with real talent. They behaved there much as they did in the salon, where they had an air of exquisite delicacy. The repertory was not greatly varied at first, but it was usually very well selected. The first representation at which I was present was composed of the *Barbier de Seville* in which M. Isabey played the rôle of Figaro and Mademoiselle Hortense that of Rosine; and the *Dépit amoureux*. Another time I saw the *Gageure imprévue* and the *Fausses Consultations* presented. Mademoiselle Hortense and M. Eugène played perfectly in this latter piece, and I yet remember vividly how, in the part of Madame Leblanc, Mademoiselle Hortense seemed prettier than ever in her old woman's costume. M. Eugène represented M. Lenoir, and M. Lauriston the charlatan. The First Consul, as I have said, confined himself to the rôle of spectator, but he appeared to take the most lively pleasure in this private, and one might say family theatre. He laughed, he applauded heartily, but also he often criticised. Madame Bonaparte was equally amused, and even if she had not been proud of the success of her children, *the first subjects of the troupe*, the fact that this was a relaxation agreeable to her husband would have been enough to make her seem pleased with it; for it was her constant study to contribute to the happiness of the great man who had united his destiny to hers.

When a day had been set for a representation, there was never a "*no performance*," but there was often a change of plays, not on account of indisposition or an actress's headache, as happens in Parisian theatres, but for much more serious motives. It often happened that M. d'Etieulette would be ordered to his regiment; that an important mission would be entrusted to Count Almaviva; but Figaro and Rosine always remained faithful at their post, and the desire to please the First Consul was, moreover, so general among all who surrounded him, that the substitutes manifested the utmost good will in the absence of the principals in their department, and the play never failed through default of an actor.[1]

---

[1] Michau, of the Comédie Française, was the instructor of the troupe; whenever any of the actors lacked ardor, Michau would shout: "*Chaud! Chaud! Chaud!*"

CHAPTER III

M. Charvet — Details anterior to the author's entering Madame Bonaparte's service — Departure for Egypt — The *Pomona* — Madame Bonaparte at Plombières — A horrible fall — Madame Bonaparte forced to remain at the baths and send for her daughter — Euphémie — Love for dainties and roguishness — The *Pomona* captured by the English — Return to Paris — Purchase of Malmaison — First plots against the First Consul's life — The marble workers — The poisoned tobacco — Schemes of abduction — Installation at the Tuileries — The horses and the sabre of Campo-Formio — The heroes of Egypt and Italy — Lannes — Murat — Eugène — Arrangement of apartments at the Tuileries — Kitchen staff of the First Consul — Chamber service — M. de Bourrienne — A game at billiards with Madame Bonaparte — The watch-dogs — Accident to a workman — The First Consul's holidays — The First Consul much loved in his own family — — *They would not dare!* — The First Consul keeping the house accounts — The yoke of misery.

I HAD not been long in Madame Bonaparte's service when I made the acquaintance of M. Charvet, the door-keeper of Malmaison. My connection with this excellent man became more intimate daily, so much so that in the end he gave me one of his daughters in marriage. I was eager to learn from him all that referred to Madame Bonaparte and the First Consul before I entered the household, and in our frequent interviews he took the greatest pleasure in satisfying my curiosity; it is to his confidences that I owe the following details concerning the mother and the daughter.

When General Bonaparte set off for Egypt, Madame Bonaparte accompanied him as far as Toulon. She even desired very much to follow him to Egypt, and when the General made objections, she reminded him that, being a Creole by birth, the warmth of the climate would be favorable rather than dangerous to her, and that, by a singular coincidence, it was on the *Pomona* that she wished to make the voyage; that is, on the same vessel that had brought her in early youth from Martinique to France. General Bonaparte, having finally acceded to his wife's wishes, promised to send her the *Pomona*, and persuaded her to go meanwhile and take the waters of Plombières. Things were settled in this way between the husband and wife, and Madame Bonaparte was enchanted to go to Plombières, which she had long desired to do, knowing, like everybody else, what was the special reputation of these waters.

Madame Bonaparte had been at Plombières but a short time, when one morning, as she was in her salon, hemming bandana handkerchiefs, and chatting with some ladies, Madame de Cambis, who was on the balcony, called her to come and see a pretty little dog that was passing in the street. All present ran out after Madame Bonaparte, and then the balcony gave way with a frightful crash. Fortunately, and one may say by a great chance, nobody was killed; but Madame de Cambis had her thigh broken, and

Madame Bonaparte was cruelly bruised, although no bones were fractured. M. Charvet, who was in a room over the salon, ran down on hearing the noise and had a sheep killed and skinned immediately, and Madame Bonaparte enveloped in the skin. She was a long time in regaining her health. Her arms and hands, especially, were so bruised that for some time she was unable to use them, and it was necessary to cut up her food and put it in her mouth, and, in a word, to render her every service ordinarily required by a child.

We have just seen that Josephine expected to rejoin her husband in Egypt, and this gave her reason to suppose that her stay at the baths of Plombières would not last long; but her accident made her conclude that it would be prolonged indefinitely, and she wished, while her health was being re-established, to have her daughter with her. Hortense was then fifteen, and was being educated at Madame Campan's boarding-school. She sent a mulatto woman after her whom she was very fond of. Euphémie, as she was called, was the foster-sister of Madame Bonaparte, and was even supposed, though I do not know whether the supposition was well founded, to be her natural sister. Euphémie set off with M. Charvet in one of Madame Bonaparte's carriages. On their arrival Hortense was enchanted with the journey she was about to make, and especially with the idea of going to her mother, for whom she had the liveliest affection. Mademoiselle Hortense was, I will not say a glutton, but excessively fond of good eating, and so M. Charvet, in relating these details, told me that in every town of the least importance the carriage was replenished with bonbons and dainties, of which Mademoiselle Hortense consumed a great many. One day when Euphémie and M. Charvet were sound asleep, they were suddenly awakened by a report which to them seemed terrible, and which gave them the greatest uneasiness, since, on awakening, they found they were passing through a dense forest. This fortuitous accident made Hortense shout with laughter, for they had hardly shown their fright before they were inundated with an odorous foam which explained where the report came from: it was that of a bottle of champagne placed in one of the pockets of the carriage, and which the heat and the motion, or more probably the roguishness of the young traveller, had uncorked with a good deal of noise. When Mademoiselle Hortense reached Plombières, her mother was nearly well, so that Madame Campan's pupil found there all the distractions and amusements suitable to her age.

One has reason to say that every mischance has its good side; for, but for the accident that happened to Madame Bonaparte, it is among the possibilities that she would have been taken prisoner by the English. She learned, in fact, that the ship *Pomona*, on which, as we have seen, she wished to make the voyage, had fallen into the hands of these enemies of France.

And as, moreover, every letter from General Bonaparte dissuaded his wife from joining him, she returned to Paris.

On her arrival Josephine bethought her of accomplishing a wish that had been expressed by General Bonaparte before his departure. He had told her that he would like to have a country house on his return, and had even commissioned his brother Joseph to take the matter in hand, which M. Joseph did not do. Madame Bonaparte, who was, on the contrary, always on the lookout for whatever might please her husband, set several people to work hunting up something that might be suitable in the environs of Paris. After hesitating long between Ris and Malmaison, she decided on the latter, and bought it from M. Lecoulteux-Dumolcy for, I think, the sum of four hundred thousand francs.

It was stories of this kind that M. Charvet was kind enough to tell me in the days when I first entered the service of Madame Bonaparte. Every one in the house liked to talk about her, and assuredly not for the sake of slandering her; for no woman was ever more loved by those around her, or deserved to be so. General Bonaparte also was an excellent man in the privacy of family life.

Since the return of the First Consul from his Egyptian campaign, several attempts had been made on his life. The police had many times warned him to be on his guard, and not to venture about alone in the neighborhood of Malmaison. The First Consul was not much inclined to be suspicious, especially before this period. But the discovery of the snares laid for him in his most intimate private life, forced him to use prudence and precaution. It has been said since then that these pretended conspiracies were mere fabrications of the police, for the purpose of making themselves necessary to the First Consul, or else (who knows?) of the First Consul himself, in order to redouble the interest attaching to his person by fear of the perils menacing his life; and the absurdity of these attempts has been alleged in proof of their falsity. I do not pretend to solve such mysteries; but it seems to me that in the matter in question, absurdity proves nothing, or, at all events, does not prove falsity. The conspirators of that epoch have given us their own measure so far as extravagance is concerned. What could be more absurd, and yet more real, than the atrocious folly of the infernal machine? However it may be, I am going to recount what happened under my own eyes during the first months of my sojourn at Malmaison. Nobody in the house had the least doubt of the reality of these attempts, or, at any rate, nobody displayed any such doubts before me.

All means to get rid of the First Consul seemed good to his enemies. They took everything into their calculations, even his recreations, as the following occurrence will prove.

There were repairs and embellishments to make in the chimneys of the First Consul's apartments at

Malmaison. The contractor who had undertaken them had sent some marble-cutters, among whom had slipped in, according to all appearances, some wretches bribed by the conspirators. The persons attached to the First Consul were constantly on the watch, and used the greatest vigilance. They thought they noticed that there were some men among these laborers who pretended to be working, but whose manner and appearance were not in keeping with their occupation. These suspicions were, unhappily, but too well founded; for when the apartments were ready to receive the First Consul, and at the moment when he came to occupy them, some one found, in making a turn about the rooms, on the desk at which he was about to seat himself, a snuff-box exactly similar to the one the First Consul was in the habit of using. It was supposed at first that this box really belonged to him and had been forgotten there by his valet, but the doubts excited by the appearance of some of the marble-cutters having taken more consistency, the snuff was examined and analyzed. It was poisoned.

Those who plotted this treachery had, so people said in those days, an understanding with other conspirators, who were to try a different means of getting rid of the First Consul. They determined to assail the guard of the château of Malmaison and forcibly abduct the head of the government. With this end in view they had uniforms made similar to those of the consular *guides* who were then on duty day and night near the First Consul, and who followed him on horseback in his excursions. In this costume, and by aid of their understanding with their accomplices within the house (the pretended marble-cutters), they might easily have approached and mingled with the guard, who were fed and lodged at the château; they might even have reached the First Consul and carried him off. This first scheme, however, was abandoned as too risky, and the conspirators flattered themselves that they could attain their object more surely and with less danger by taking advantage of the First Consul's frequent journeys to Paris. Aided by their disguise, they were to mingle with the *guides* of the escort and kill them. Their rallying-point was to be the quarries of Nanterre. Their plot was discovered for the second time. There was a rather deep quarry in the park at Malmaison, and as it was feared that it might be taken advantage of as a hiding-place whence violence might be done to the First Consul in one of his solitary walks, an iron door was put there.

At one o'clock in the afternoon of February 19, the First Consul repaired in state to the Tuileries, which was then styled the Palace of the Government, in order to install himself there with all his household. His two colleagues were with him, one of whom, the Third Consul, was to occupy the same residence and establish himself in the Pavilion of Flora. The carriage of the consuls was drawn by six white horses presented to the conqueror of

Italy by the Emperor of Germany after the signatures had been affixed to the treaty of Campo-Formio. The magnificent sabre worn by the First Consul at this ceremony had also been given him by that monarch on the same occasion. A remarkable thing about this formal change of domicile was that the acclamations and regards of the crowd, and even of the most distinguished spectators who thronged the windows of the rue Thionville and the quai Voltaire, were addressed only to the First Consul and the young warriors of his brilliant staff, still all bronzed by the sun of the Pyramids or of Italy. In the first rank marched Generals Lannes and Murat, the first easy to recognize by the audacity of his appearance and his thoroughly military manners; the second by the same qualities and, in addition, by a very punctilious elegance in his costume and his weapons. His new title of brother-in-law to the First Consul likewise contributed powerfully to fix universal attention on him. For my part, all mine was absorbed by the principal person in the procession, whom, like all the people who surrounded me, I never looked at without a sort of religious admiration, and by his stepson, the son of my excellent mistress and himself my former master, the brave, modest, and good Prince Eugène, who at that time was not yet a *prince*. On arriving at the Tuileries, the First Consul took possession at once of the apartment he always occupied thereafter, and which formed part of what had been the royal apartments. This suite was composed of a bedroom, bath-room, a cabinet, and a salon in which he gave audience in the morning, a second salon where the aides-de-camp on duty remained, and which served him as a dining-room, and of a vast antechamber. Madame Bonaparte had her own apartments on the ground-floor, the same she occupied when Empress. Over the part of the building inhabited by the First Consul was the lodging of M. de Bourrienne, his secretary, communication between them being established by means of a private stairway.

Although he already had courtiers at this period, he had as yet no court. The etiquette was of the simplest description. As I have said before, the First Consul slept in the same bed as his wife. They inhabited together sometimes the Tuileries and sometimes Malmaison; as yet neither grand marshal, chamberlains, prefects of the palace, nor ladies of honor, tiring women and pages were to be seen. The household of the First Consul comprised merely M. Pfister, the steward, M. Venard, chief cook, MM. Gaillot and Dauger, superintendents, and Colin, chief of the kitchen and its dependencies. M. Ripeau was librarian, and the elder M. Vigogne, equerry. The persons engaged in private service were the first valet de chambre, M. Hambart; Hébert, ordinary valet; and Roustan, the First Consul's Mameluke. There were besides some fifteen persons employed in subordinate offices. M. de Bourrienne governed the entire force and checked the expenditures; although very quick-tempered, he had been able to conciliate universal respect and affection; he was kind, obliging, and above all very just. Hence, at the time of his disgrace, the whole household was grieved about it; for my part, I have retained a sincere and respectful memory of him, and I hope that, if he has had the misfortune to find enemies among the great, he has at least met among his inferiors none but grateful hearts which have keenly regretted him.

Some days after this installation, there was a reception of the diplomatic corps at the château; the details I am about to give concerning it will show how simple was the etiquette at this time of what was already styled *the Court*.

By eight o'clock in the evening the apartments of Madame Bonaparte, situated as I have said, in the part of the ground-floor overlooking the garden, were thronged with people; there was an incredible profusion of feathers, diamonds, and dazzling toilets; such a crowd was present that it was necessary to open the door of Madame Bonaparte's bedroom, for the two salons were so full that it was impossible to move around in them.

When all these people had taken their places as well as they could, after a good deal of embarrassment and trouble, Madame Bonaparte was announced, and entered, conducted by M. de Talleyrand. She wore a white muslin robe with short sleeves, and a pearl necklace. Her head was bare, and her braided hair kept in place by a shell comb with a most charming negligence; her ears must have been agreeably struck by the flattering murmurs that greeted her entrance. Never, I think, had she more grace and majesty.

M. de Talleyrand, still giving his hand to Madame Bonaparte, had the honor of presenting to her in succession the members of the diplomatic corps, not by their own names but by those of their courts. Afterwards he made the round of the two salons with her. The review of the second salon was half over when, without having himself announced, the First Consul entered, in an extremely simple uniform, with a tricolored scarf of silk, with fringe of the same material, tied round him. He wore white cashmere tights, with top boots, and carried his hat in his hand. This unelaborate costume appearing in the midst of the embroidered coats, overloaded with ribbons and jewels, which were worn by the ambassadors, formed a contrast at least as imposing as did the toilet of Madame Bonaparte with those of the ladies invited.

Before relating how it was that I left Madame Bonaparte's service for that of the head of the State, and the abode of Malmaison for the second campaign in Italy, I think it well to stop, give a glance behind me, and set down here one or two souvenirs of the time when I still belonged to Madame Bonaparte. In the evenings, when nearly everybody had retired, she was fond of sitting up to play a game of billiards

VOL. I.— E

and oftener still of backgammon. It happened once that, having dismissed all her company, and being still disinclined to sleep, she asked me if I knew how to play billiards. On my reply, which was affirmative, she asked me with charming kindness to have a game with her, and I had the honor of playing several. Although I have a certain skill, I managed so as to let her win frequently, which amused her very much. If this was flattery, I must own myself guilty of it, but I think I would have acted in the same way with any other woman, whatever her rank and position in relation to me, even though she were not half so amiable as Madame Bonaparte.

The porter of Malmaison, who had the entire confidence of his masters, among other means of defence and surveillance which he had devised in order to guard the house and person of the First Consul from an unexpected attack, had obtained a number of enormous watch-dogs, two of which were very fine Newfoundlands. The embellishments of Malmaison were constantly in progress, and a crowd of workmen spent the nights there, all of whom had been warned not to go out of doors alone. One night when several of these watch-dogs were inside the house with the workmen, and allowing themselves to be caressed, their apparent gentleness inspired one of these men with so much courage, or rather imprudence, that he was not afraid to go out alone. He even thought that, to avoid all danger, he could not do better than put himself under the protection of one of these terrible animals. So he took one with him, and they went together, very amicably, through the doorway; but hardly was he outside when the dog sprang upon his unlucky companion and threw him down. The cries of the poor workman awakened several of the men-servants and they ran to his rescue. It was time, for the dog was keeping him down and choking him cruelly; he was picked up, badly wounded. Madame Bonaparte, on learning this incident, had the man who so narrowly escaped being a victim cared for until he was perfectly cured, and gave him a large gratuity, at the same time recommending him to be more prudent in future.

Every moment that the First Consul could snatch from affairs he spent at Malmaison: the eve of each *décadi*[1] was a festival looked forward to by every one in the château. Madame Bonaparte used to send domestics afoot and on horseback to meet her husband, and even went herself frequently with her daughter and the intimates of Malmaison. When I was not on duty I took the same direction myself, and all alone; for we all had an equal affection for the First Consul and experienced the same anxiety about him. Such was the bitterness and the audacity of the enemies of the First Consul, that the road, though not very long, between Paris and Malmaison was strewn with snares and dangers; we knew that

---

[1] The tenth and last day in the Republican calendar.

several attempts to abduct him while passing over it had been made and might be repeated. The passage most suspected was that of the quarries of Nanterre, which I have mentioned already; hence they were carefully visited and inspected by the men of the household on the days of the First Consul's visits; in the end they filled up the holes that were nearest the road. The First Consul was pleased with our devotion and let us see his satisfaction, but for his own part seemed always fearless and without anxiety; in fact, he often mocked at us for ours, and would tell the good Josephine very seriously that he had had a fine escape on the road; that men with sinister faces had shown themselves many a time while he was passing; that one of them had had the audacity to take aim at him, etc.; and when he saw her very frightened, he would burst out laughing and give her several taps or kisses on the cheek or neck and say: "Don't be afraid, you great ninny, *they would not dare.*"

He busied himself on these holidays, as he himself called them, more with his private affairs than with those of the State. But he could never remain idle; he was always demolishing, restoring, building, enlarging, planting, pruning in the château and in the park, examining the expense accounts, calculating his income, and prescribing economies. Time passed quickly in all these occupations, and the moment soon came when he must go, as he used to say, to resume the *yoke of misery.*

CHAPTER IV

The First Consul takes the author into his service — Forgotten — Chagrin — Consolations offered by Madame Bonaparte — Reparation — Constant's departure for the First Consul's headquarters — Enthusiasm of the soldiers starting for Italy — The author rejoins the First Consul — Hospice of Mont Saint-Bernard — Passage — The slide — Humanity of the monks and generosity of the First Consul — Passage of Mont Albaredo — The First Consul's glance — Taking of Fort de Bard — Entry of Milan — Joy and confidence of the Milanese — Constant's colleagues — Hambard — Hébert — Roustan — Ibrahim-Ali — An Arab's anger — The poniard — The surprise bath — Sequel of the Italian campaign — Combat of Montebello — Arrival of Desaix — Long interview with the First Consul — Desaix's anger against the English — Battle of Marengo — Painful uncertainty — Victory — Death of Desaix — The First Consul's sorrow — The aides-de-camp of Desaix become the aides-de-camp of the First Consul — MM. Rapp and Savary — Tomb of Desaix on Mont Saint-Bernard.

TOWARD the end of March, 1800, five or six months after my entering the service of Madame Bonaparte, the First Consul kept his eyes on me one day while eating his dinner, and having weighed and measured me from top to toe: "Young man," said he to me, "would you like to follow me to the campaign?" I replied with much emotion that I would ask nothing better. "Very well, then, you shall follow me;" and on rising from the table he ordered M. Pfister, the steward, to put me on the list of those belonging to the household who were to take the journey. My preparations did not take long; I was enchanted at the notion of being attached to the personal service of so great a man, and I already beheld myself on the other side of the Alps. . . . The First Consul went away without me! M. Pfister, through a possibly premeditated forgetfulness, had omitted to inscribe me on the list. I was in despair, and went crying to my excellent mistress to relate my misadventure, and she kindly endeavored to console me by saying: "Oh well, Constant, all is not lost, my friend: you will stay with me and go hunting in the park to divert yourself, and perhaps in the end the First Consul will ask you again." Nevertheless Madame Bonaparte did not expect this; for she thought as I did, though out of kindness she would not tell me so, that the First Consul, having changed his mind and no longer desiring my services in the campaign, had himself countermanded his order. I soon obtained direct proof to the contrary. On the way to Dijon, in his march toward Mont Saint-Bernard, the First Consul, who thought I was in his suite, asked for me and learned then that I had been forgotten. He showed some dissatisfaction and desired M. de Bourrienne to write immediately to Madame Bonaparte and beg her to send me along without delay. One morning when my vexation had returned, more keen than ever, Madame Bonaparte summoned me and said, with M. de Bourrienne's letter in her hand: "Constant, since you are resolved to quit us to make your campaigns, you may rejoice and be glad, for you are going to start; the First Consul has sent for you. Call on M. Maret and inquire whether he is not to send a courier very soon; you can travel along with him." At this good news I was in a state of inexpressible rapture which I did not try to hide. "Then you are very glad to get away from us?" observed Madame Bonaparte with a kindly smile. "No, Madame," I replied; "but to come nearer the First Consul is not to go further from Madame." — "I hope so, truly," she returned. "Go, Constant, and take good care of him." If there had been any need of it, this recommendation from my noble mistress would have augmented the zeal and vigilance with which I had determined to fill my new position.

I ran without delay to the house of M. Maret, the Secretary of State, who knew me and had shown me much kindness. "Get ready at once," he said to me; "a courier will be starting this evening or to-morrow morning." I returned in haste to Malmaison to announce my near departure to Madame Bonaparte. She instantly had a good post-chaise prepared for me, and Thiébaut (that was the name of the courier I was to accompany) was charged to provide horses for me all along the road. M. Maret gave me eight hundred francs for my travelling expenses. This sum, which I was far from expecting, made me open my eyes; never had I beheld myself so rich. At four o'clock in the morning a messenger came from Thiébaut to notify me that everything was ready. I went to his house, where the post-chaise was waiting, and we set off.

I travelled very agreeably, sometimes in the post-chaise and sometimes as courier; in the latter case I took Thiébaut's place and he mine. I expected to rejoin the First Consul at Martigny, but his march had been so rapid that I only came up with him at the convent of Mont Saint-Bernard. On our way we were continually passing regiments on the march, and officers and soldiers who were hastening to rejoin their several corps. Their enthusiasm was inexpressible. Those who had made the Italian campaigns, rejoiced at returning to so beautiful a country; those who did not know it as yet, were burning to see the battlefield immortalized by French valor and the genius of the hero still marching at their head. They all acted as if going to a feast, and climbed the Valais mountains, singing. It was eight o'clock in the morning when I arrived at headquarters. Pfister announced me, and I found the Commander-in-Chief in the great lower hall of the hospice. He was taking his breakfast standing, along with his staff. As soon as he caught sight of me: "Ah! there you are, then, you rogue! Why didn't you come with me?" said he. I excused myself, saying that, to my great regret, I had received a countermand, or at least had been left behind at the moment of departure. "Lose no time, my friend," he added, "eat a mouthful quickly; we are going to start." From that moment I was attached to the special service of the First Consul in the capacity of ordinary valet de chambre, that is, in my turn. This service gave me very little to do. M. Hambart, chief valet de chambre of the First Consul, was in the habit of dressing him from head to foot.

Directly after breakfast we began to descend the mountain. Several persons slid down on the snow, very much as people roll down from the top of the Russian mountains in the Beaujon garden. I followed their example. They called it making a sledge. The Commander-in-Chief also slid down an almost perpendicular glacier in this way. His guide was an alert and courageous peasant whose future the First Consul assured for the rest of his life. Some young soldiers who had gone astray in the snow had been discovered, almost dead with cold, by the dogs of the religious, and transported to the hospice, where they had received all imaginable care and been speedily returned to life. The First Consul manifested his gratitude to the good fathers for such active and generous charity. Before quitting the hospice, where tables loaded with provisions were prepared for the soldiers as they climbed up, he left the pious monks, in recompense for the hospitality he and his companions had received, a considerable sum of money, and the vouchers for an annuity for the support of their convent.

That same day we scaled Mont Albaredo; but as this passage would have been impracticable for the cavalry and artillery, they were sent by way of the town of Bard, under the batteries of the fort. The First Consul had ordered them to pass it by night and on the gallop, and had had the wheels of the artillery wagons and the horses' feet wrapped in straw. These precautions were not sufficient completely to prevent the Austrians from hearing our troops, and the cannons of the fort never stopped firing grape-shot. But, luckily, the houses of the town sheltered our soldiers from the fire of their enemies, and more than half the army traversed the city without having much to suffer. As to the household of the First Consul, commanded by General Gardanne, and of which I was one, it went around the Fort of Bard. May 23, we forded a torrent which flowed between the town and the fort, with the First Consul at our head. He climbed afterwards, followed by General Berthier and several officers, a footpath up the Albaredo which commanded the fort and city of Bard. There, turning his pocket-glass on the opposing batteries, against whose fire nothing protected him but some bushes, he found fault with the disposal of the troops made by the officer charged with commanding the siege, and ordered new ones, whose effect would be, as he said himself, to make the place fall into his hands within a very short time, and rid him, henceforward, of the trouble given him by this fort, which, said he, had hindered him from sleeping the two days he had spent at the convent of Saint-Maurice. Then, extending himself at the foot of a fir tree, he fell into a sound slumber, the army meanwhile continuing its passage. Refreshed by this brief instant of repose, the First Consul went down the mountain again, continued his march, and we went to bed at Yorée, where he was to pass the night. The brave General Lannes, who commanded the vanguard, acted after a fashion as our quartermaster, seizing by main force every place that barred the road. It was only a few hours after he had forced his way into Yorée that we entered it.

Such was this miraculous passage of Mont Saint-Bernard. Horses, cannons, artillery wagons, immense stores, were all dragged or carried over glaciers which seemed inaccessible, and by roads apparently impracticable even for a single man. The Austrian cannons succeeded no better than the snow and ice in arresting the French army; so true it is that the genius and perseverance of the First Consul had communicated themselves, so to say, even to the least of his soldiers, and inspired them with a courage and force the results of which will one day seem fabulous.

June 2, which was the morrow of the passage of the Tessin, and the very day of our entrance into Milan, the First Consul learned that the Fort of Bard had been taken the day previous. Hence his arrangement of troops had promptly produced its effect, and the route of communication by way of the Saint-Bernard was cleared.

The First Consul entered Milan without having

encountered much resistance. The whole population had thronged about his passage and he was received with a thousand acclamations. The confidence of the Milanese was redoubled when they learned that he had promised the assembled clergy to maintain the Catholic worship and clergy as they were established, and had made them take an oath of fealty to the Cisalpine Republic.

The First Consul remained some days in this capital, and I had time to cement a more intimate acquaintance with my colleagues. They were, as I have said, MM. Hambart, Roustan, and Hébert. We relieved each other every twenty-four hours at noon precisely. My first care, as it has always been when I have had to live with new faces, was to observe, as closely as I could, the character and temper of my comrades, so as to draw conclusions from them which would afterwards regulate my conduct where they were concerned, and to know in advance pretty much what I might have to hope or to fear from their acquaintance.

Hambart had an unlimited devotion to the First Consul, whom he had followed to Egypt; but he unfortunately had a sombre and misanthropic character, which made him extremely cross and disagreeable. The favor enjoyed by Roustan had probably contributed not a little toward augmenting this gloomy disposition. In his species of mania, he imagined himself the object of an altogether special surveillance. As soon as his service was ended, he would shut himself up in his room, and pass his entire leisure in the most doleful solitude. When the First Consul was in good humor he would joke him about this unsociability, and laughingly call him *Mademoiselle* Hambart. "Well, Mademoiselle, what are you doing all alone this way in your room? You are reading some bad novels there, no doubt, some worthless old books treating of princesses abducted and *held in surveillance* by a barbarous giant." To this poor Hambart would reply with a churlish air: "General, you doubtless know better than I do what I am doing," intending by these words an allusion to the espionage by which he believed himself surrounded. In spite of this unhappy disposition, the First Consul was very good to him. At the time of the journey to the camp of Boulogne he refused to follow the Emperor, who retired him with the post of porter to the palace of Meudon. Here he committed a thousand follies. His end was lamentable. During the Hundred Days, after an audience with the Emperor, he was seized with one of his spells, and threw himself with such force on a kitchen knife that the blade protruded two inches through his back. As it was thought in those days that I had the Emperor's wrath to dread, the rumor spread that it was I who had committed suicide, and this tragic death was announced as mine in several journals.

Hébert, *valet de chambre ordinaire*, was a very gentle young man, but excessively timid. Like all the rest of the household, he had the most devoted affection for the First Consul. It happened one day, in Egypt, that the latter, who had never been able to shave himself (it was I, as I shall relate hereafter with some details, that taught him how to do so), called for Hébert in the absence of Hambart, who usually shaved him, to perform that duty. As it had sometimes happened to Hébert, as a result of his great timidity, to cut his master's chin, the latter, who had a pair of scissors in his hand, said to Hébert as he approached, holding his razor: "Take good care, you rogue; if you cut me, I will poke my scissors into your belly." This threat, made with an air that was almost serious, but which was really nothing but a joke, such as I have repeatedly noticed the Emperor loved to make, produced such an impression on Hébert that he was unable to finish his work. He was seized with a convulsive trembling, his razor fell from his hands, and it was useless for the Commander-in-Chief to stretch out his neck and repeat with a laugh: "Come, finish then, you coward!" Hébert was not only obliged to stop there, but from that time forward he was obliged to relinquish the office of barber. The Emperor disliked this excessive timidity in those who served him; but that did not prevent him, when he had the château of Rambouillet renovated, from giving the place of porter there to Hébert, who had asked for it.

Roustan, so well known under the name of the Emperor's Mameluke, belonged to a good Georgian family. Carried off at the age of six or seven years and taken to Cairo, he had been brought up among the young slaves who serve the Mamelukes while awaiting the time when they shall be old enough to enter that warlike militia themselves. The Sheik of Cairo, when giving General Bonaparte a magnificent Arabian steed, had also given him Roustan and Ibrahim, another Mameluke who was afterwards attached to Madame Bonaparte's service under the name of Ali. It is known that Roustan became an indispensable accompaniment on every occasion when the Emperor appeared in public. He was a part of every journey, every cortège, and, what was most honorable of all, of every battle. In the brilliant staff which followed the Emperor, he shone above all the rest by the glitter of his rich Oriental costume. The sight of him produced a prodigious effect, especially on the common people and in the provinces. He was supposed to be in high credit with the Emperor, and this arose, according to certain credulous persons, from the fact that Roustan had saved his master's life by throwing himself between him and the sabre of an enemy about to strike him. I believe that this was an error. The altogether special favor of which he was the object was sufficiently accounted for by the habitual kindness of His Majesty for all those who were in his service. Moreover, this favor did not extend beyond the circle of the domestic relations. M. Roustan married a young and pretty Frenchwoman, named Mademoiselle Douville, whose father was the Empress Josephine's valet de chambre. When, in 1814 and 1815, some journals reproached him somewhat because he had not followed to the end the fortunes of him to whom he had always professed the greatest devotion, he replied that the family ties he had contracted forbade his leaving France, and that he could do nothing to disturb the happiness he enjoyed in his domestic life.

Ibrahim took the name of Ali on passing into Madame Bonaparte's service. He was of a more than Arabian ugliness and had a wicked glance. I recall a little circumstance concerning him which happened at Malmaison, and may give a notion of his character. One day when we were playing on the lawn of the château, I unintentionally caused him to fall, while running. Furious at his tumble, he picked himself up, drew his poniard which he never laid aside, and sprang toward me to strike me with it. I had laughed at first, like every one else, at his accident, and amused myself by making him run. But warned by the cries of my comrades, and turning round to see how near he was, I perceived at once both his weapon and his anger. I stopped instantly, my foot firm and my eye fixed on his poniard, and I was lucky enough to avoid the thrust, although it just brushed against my breast. Furious in my own turn, as may be readily believed, I seized him by his wide trousers and threw him ten feet away from me into the Malmaison river, which was barely two feet deep. The plunge quieted his senses in the first place, and, besides, his poniard had sunk to the bottom of the water, which rendered my man much less redoubtable. But he began to scream so loudly in his disappointment that Madame Bonaparte heard him, and as she overflowed with kindness for her Mameluke, I was roundly scolded. Nevertheless this poor Ali had such an unsociable temper that he quarrelled with everybody in the house, and was finally sent to Fontainebleau as château messenger.

I return to our campaign. June 13, the First Consul slept at Torre-di-Galifolo, where he had established his headquarters. The march of the army had not slackened since the day we entered Milan. General Murat had crossed the Po and seized Plaisance. General Lannes, although pushing ahead with his brave vanguard, had delivered a bloody battle at Montebello, a name he was afterwards to render illustrious by bearing it. The very recent arrival of Desaix, who came from Egypt, overwhelmed the Commander-in-Chief with joy and also gave additional confidence to the soldiers, by whom the brave and modest Desaix was adored. The First Consul had received him with the most frank and cordial friendship, and they immediately spent three consecutive hours alone together. At the close of this conference an order of the day announced to the army that General Desaix would take command of the Boudet division. I heard several persons belonging to the suite of General Desaix remark that his patience and evenness of temper had been put to rude tests during his voyage by adverse winds, forced delays, the tediousness of quarantine, and especially by the malicious proceedings of the English, who had for some time kept him prisoner on their fleet, in sight of the coast of France, notwithstanding that he was the bearer of a passport signed in Egypt by the English authorities, as a result of a capitulation reciprocally accepted. His resentment against them, therefore, was of the most ardent sort, and he said he keenly regretted that the enemies he would have to fight were not English. In spite of the simplicity of his tastes and habits, nobody was more athirst for glory than this brave General. All his wrath against the English sprang from the fear he had that he would not arrive in time to reap new laurels. He arrived but too soon, to find a glorious death, but alas! one so premature!

The celebrated battle of Marengo was delivered June 14. It began early and lasted all day. I remained at the quarters, with all the General's household. We were in a manner within reach of the cannon of the battle-field, and contradictory reports were all the time arriving. One would represent the battle as entirely lost, the next would give us the victory; there was a moment when the increase in the number of our wounded and the redoublement of the Austrian firing would make us believe for an instant that we were beaten; then all of a sudden some one would come to tell us that this apparent defeat was merely the result of a bold manœuvre of the First Consul, and that a charge made by General Desaix had assured the winning of the battle. But the victory cost France and the heart of the First Consul dear. Desaix, struck by a ball, had fallen dead on the instant, and the grief of his men having only exasperated their courage, they had routed the enemy at the point of the bayonet, the latter having been badly cut up already by a brilliant charge of General Kellermann.

The First Consul slept on the field of battle. In spite of the decisive victory just gained, he was full of sadness, and in the evening, before Hambart and me, he said several things which proved the profound affliction he experienced from the death of General Desaix: "That France had just lost one of her best defenders and he his best friend; that no one knew all the virtue there was in Desaix's heart and what genius in his head." Thus he consoled himself for his grief by eulogizing to everybody the hero who had just died on the field of honor. "My brave Desaix," he said again, "had always desired to die like this." Then he added, almost with tears in his eyes: "But need death have been so quick to grant his prayer!" There was not a soldier in our victorious army who did not share so justifiable an affliction. Rapp and Savary, the General's aides-de-camp, remained in the bitterest despair beside the body of their chief, whom, in spite of his youth, they called their father, more to express his inexhaustible kindness toward them than on account of the gravity of his character. As a consequence of his respect for his friend's memory, the Commander-in-Chief, although his staff was complete, attached these young officers to himself as aides-de-camp.

Commander Rapp (that was his rank then) was at this time what he has been all his life, good, full of courage, and universally beloved. His frankness, though sometimes a little rude, was pleasing to the Emperor. I have heard the latter eulogize his aide-de-camp a thousand times; he always called him *my brave Rapp*. This worthy General was not lucky in battles, and seldom took part in an affair without receiving some wound. Since I am already anticipating the course of events, I will say here that in Russia, on the eve of the battle of Moscow, I heard the Emperor say to General Rapp, who had arrived from Dantzic: "Attention, my hero; we are going to fight to-morrow; look out for yourself, fortune does not spoil you." "That is one of the perquisites of the trade," replied the General. "Rely on it, Sire, I will not do less than my best."

M. Savary maintained toward the First Consul that ardent zeal and boundless devotion which had attached him to General Desaix. If he lacked any one of General Rapp's qualities, it was certainly not that of bravery. Of all the men who surrounded the Emperor, not one was more absolutely devoted to his slightest will. I shall doubtless have occasion, during the course of these Memoirs, to recall some traits of this unexampled devotion, for which the Duke de Rovigo was so magnificently rewarded; but it is just to say that he at least did not wound the hand that had elevated him, and that he gave to the very end, and after the end of his former master (it is thus that it pleased him to style the Emperor), the not very well followed example of gratitude.

A decree of the government, in the following June, provided that the body of Desaix should be transported to the convent of the great Saint-Bernard, and a monument for him raised there in attestation of the regrets of France, and especially of those of the First Consul, in a spot where he had covered himself with immortal glory.[1]

---

[1] Two monuments have been raised in Paris to the brave Desaix: a statue on the Place des Victoires and a bust on the Place Dauphine. The statue affected a theatrical pose which scarcely accorded with the serious manners and perfect simplicity of him whose image it was supposed to reproduce. Moreover, being perfectly nude, except as it was badly veiled by a sword-belt, it shocked all eyes and provoked scurrilous jests. The great victor of Waterloo was represented, during his lifetime, in Hyde Park, as an enormous Achilles, and His Grace (at least the statue of His Grace) is executed in such a manner that the curious lose not a single line, a single muscle of his heroic person. That nothing might be wanting to this parody, it was the English *ladies,* so susceptible on the point of decency and dignity, who raised this monument to My Lord Duke.

To come back to Desaix (it is to come very far back), the statue raised to him on the Place des Victoires was removed under the Empire by order of the government. As to the bust which may still be seen on the Place Dauphine, it would be difficult to imagine anything more shabby, blackened up, or neglected. That is the way that Desaix's bust is treated. On the other hand, Pichegru has statues of bronze.

CHAPTER V

Return to Milan, on march to Paris — The Singer Marchesi and the First Consul — Impertinence and several days in prison — Madame Grassini — Entering France by way of Mont Cenis — Triumphal arches — Procession of young girls — Entry of Lyons — Couthon and the demolishers — The First Consul causes the houses on the Place Belcour to be rebuilt — The overset carriage — Illuminations at Paris — Kléber — Calumnies against the First Consul — Fall of Constant's horse — Kindness of the First Consul and Madame Bonaparte toward Constant — Generosity of the First Consul — The author's emotion — The Emperor outrageously misunderstood — The First Consul, Jérôme Bonaparte, and Colonel Lacuée — The First Consul's love for Madame D. — Madame Bonaparte's jealousy and the First Consul's precautions — Indiscreet curiosity of a chambermaid — Threats and forced discretion — The small house in the Allée des Veuves — The First Consul's consideration for his wife — The First Consul's morals and his manners with women.

THIS victory of Marengo had assured the conquest of Italy; hence the First Consul, judging his presence more necessary in Paris than at the head of his army, gave the chief command to General Masséna and made ready to recross the mountains. We returned to Milan, where the First Consul was received with still more enthusiasm than during our first visit. The establishment of a republic crowned the wishes of the majority of the Milanese, and they styled the First Consul their saviour for having delivered them from the Austrian yoke. Nevertheless there was a party which detested equally the changes, the French army which had been the instrument of them, and the young chief who was their author. In this party figured a celebrated artist, Marchesi the singer; when we first went through, the First Consul had sent for him, and the musician had begged to be excused from inconveniencing himself; he finally came, but with all the importance of a man who felt his dignity wounded. The very simple costume of the First Consul, his short figure and his pale and not very good-looking visage, were not calculated greatly to impress the heroes of the theatre. Hence the Commander-in-Chief having received him well and very politely asked him to sing an air, he had responded by this bad pun, delivered in an impertinent tone which his Italian accent heightened: "Signor Zeneral, if it is a good air you want, you will find an excellent one by taking a little turn in ze zarden." For this pretty performance Signor Marchesi was instantly turned out of doors and that very evening an order had been sent to put him into prison. On his return, when the cannonading of Marengo had doubtless silenced his resentment against Marchesi, and when he thought, moreover, that the artist's penance for a wretched quibble had been long enough, the First Consul sent for him and again begged him to sing. This time Marchesi was polite and modest, and sang in an enchanting manner. After the concert, the First Consul applauded him, shook his hand warmly, and complimented him in the most affectionate tone. From that moment peace was concluded between the two powers, and Marchesi did nothing but chant the praises of the First Consul thereafter.

At this same concert, the First Consul was struck by the beauty of a famous songstress, Madame Grassini. He did not find her cruel, and at the end of a few hours the conqueror of Italy counted an additional conquest. She breakfasted next morning with the First Consul and General Berthier in the chamber of the former. General Berthier was commissioned to provide for the journey of Madame Grassini, who was sent to Paris, and attached to the concerts of the court. . . .

The First Consul left Milan June 24, and we re-entered France by way of Mont Cenis. We travelled with the greatest rapidity. The First Consul was received everywhere with an enthusiasm difficult to describe. Triumphal arches had been erected at the entrance of every town, and in each canton a deputation of notables came to harangue and compliment him. Long files of young girls, dressed in white and crowned with flowers, with flowers in their hands and throwing flowers into the First Consul's carriage, were his only escort, surrounding, following, and preceding him until he had passed, or, whenever he alighted, until he set foot to the ground. Hence this journey was throughout a perpetual festival. At Lyons it was a delirium: the whole city came out to meet him. He entered it in the midst of an immense crowd and the noisiest acclamations, and alighted at the Hôtel des Célestins. During the Terror, and when the Jacobins had wreaked their whole fury on the city of Lyons, which they had sworn to ruin, the fine edifices which ornamented the Place Belcour had been razed from top to bottom, and the hideous cripple Couthon had been the first to carry the sledge-hammer thither, at the head of the vilest rabble of the clubs. The First Consul detested the Jacobins, who, on their side, hated and feared him, and it was his most unceasing care to destroy their work, or, better, to raise up again the ruins with which they had covered France. He thought then, and rightly, that he could not better respond to the affection of the Lyonnese than by encouraging with all his might the reconstruction of the buildings on the Place Belcour, and he laid the first stone himself before his departure. The city of Dijon gave the First Consul a reception not less brilliant.

Between Villeneuve and Sens, at the descent of the bridge of Montereau, the eight horses plunged forward at a gallop, dragging the carriage very swiftly (the First Consul already travelled in royal style), and the screw of one of the front wheels came out. The people living along the road, witnessing this accident and foreseeing what would be the result of it, shouted with all their might to the postilions to stop; but the latter could not manage it. The carriage was rudely overturned. The First Consul received no damage; General Berthier's face was somewhat scratched by the broken glass of the windows; two footmen who were on the seat were thrown violently to a distance and rather badly bruised. The First Consul came out, or rather was hauled out through one of the doors; however, this accident did not stop him; he got at once into another carriage and reached Paris without any further mishap. He alighted at the Tuileries in the night of July 2; and when the news of his return had gone the rounds of Paris the next day, the entire population thronged the courts and garden. They crowded beneath the windows of the Pavilion of Flora, hoping to get a glimpse of the saviour of France, the liberator of Italy. In the evening there was neither rich nor poor who did not illuminate his mansion or his garret.

It was shortly after his arrival in Paris that the First Consul learned the death of General Kléber. Suleyman's poniard had immolated this great captain the same day that the cannon of Marengo brought low another hero of the army of Egypt. This assassination afflicted the First Consul very keenly. I witnessed this and can affirm it, and yet his calumniators have dared to say that he rejoiced at an event which, even to consider it merely on its political side, caused him the loss of a conquest which had cost him so many efforts and France so much expense and blood. Other wretches, still more infamous and stupid, have gone so far as to imagine and to circulate the rumor that the First Consul had commanded the assassination of his companion in arms, of him whom he had put in his own place at the head of the army of Egypt. I know of but one answer to make to such people, if any answer is needed: it is that they never knew the Emperor.

After his return the First Consul often went with his wife to Malmaison, where he sometimes remained for several days. At this period the valet on duty followed the carriage on horseback. One day as he was going to Paris, the First Consul perceived, when about a hundred paces from the château, that he had forgotten his snuff-box; he told me to go and find it. I wheeled and set off at a gallop, and having found the snuff-box on the First Consul's bureau, I set off at the same pace on his track. I did not come up with his carriage till we reached Ruelle. But just as I was about to do so, my horse's foot slipped on a pebble; he fell and threw me over into a ditch. The fall was severe; I remained stretched out on the spot, a shoulder dislocated and an arm badly bruised. The First Consul had his horses stopped at once, gave himself the orders necessary for taking me up, and indicated the attentions which must be given me in my condition; I was carried, in his presence, to the Ruelle barracks, and before continuing his route he assured himself that I was in no danger. The family doctor was summoned to Ruelle, where he set my shoulder and dressed my arm. From there I was taken, as gently as possible, to Malmaison.

The excellent Madame Bonaparte was so kind as to visit me, and had all possible attentions lavished on me.

On the day when I resumed my service, after my recovery, I was in the First Consul's antechamber just as he was leaving his cabinet. He came up to me and asked with much interest how I was. I answered him that, thanks to the care my excellent masters had caused to be given me, I was completely cured. "So much the better," said the First Consul to me. " Constant, make haste to regain your former strength. Continue to serve me well, and I will take care of you. Here," added he, putting three little papers in my hand, "this is to replenish your wardrobe;" and he passed on without listening to the thanks I was addressing to him with much emotion, far more for the benevolence and the interest he had deigned to display, than for his present; for I did not know in what that consisted. When he was gone, I unrolled my *chiffons;* they were three bank-notes of a thousand francs each! I was affected to tears by so perfect a kindness. It must be remembered that at this time the First Consul was not rich, although he was the first magistrate of the Republic. Hence the recollection of this generous deed still moves me profoundly even now. I do not know whether any one will be interested by details so personal to me; but I think them calculated to make known the character of the Emperor, so outrageously misapprehended, and his habitual manner with the people of his household; they will at the same time afford grounds for a conclusion as to whether the rigid economy he required in his family, and of which I shall myself have occasion to speak elsewhere, was, as it has been called, a sordid avarice, or not rather a rule of prudence which he willingly departed from when urged to do so by his kindness or his humanity.

I do not know whether my memory deceives me in making me set down here a circumstance that proves the esteem the First Consul had for the heroes of his army, and which he liked to display to them on every occasion. I was in his bedroom one day, at the usual hour for his toilet, and was on that day fulfilling the duties of first valet de chambre, Hambert being either absent or in some way hindered. There was no one in the apartment, apart from the attendants, except the brave and modest Colonel Gérard Lacuée, one of the First Consul's aides-de-camp. M. Jérôme Bonaparte, then hardly seventeen years old, was introduced. This young man was giving his family frequent subjects for complaint, and feared nobody but his brother Napoleon, who reprimanded, preached to, and scolded him as if he had been his son. There was a question at the time of making him a sailor less for the sake of a career than to remove him from the seductive temptations which the lofty fortune of his brother caused to spring up under his feet, and which he was very far from resisting. One can understand that it cost him something to relinquish pleasures so easy and so intoxicating to a young man. Hence he never failed to proclaim his inaptitude for the naval service on every occasion, going so far, it was said, as to allow himself to be rejected by the marine examiners, although, with a little study and good will, it would have been easy for him to answer their questions. However, the will of the First Consul had to be obeyed, and M. Jérôme was obliged to embark. On the day I am speaking of, after some minutes of conversation and of grumbling, always on the subject of the marine, M. Jérôme said to his brother: "Instead of sending me to die of ennui at sea, you ought to take me for aide-de-camp." "You *greenhorn!*" his brother responded briskly; "wait until a ball shall have ploughed up your face, and then we will see;" and at the same time he glanced toward Colonel Lacuée, who reddened and cast down his eyes like a young girl. To understand how flattering to him this answer was, one should know that his face was scarred by a ball. This brave colonel was killed in 1805, before Guntzbourg. The Emperor keenly regretted him. He was one of the most intrepid, most learned men in the army.

It was, I think, about this epoch that the First Consul was smitten with a strong passion for a young lady full of wit and grace, Madame D——. Madame Bonaparte, suspecting this intrigue, showed that she was jealous of it, and her husband did all he could to allay the conjugal suspicions. He waited until everybody was asleep before going to his mistress, and even carried precaution so far as to make the transit between the two apartments in night-drawers, minus either shoes or stockings. I once saw the day break before he returned, and, dreading scandal, I went, according to the orders given me by the First Consul himself, in case such a thing should happen, to warn Madame D——'s waiting-woman, so that, on her part, she could go and tell her mistress the hour. Hardly five minutes after this prudent warning had been given, I saw the First Consul returning in considerable agitation, of which I presently learned the cause: he had caught sight, as he was coming back, of one of Madame Bonaparte's women, who was spying on him through the window of a cabinet opening on the corridor. The First Consul, after a vigorous outburst against the curiosity of the fair sex, sent me to the young *scout* of the enemy's camp, to notify her of the order to hold her tongue if she did not want to be dismissed, and not to repeat her indiscretion in future. I do not know whether he did not add some gentler argument to these terrible threats, in order to *buy* her silence; but whether through fear or favor, she had the good sense to keep quiet. Nevertheless the successful lover, fearing some new surprise, ordered me to hire a little house in the Allée des Veuves, where he and Madame D—— met from time to time.

This was the way in which the First Consul always acted toward his wife. He was full of consideration for her, and took every imaginable means of preventing his infidelities from reaching her knowledge. Moreover, these passing infidelities detracted nothing from his tenderness for her, and although other women may have inspired him with love, none had his confidence and friendship to the same extent as Madame Bonaparte. It is the same with the Emperor's severity and brutality toward women as it is with the thousand and one other calumnies of which he was the object. He was not always courtly, but no one ever saw him coarse, and however singular this observation may appear after what I have just narrated, he professed the greatest veneration for a well-conducted woman, praised faithful marriages, and did not like indecency either in morals or language. Although he had several secret liaisons, it was not his fault that they were not carefully concealed.

CHAPTER VI

The *infernal machine* — The most disabled of architects — The happy chance — Precipitation and delay alike salutary — Hortense slightly wounded — Fright of Madame Murat and its consequences — Germain the coachman — How he got the name of Cæsar — Inexactitudes respecting him — Banquet offered him by five hundred cabmen — The author at the Feydeau during the explosion — Alarm — Runs without a hat — Inflexible sentinels — The First Consul re-enters the Tuileries — The First Consul's remarks to Constant — The consular guard — The First Consul's household placed under surveillance — Unalterable fidelity — The Jacobins innocent and the Royalists guilty — Grand review — Joy of soldiers and people — Universal peace — Public rejoicings and improvised feasts — Reception of the military corps and of Lord Cornwallis — Military luxury — The *Regent* diamond.

THE 3d Nivose, year IX. (December 21, 1800), the Opera gave, *by command*, Haydn's *Creation*, and the First Consul had announced that he would go with all his family to hear the magnificent oratorio. He dined that day with Madame Bonaparte, her daughter, and Generals Rapp, Lauriston, Lannes, and Berthier. I was just then on duty; but as the First Consul was going to the Opera, I thought my presence at the château would be superfluous, and determined to go for my own part to the Feydeau, where Madame Bonaparte provided us with a box situated beneath her own. After dinner, which the

First Consul expedited with his usual promptness, he rose from table, followed by his officers, excepting General Rapp, who remained with Mesdames Josephine and Hortense. Toward seven o'clock the First Consul entered a carriage along with MM. Lannes, Berthier, and Lauriston, to go to the Opera; on reaching the middle of the rue Saint-Nicaise, the outrider who preceded the carriage found the way obstructed by what seemed to be an abandoned cart, on top of which a cask was strongly attached by cords. The head of the escort had this cart shoved alongside the houses on the right, and the First Consul's coachman, who had become impatient at this brief delay, whipped up his horses, which started off like a flash. It was not more than two seconds after they started when the barrel on the cart exploded with a frightful noise. None of the escort and suite of the First Consul were killed, but several received injuries. The fate of those who, either living in the street or passing through it, found themselves near the horrible machine was much more afflicting; more than twenty of them perished, and more than sixty were grievously wounded. M. Trepsat, architect, had a thigh broken; the First Consul afterwards decorated him and appointed him architect of the Invalides, saying to him that he had long been the most disabled of architects. All the window panes in the Tuileries were broken; several houses fell down; all those on the rue Saint-Nicaise and even some on adjacent streets were badly damaged.[1] Some of the debris flew as far as the house of Consul Cambacérès. The windows of the First Consul's carriage were broken in pieces.

By the luckiest of chances, the carriages of the suite, which were to have been immediately behind that of the First Consul, were far enough behind, and this is why: After dinner, Madame Bonaparte had sent for a shawl to wear to the Opera; when it was brought, General Rapp gayly criticised the color of it and urged her to choose another. Madame Bonaparte defended her shawl, and said to the Gen-

---

[1] The prefect of police sent a report to the consuls in which, after having recounted the details of this frightful event, he gave the list of killed and wounded. There were eight of the former and twenty-eight of the latter.

"Forty-six horses," adds the report, "were extremely damaged."

"The damage to real estate is estimated at the sum of 40,845 francs."

"To furniture, at 123,645 francs."

"The national buildings are not comprised in this estimate."

"The horse, the remains of the vehicle, and several portions of the casks were taken to the prefecture."

"These remains have been scrupulously collected. A description of the horse has been drawn up with the greatest care."

M. Dubois had thought it his duty to end his report by a compliment to the First Consul, in which there was, notwithstanding, considerable truth; viz., that the attempt of the 3d Nivose had redoubled the attachment of the French to the head of the State. Here is the last paragraph but one of the report:

"From the very first moment of the explosion an inquest was made on the spot. Declarations were received; and even amidst the cries of anguish uttered by the wretched victims of the most atrocious of outrages, the heart could still experience an agreeable sensation; these unfortunates forgot themselves to think only of the First Consul; it was for him that they demanded vengeance."

eral that he knew as much about attacking a toilet as she did about attacking a redoubt. This friendly discussion was carried on for some time in the same tone. During this interval, the First Consul, who never waited, started in advance, and the miserable assassins who were authors of the plot set off their infernal machine. If the First Consul's coachman had been in less of a hurry, and had delayed only two seconds longer, it would have been all up with his master; if, on the contrary, Madame Bonaparte had made haste to follow her husband, it would have been all over with her and her suite; it was, in fact this momentary delay which saved her life and her daughter's, that of Madame Murat, her sister-in-law, and those of all who were to accompany her. The carriage containing these ladies, instead of being in line with that of the First Consul, had come out on the Place du Carrousel at the moment when the machine exploded; its windows were broken also. Madame Bonaparte received nothing but a great fright; Mademoiselle Hortense was slightly wounded in the face by a splinter of glass; Madame Caroline Murat, who was then far advanced in pregnancy, was seized by such a fear that they were obliged to take her back to the château. This catastrophe had a great effect also on the health of her child. I have been told that Prince Achille Murat is still subject to frequent attacks of epilepsy. It is known that the First Consul went on to the Opera, where he was received with indescribable acclamations, and where the calmness imprinted on his countenance contrasted strongly with the pallor and agitation of Madame Bonaparte, who had trembled, not for herself, but for him.

The coachman who thus fortunately conducted the First Consul was called Germain; he had gone with him to Egypt, and during an affray had killed an Arab with his own hands under the eyes of the Commander-in-Chief, who, amazed at his courage, had exclaimed: "The devil! there's a hero! He is a Cæsar!" The name stuck to him. It has been pretended that this worthy man was drunk at the time of the explosion. That is an error which his very address in this circumstance contradicts in a positive manner. Whenever the First Consul, after becoming Emperor, went out incognito in Paris, it was Cæsar who drove him, but never in livery. It will be found in the *Memorial of Saint Helena* that the Emperor, speaking of Cæsar, says that he was in a state of complete intoxication; that he took the detonation for a salute of artillery, and did not know until the next morning what had happened. All that is inexact, and the Emperor had been badly informed with respect to his coachman. Cæsar drove the First Consul very fast because the latter had charged him to do so, and because he thought, for his own part, that it concerned his honor not to be late on account of the obstacle interposed by the infernal machine before the explosion. I saw Cæsar the evening of the event, who was perfectly *recent*, and who related to me some of the events I have just told. Some days afterward, four or five hundred Parisian hackmen clubbed together and offered him a magnificent dinner, at twenty-four francs a head.

While the infernal conspiracy was being carried out and costing the lives of so great a number of innocent citizens, yet without attaining the end proposed by the assassins, I was, as I have said, at the Feydeau theatre, where I was preparing to enjoy at leisure one evening's liberty and the pleasure of seeing a play, a thing for which I have all my life had a real passion. But hardly was I squarely installed in the box, when the doorkeeper entered suddenly and in the greatest disorder: "Monsieur Constant," cried she, "they say the First Consul has just been blown up; everybody has heard a frightful noise; they declare that he is dead." These terrible words were like a thunderclap to me; not knowing what I was about, and not thinking to take my hat, I ran like a madman to the château. I saw no extraordinary commotion while passing through the rue Vinvienne and the Palais-Royal, but in the rue Saint-Honoré the tumult was extreme. I saw them carrying on stretchers some dead bodies and some wounded who had at first been sheltered in neighboring houses in the rue Saint-Nicaise; a thousand groups had assembled, and were cursing with one voice the still unknown authors of this execrable attempt. Some were accusing the Jacobins, who, three months earlier, had put poniards in the hands of Ceracchi, Aréna, and Topino-Lebrun; while others, though not so many, named the aristocrats, the Royalists, as alone guilty of this atrocity. I lent no further ear to these various accusations than the time required to force my way through a dense and enormous crowd; as soon as I could I resumed my course, and in two seconds was at the Carrousel. I sprang toward the wicket, but at the same moment the two sentinels crossed bayonets on my breast. It was of no use for me to cry that I was the First Consul's valet de chambre; my bare head, my distracted air, the disorder of my whole person and of my ideas, seemed suspicious to them, and they obstinately and most energetically refused to let me enter. I then begged them to summon the concierge of the château; he came, and I was introduced, or rather I precipitated myself into the château, where I learned what had just occurred. Soon after, the First Consul arrived and was at once surrounded by all his officers and his entire household; there was not a soul present who was not in the greatest anxiety. When the First Consul alighted from the carriage, he seemed very calm and was smiling; he even seemed amused. On entering the vestibule, he said to his officers, rubbing his hands: "Eh well! gentlemen, we have had a fine escape!" The latter were shuddering with wrath and indignation. Then he entered the large salon on the ground-floor, where a great number of councillors of state, and officials, were already assembled; they had barely commenced to offer him their congratulations when he began to speak, and in a tone so loud that his voice could be heard outside the salon. We were told after this council that he had had a lively altercation with M. Fouché, minister of police, whom he had reproached with his ignorance of this conspiracy, and that he had loudly accused the Jacobins of being the authors of it.

When he was going to bed that evening, the First Consul laughingly asked me if I had been frightened. "More than you were, General," I answered; and I told him how I had learned the bad news at the Feydeau, and how I had run without a hat to the wicket of the Carrousel, where the sentinels had been determined not to let me enter. He was amused by the oaths and unflattering epithets with which they had accompanied their refusal, and ended by saying to me: "After all, my dear Constant, you must bear them no ill will for it; they were only doing their duty. They were honest men, on whom I can rely." The fact is that the consular guard was not less loyal at this epoch than when it afterwards received the title of imperial guard. At the first rumor of the danger incurred by the First Consul, all the soldiers of this faithful troop had spontaneously assembled in the court of the Tuileries.

After this fatal catastrophe, which disturbed all France and put so many families in mourning, the entire police force was actively employed in searching for its authors. The household of the First Consul was at once placed under surveillance. We were incessantly spied upon, without our suspecting it. All our proceedings, all our visits, all our comings and goings, were known; and likewise our friends and connections, and we ourselves were under inspection. But such was the devotion of each and all of us to the person of the First Consul, so great was the affection he could inspire in those about him, that not one of those in his service was suspected for an instant of being implicated in this infamous attempt. Neither then, nor in any affair of the sort, were the people of his own household ever compromised, and never has the name of the least of the Emperor's servants been found mixed up in criminal schemes against a life so dear and glorious.

The minister of police suspected the Royalists of this outrage. The First Consul accused nothing but the conscience of the Jacobins, heavy enough already, it must be owned, with crimes as odious. One hundred and thirty of these men, the most prominent of the party, were transported merely on suspicion and without trial. It is well known that the discovery, trial, and execution of Saint-Régent and Carbon, the real criminals, proved that the suspicions of the minister were better founded than those of the head of the State.

The 4th Nivose, at noon, the First Consul held a grand review on the Place du Carrousel. An innumerable crowd of citizens were assembled there to see him and testify their affection for his person and their indignation against enemies who dared attack him only by assassination. Hardly had he turned his horse toward the first line of grenadiers of the consular guard, when the air was rent with countless shouts. He rode very slowly through all the ranks, exhibiting much feeling, and responding by several simple and affectionate salutes to this outburst of popular joy. The cries of "Long live Bonaparte! Long live the First Consul!" did not cease until after he had returned to his apartments.

The conspirators who persevered with such bitterness in their attempts on the life of the First Consul, could have chosen no time more unfavorable to their schemes than 1800 and 1801; for at that period the First Consul was loved not only for his great military achievements, but also, and above all, for the hopes of peace that he gave to France. These hopes were speedily realized. At the first rumor that peace had been concluded with Austria, the majority of the inhabitants of Paris assembled underneath the windows of the Pavilion of Flora. Benedictions and cries of gratitude and joy resounded there; then musicians assembled to serenade the head of the State, ended by forming into orchestras, and dancing was kept up all night. I have never seen anything more singular and joyful than this improvised festival.

And when, in October, the Peace of Amiens having been concluded with England, France found herself delivered from all the wars she had sustained for so many years and at the price of so many sacrifices, no idea can be formed of the transports which broke forth on every side. The decrees ordaining either the disarmament of war vessels or the reorganization of strongholds on a peace footing, were welcomed as pledges of happiness and security. On the day of the reception of Lord Cornwallis, the English ambassador, the First Consul displayed the greatest pomp. "We must show these haughty Britons," he said the evening before, "that we are not reduced to beggary." The fact is that the English, before touching French soil, had expected to find nothing but ruins, dearth, and poverty in all directions. France had been described to them in the most sombre colors, and they imagined themselves about to land in Barbary. Their surprise was extreme when they saw how many evils the First Consul had repaired in so short a time, and the improvements he still proposed to make. They spread the news in their own country of what they called the First Consul's prodigies, and thousands of their compatriots hastened over to see and judge them with their own eyes. At the moment when Lord Cornwallis entered the hall of ambassadors with his suite, these Englishmen must have been struck by the aspect of the First Consul, surrounded by his two colleagues, the entire diplomatic corps, and an already brilliant military court. Amidst all these rich uniforms his own was remarkable for its simplicity; but the diamond called the *Regent*, which had been pawned by the Directory, and redeemed within a few days by the First Consul, glittered in the hilt of his sword.

CHAPTER VII

The King of Etruria — Madame de Montesson — The monarch not industrious — Conversation about him between the First and Second Consuls — A joke about the return of the Bourbons — Intelligence and conversation of Don Louis — Singular traits of economy — A present worth a hundred thousand écus and a royal gratuity of *six francs* — The severity of Don Louis toward his attendants — Hauteur towards a diplomat, and disgust for serious occupations — The King of Etruria installed by the future King of Naples — The Queen of Etruria — Her lack of taste in dress — Her good sense — Her kindness — Her fidelity in the fulfilment of her duties — Magnificent fêtes at the house of M. de Talleyrand — At the house of Madame de Montesson — At that of the minister of the interior on the anniversary of the battle of Marengo — Departure of Their Majesties.

IN May, 1801, the Prince of Tuscany, Don Louis I., whom the First Consul had just made King of Etruria, arrived in Paris to go from there into his new kingdom. He travelled under the name of the Count of Leghorn, with his wife, the Infanta of Spain, Marie Louise, third daughter of Charles IV. Notwithstanding the incognito he seemed to wish to maintain, judging from the modest title he had assumed, possibly on account of the insignificant appearance of his little court, he was received and treated at the Tuileries in kingly style. This prince was in rather bad health and suffered, so they said, from epilepsy. He had been lodged at the hotel of the Spanish Embassy, formerly the hotel Montesson, and he had begged Madame de Montesson, who lived next door, to allow him to restore a way of communication long since closed up. He took great pleasure, as the Queen of Etruria did also, in the company of this lady, the widow of the Duke of Orleans, and spent several consecutive hours there almost every day. A Bourbon himself, he doubtless liked to hear all the details that could be given him by a person who had lived at their court and in the intimacy of their family, to which she belonged herself by ties which were none the less legitimate and avowed for being officially unrecognized. Madame de Montesson received at her house all the most distinguished people in Paris. She had reunited the remains of social circles formerly most sought after, and which the Revolution had dispersed. A friend of Madame Bonaparte, she was liked and venerated by the First Consul, who desired that people should think and speak well of him in the most noble and most elegant salon of the capital. Moreover, he relied on the souvenirs and the exquisite tone of this lady to establish in his own palace and society, of which he already dreamed of making *a court*, the usages and etiquette practised in those of sovereigns.

The King of Etruria was not a great worker, and, in this respect, he did not greatly please the First Consul, who could not endure idleness. I heard him one day, in conversation with his colleague,

M. Cambacérès, treat his royal protégé (absent, as there is no need to say) very severely. "There is a good prince," said he, "who does not concern himself much about his very dear and beloved subjects. He spends his time cackling with old women, to whom he says aloud a great many good things about me, while he grumbles in an undertone at having to owe his elevation to the head of this cursed French Republic. That fellow occupies himself with nothing but promenades, hunting, balls, and plays." "They say," observed M. Cambacérès, "that you intended to disgust the French with kings by showing them such a specimen, just as the Spartans disgusted their children with drunkenness by making them see a slave drunk." — "Not at all, not at all, my dear fellow," returned the First Consul; "I am not anxious to disgust them with royalty; but the sojourn of His Majesty the King of Etruria will dissatisfy that considerable number of worthy people who are laboring to revive the taste for the Bourbons."

Don Louis did not deserve, perhaps, to be treated so severely, though, it must be owned, he was endowed with very little wit and still less charm. When he dined at the Tuileries he could not answer the simplest questions put to him by the First Consul without embarrassment; beyond rain and fine weather, horses, dogs, and other subjects of equal importance, there was nothing to which he could give a satisfactory response. The Queen, his wife, often made signs to put him on the right track, and even whispered to him what he ought to do or say; but that only made his absolute lack of presence of mind more shocking. People in general made a good deal of fun at his expense, but they took care, however, not to do it in the presence of the First Consul, who would not have suffered a failure in respect toward a guest to whom he himself showed much.

During his stay the First Consul sent him several times some magnificent presents, Savonnerie carpets, Lyons stuffs, Sèvres porcelains. On such occasions, His Majesty refused nothing, unless it were to give some trifling gratuity to the bearers of all these precious objects. One day they brought him a vase of the greatest value (it cost, I think, a hundred thousand écus); it took a dozen workmen to place it in the King's apartment. Their work finished, the men were waiting for His Majesty to testify to them his satisfaction, and flattered themselves on beholding him display a truly royal generosity. However, time slipped by and they did not see the hoped-for recompense arriving. At last they addressed themselves to one of the chamberlains, and begged him to lay their just claims before the King of Etruria. His Majesty, who was still in ecstasies over the beauty of the gift and the munificence of the First Consul, could not have been more surprised than he was at such a demand. This was a present; then what he had to do was to receive, not to give. It was only after a good deal of urging that the chamberlain obtained for each of these workmen an écu of six francs, which the good fellows refused.

The members of the Prince's suite claimed that to this exaggerated aversion to expense, he joined an extreme severity toward them. However, the first of these two dispositions probably induced the attendants of the King of Etruria to exaggerate the second. Masters who are much too economical never fail to be adjudged severe, and at the same time to be severely judged by their servants. It is perhaps (be it said in passing) on account of judgments of this nature that certain persons have credited the calumnious report which represented the Emperor as often inclined to thrash people; and yet the economy of the Emperor Napoleon was nothing but a love of the most perfect order in his household expenses. What is certain about the King of Etruria is that he did not really feel either all the enthusiasm or all the gratitude that he professed for the First Consul. The latter had more than one proof of this; so much for his sincerity. As for his talent for governing and reigning, the First Consul said on rising to M. Cambacérès, in the same interview of which I just now recounted a few words, that the Spanish ambassador complained of the haughtiness of the Prince towards him, of his complete ignorance, and of the disgust with which every sort of serious occupation inspired him. Such was the king who was to govern a part of Italy. It was General Murat who installed him in his kingdom, without suspecting, according to all appearance, that a throne was reserved for him also, within a few leagues of that on which he had just seated Don Louis.

The Queen of Etruria was, in the judgment of the First Consul, much better and more prudent than her august spouse. This princess shone neither by grace nor elegance; she had herself dressed in the morning for the whole day, and promenaded in the garden with a diadem, or flowers on her head, and in a robe with a train that swept the sand of the alleys. More often than not she carried in her arms one of her children still in swaddling-clothes and subject to all the inconveniences of such a baby. One can understand that by evening Her Majesty's toilet was somewhat in disorder. Besides, she was far from being pretty, and had not the manners befitting her rank. But, which certainly more than compensated for all this, she was very good, very much loved by her attendants, and fulfilled scrupulously all her duties as wife and mother; hence the First Consul, who esteemed the domestic virtues so highly, professed the highest and most sincere esteem for her.

There was a constant succession of fêtes during the whole month that Their Majesties stayed in Paris. M. de Talleyrand offered them one at Neuilly of admirable opulence and splendor. I was on duty, and I attended the First Consul there. The château and the park were illuminated by a brilliant profusion of colored glass. There was a concert in the first place, at the end of which the back of the hall was lifted like the curtain at a theatre, and displayed the principal place in Florence, the ducal palace, a fountain of gushing water, and the Tuscans indulging in the games and dances of their country and chanting couplets in honor of their sovereigns. M. de Talleyrand came to beg Their Majesties to deign to mingle with their subjects; and they had hardly set foot in the garden when they found themselves as it were in fairyland: luminous bombs, rockets, Bengal lights, went off in every direction and in every form; colonnades, triumphal arches, and flaming palaces rose, were eclipsed, and succeeded each other without a break. Several tables were laid in the apartments and in the gardens, and all the spectators were able to seat themselves in succession. Finally a magnificent ball worthily crowned this evening of enchantments; it was opened by the King of Etruria and Madame Leclerc (Pauline Borghese).

Madame de Montesson also offered Their Majesties a ball, at which all the family of the First Consul were present. But of all these diversions, that which I have remembered best is the truly marvellous soirée given by M. Chaptal, minister of the interior. The day he selected was the 14th of June, anniversary of the battle of Marengo. After the concert, the play, the ball, a new representation of the city and the inhabitants of Florence, a splendid supper was served in the garden, under military tents, decorated with flags, sheaves of arms, and trophies. Each lady was accompanied and served at table by an officer in uniform. When the King and Queen of Etruria came out of their tent a balloon was sent up, which carried into the air the name of MARENGO in letters of fire.

Their Majesties wished to visit the principal public establishments before departing. They went to the Conservatory, to a session of the Institute, where they looked as if they comprehended very little, and to the Mint, where a medal was struck in their honor. M. Chaptal received the thanks of the Queen for the manner in which he had received and treated the noble guests, as a savant of the Institute, as a minister in his own house, and in the visits they had made to the different establishments of the capital. The day before his departure, the King had a long secret interview with the First Consul. I do not know what took place; but neither of them looked satisfied on coming out of it. Nevertheless Their Majesties must, on the whole, have carried away with them the most favorable idea of the reception accorded them.

CHAPTER VIII

A madman's passion for Mademoiselle Hortense — Marriage of M. Louis Bonaparte and Hortense — Vexations — Character of M. Louis — Atrocious calumny against the Emperor and his stepdaughter — Inclination of Hortense before her marriage — General Duroc marries Mademoiselle Hervas d' Alménara — Portrait of this lady — The broken piano and the smashed watch — Marriage and sadness — Misfortunes of Hortense before, during, and after her grandeurs — The First Consul's journey to Lyons — Fêtes and felicitations — Soldiers of the army of Egypt — The Pope's legate — The deputies of the council — Death of the Archbishop of Milan — Occasional verses — Poets of the Empire — The First Consul and his writing master — M. l'Abbé Dupuis, librarian of Malmaison.

IN all the fêtes offered by the First Consul to Their Majesties, the King and Queen of Etruria, Mademoiselle Hortense had shone with that splendor of youth and grace which made her the pride of her mother and the most beautiful ornament of the budding court of the First Consul.

About this time she inspired the most violent passion in a gentleman of very good family, but whose brain was already, I think, somewhat deranged before he took this foolish love into his head. This unfortunate incessantly prowled about Malmaison; and as soon as Mademoiselle came out, he would run to the side of the carriage and, with the liveliest demonstrations of affection, throw flowers, locks of his hair, and verses of his composition in through the door. Whenever he met Mademoiselle on foot, he would throw himself on his knees before her with a thousand passionate gestures, and call her by the most touching names. In spite of everybody, he followed her even into the court of the château, and gave himself up to all his folly. At first, Mademoiselle, being young and gay, amused herself with the affectations of her adorer. She read the verses he sent her, and gave them to the ladies who accompanied to read also. Such poetry was calculated to produce laughter; hence she found no fault with it at first; but after these first transports of gaiety, Mademoiselle Hortense, who, like her mother, was good and charming, never failed to say, with a compassionate look and accent: "That poor man is very much to be pitied!" In the end, however, the importunities of this wretched madman multiplied so that they became insupportable. In Paris he would stand at the door of the theatres whenever Mademoiselle Hortense was to go there, and prostrate himself at her feet, supplicating, weeping, laughing, and gesticulating all at once. This spectacle amused the crowd too much to continue to amuse Mademoiselle de Beauharnais any longer; Carrat was ordered to get rid of the unfortunate man, who was, I think, placed in an asylum.

Mademoiselle would have been only too happy if she had never known love except through the burlesque effects it produced in a deranged brain. In that case she would have seen it only on its comic and amusing side. But the moment came when she had to feel all the sorrow and bitterness there is in the disappointments of this passion. In January, 1802, she was married to M. Louis Bonaparte, brother of the First Consul. This alliance was suitable as far as age was concerned. M. Louis was hardly twenty-four, and Mademoiselle de Beauharnais not more than eighteen; and yet it was the source of long and interminable vexations to both of them. M. Louis was, however, good and sensible, full of benevolence and wit, studious and a friend of letters, like all his brothers except one; but his health was poor, he was ill almost constantly, and had a melancholy disposition. All of the First Consul's brothers resembled him more or less, and M. Louis more than the others, especially in the days of the consulate, and before the Emperor Napoleon grew fat. At the same time, not one of his brothers had that incisive and imposing glance, and that rapid and imperious gesture which came to him at first by instinct and afterwards through the habit of command. M. Louis had peaceful and modest tastes. It has been claimed that at the time of his marriage he had a keen attachment for a person whose name could not be discovered and is, I believe, a mystery still. Mademoiselle Hortense was extremely pretty, with a charming and mobile countenance. Moreover, she was full of grace, talents, and affability; benevolent and lovable like her mother, she had not that excessive facility, or, better, that feebleness of character which sometimes detracted from Madame Bonaparte. Yet this is the woman whom the evil rumors spread abroad by wretched libellers have so outrageously calumniated! One's gorge rises with disgust and indignation when such revolting absurdities are told and repeated. If these worthy fabricators are to be believed, the First Consul must have seduced his wife's daughter before giving her in marriage to his own brother. One has only to put such a thing into words to make its falsity comprehended. I know the love affairs of the Emperor better than anybody; in that sort of clandestine connections he dreaded scandal and hated the boastings of vice, and I can affirm on my honor that the infamous desires which have been attributed to him never germinated in his heart. Like all those, and even better than all those who approached Mademoiselle de Beauharnais, because he knew his stepdaughter more intimately, he had the tenderest affection for her; but this sentiment was entirely paternal, and Mademoiselle responded to it with that respectful fear which a well-bred girl experiences in the presence of her father. She could have obtained all she desired from her stepfather if extreme timidity had not prevented her from asking; but, instead of addressing herself directly to him, she would in the first place have recourse to the secretary and attendants of the Emperor. Would she have acted in this way if the evil rumors scattered by her enemies and those of the Emperor had had the least foundation?

Before this marriage Mademoiselle had an inclination for General Duroc. He was barely thirty, well made, and a favorite of the head of the State, who, knowing him to be prudent and reserved, had entrusted several important missions to him. An aide-de-camp of the First Consul, a general of division, and governor of the Tuileries, he had long been living in intimate familiarity with Malmaison and the home of the First Consul. During his obligatory absences he kept up a regular correspondence with Mademoiselle Hortense, and yet the indifference with which he allowed her marriage with M. Louis proves that he shared but feebly in the affection which he had inspired. It is certain that he might have had Mademoiselle de Beauharnais for his wife if he had been willing to accept the terms on which the First Consul offered him his stepdaughter's hand. But he expected something better, and his usual prudence failed at the moment when it might have shown him a future easy to foresee, and calculated to crown the wishes of an ambition more exalted than his own. Hence he flatly refused, and the entreaties of Madame Bonaparte, which had already shaken her husband, took decidedly the upper hand. Madame Bonaparte, who found herself not treated in a very friendly manner by the brothers of the First Consul, sought to create a support for herself in this family against the troubles constantly accumulated around her by those who sought to deprive her of her husband's affection. It was with this end in view that she did all she could to bring about a marriage between her daughter and one of her brothers-in-law.

General Duroc probably repented in the end of the precipitancy of his refusal when crowns began to rain into the august family with which he might have allied himself; when he saw Naples, Spain, Westphalia, Upper Italy, the duchies of Parma, Lucca, etc., becoming the appanages of the new imperial dynasty; when the beautiful and gracious Hortense herself, who had loved him so much, ascended the throne which she would have been so happy to share with the object of her first affections. As for him, he married Mademoiselle Hervas d'Alménara, daughter of the banker of the court of Spain, a little woman, very brown, very thin, and not very graceful; but, on the other hand, of the most vixenish, haughtiest, most exacting and capricious temper. As she was to have an enormous dowry in marriage, the First Consul asked her hand for his first aide-de-camp. I have been told that Madame Duroc forgot herself so far as to beat her servants, and even to fly into the strangest passions with people in nowise dependent on her. When M. Dubois came to tune her piano, if she was unfortunately present, as she could not endure the noise required by this operation, she would drive the tuner away with the utmost violence. In one of these singular fits, she one day broke all the keys of her instrument; at another time, M. Mugnier, clockmaker to the Emperor, and the first artist in Paris of his profession, with M. Bréguet, having brought her a very costly watch, which had been ordered by the Duchess de Frioul herself, this bijou did not please her, and in her rage she threw the watch on the floor, began to dance on it, and broke it into pieces in M. Mugnier's presence. She would never pay for it, and the Marshal was obliged to settle the bill himself. Thus the mistaken refusal of General Duroc and the not very disinterested calculations of Madame Bonaparte caused the misery of two households.

For the rest, the portrait I have just drawn, and which I think true, although not much flattered, is simply that of a young woman spoiled like an only daughter, harsh-tempered like a Spaniard, and brought up with that indulgence and even with that absolute negligence which injures the education of all the compatriots of Mademoiselle d'Alménara. Time has calmed this vivacity of youth, and Madame the Duchess de Frioul has since given an example of the most tender devotion to all her duties, and of a great strength of soul in the frightful misfortunes she has had to endure. For the loss of her husband, most sorrowful though it was, glory had at least some consolations to offer to the widow of the grand marshal. But when a young girl, sole heiress to a great name and an illustrious title, is suddenly carried away by death from all the hopes and all the love of her mother, who would dare to speak to her of consolations? If there could be any (which I do not believe), it must needs be the remembrance of the cares and tenderness lavished to the end by a maternal heart. This memory, the bitterness of which is mingled with a certain sweetness, cannot be lacking to Madame the Duchess de Frioul.

The religious ceremony of the marriage took place January 7, in the house on the rue de la Victoire, and the marriage of General Murat with Mademoiselle Caroline Bonaparte, which had only been contracted before the officer of the civil law, was consecrated the same day. The two spouses (M. Louis and his wife) were very melancholy: the latter wept bitterly during the ceremony, and her tears were not stanched afterward. She was far from seeking her husband's eyes, and on his side, he was too proud and too embittered to pursue her with his attentions. The good Josephine did all she could to unite them. Feeling that this union which commenced so badly was her work, she would have liked to reconcile her own interest, or at least what she considered such, with the happiness of her daughter. But her efforts, like her advice and entreaties, accomplished nothing. I have a hundred times seen Madame Louis Bonaparte seek the solitude of her own apartment and the bosom of a friend to shed her tears there. They escaped from her even in the salon of the First Consul, where one sorrowfully beheld this brilliant and gay young woman, who had often done the honors and relaxed the stiffness of etiquette so graciously, now retiring into a corner, or into the embrasure of a window, with some person in whom she trusted, to confide her troubles to her. During this interview, from which she emerged with red and humid eyes, her husband kept himself, pensive and taciturn, at the opposite end of the salon.

People have greatly censured the errors of Her Majesty the Queen of Holland, and all that has been said or written against this princess bears the marks of gross exaggeration. So lofty a fortune drew all eyes upon her and excited a jealous malevolence; and yet those who have envied her would not have failed to pity themselves if they had been put in her place on condition of sharing her afflictions. The misfortunes of Queen Hortense began with her life. Her father dead on the revolutionary scaffold, her mother thrown into prison, she found herself, when yet a child, isolated and without other support than the fidelity of the former servants of the family. Her brother, the noble and worthy Prince Eugène, had been obliged, they say, to apprentice himself to a trade; she had some years of happiness, or at least of repose, during the time that she was confided to the motherly cares of Madame Campan, and also after leaving her boarding school. But fate was now released from obligations: her inclinations thwarted, an unhappy marriage opened for her a new train of misfortunes. The death of her first son, whom the Emperor had intended to adopt, and whom he had designated as his successor to the Empire, the divorce of her mother, the cruel death of her dearest friend, Madame de Brocq,[1] who fell down a precipice before her eyes, the overthrow of the imperial throne which caused her to lose her title and her rank as queen, a loss which she felt much less sensibly than she did the misfortune of him whom she regarded as her father; finally, the continual annoyances of her domestic disputes, the vexatious trial, and her sorrow at beholding her eldest son taken from her by her husband's order; such have been the principal catastrophes of a life which one might have thought destined to much happiness.

On the day after the marriage of Mademoiselle Hortense, the First Consul started for Lyons, where the deputies of the Cisalpine Republic, assembled for the election of a president, were awaiting him.

---

[1] Mademoiselle Adèle Anguié, sister of Madame la Marechale Ney, married General de Brocq, grand marshal of the court of Holland. Her Majesty Queen Hortense, being at the baths of Aix in Savoy, took pleasure in making excursions with her friend, on the most craggy mountains. On one of these they found a torrent in their path, bridged only by a fragile plank. The Queen, conducted by her equerry, crossed first, and was turning to encourage Madame de Brocq, when she saw her slip and fall headlong down the precipice. At this horrible sight the Queen uttered piercing shrieks. But her despair did not deprive her of presence of mind. She gave orders and multiplied prayers and promises. But all aid was useless. The body had been shattered in the fall, and a certain time elapsed before the cold and mutilated corpse could be withdrawn from the water. These sad remains were brought back to Saint-Leu, all of whose inhabitants were plunged into profound grief. Madame de Brocq's duty was to distribute the numerous charities of the Queen. She merited the tears called forth by her death.

Everywhere along his passage he was received amidst fêtes and by the felicitations which people were eager to express to him on the miraculous manner in which he had escaped from the plots of his enemies. This journey did not differ in any way from those he made afterward as emperor. On arriving in Lyons, he received the visit of all the authorities of the constituted bodies, deputations from the neighboring departments, and members of the Italian council. Madame Bonaparte, who went on this journey, accompanied her husband to the theatre, and shared with him the honors of the magnificent fête offered him by the city of Lyons. The day when the council elected and proclaimed the First Consul president of the Italian republic, he reviewed the troops of the garrison on the Place des Brotteaux, and recognized several soldiers of the army of Egypt, with whom he talked for some time. On all these occasions the First Consul wore the same costume which he did at Malmaison, and which I have described elsewhere. He rose early, mounted his horse, and visited the public works, among others those of the Place Belcour, the first stone of which he had laid on his return from Italy, He went through the Brotteaux, inspecting and examining everything, and, always indefatigable, worked on coming in again as if he had been at the Tuileries. He seldom changed his dress; that only happening when he received the authorities at his table or the principal inhabitants. He received all requests kindly. Before leaving he presented the mayor of the city with a scarf of honor, and the Pope's legate with a rich snuff-box ornamented with his portrait. The deputies of the council also received presents, and were not backward in returning them. They offered Madame Bonaparte some magnificent ornaments in diamonds and precious stones and the most costly jewels.

The First Consul, on arriving in Lyons, had been keenly afflicted by the sudden death of a worthy prelate whom he had known in his first Italian campaign. The Archbishop of Milan had come to Lyons, in spite of his great age, to see the First Consul whom he loved tenderly; so much so that in conversation the venerable old man had been heard to address the young General as "my son." The peasants of Pavia having revolted, because they had been fanaticized by being told that the French wished to destroy their religion, the Archbishop of Milan, to prove to them that their fears were groundless, had often shown himself in the carriage with General Bonaparte.

This prelate had stood the journey perfectly. M. de Talleyrand, who had arrived in Lyons some days before the First Consul, had given a dinner to the Cisalpine deputies and the principal notabilities of the city. The Archbishop of Milan was on his right. Hardly seated, and as he was bending toward M. de Talleyrand to speak to him, he died in his chair.

January 12, the city of Lyons offered to the First

Consul and Madame Bonaparte a magnificent ball, preceded by a concert. At eight o'clock in the evening, the three mayors, accompanied by the commissioners of the fête, came to seek their guests at the government palace. I seem still to see that immense amphitheatre, magnificently decorated, and illuminated by chandeliers and candles without number; those seats draped with the richest tapestries from the manufactories of the city, and covered with thousands of brilliant women, some of them young and beautiful, and all of them ornamental. The theatre had been selected as the place for the entertainment. At the entry of the First Consul and of Madame Bonaparte, who came forward giving an arm to one of the mayors, there rose a thunder of applause and acclamations. All at once the theatrical decorations disappeared and gave way to the Place Bonaparte (the former Place Belcour), such as it had been restored by order of the First Consul. In the middle of it arose a pyramid surmounted by the statue of the First Consul, who was represented as leaning on a *lion*. Trophies of arms and of bas-reliefs figured on one of the faces the battle of Arcola, and on the other that of Marengo.

When the first transports excited by this spectacle, which simultaneously recalled the good deeds and the victories of the hero of the fête, had quieted down, a great silence fell, and then delightful music, blended with chants all celebrating the glory of the First Consul, his wife, the warriors surrounding him, and the representatives of the Italian republics, was heard. The singers and players were all of them amateurs of Lyons. Mademoiselle Longue, M. Gerbet, postoffice director, and M. Théodore, a merchant, each of whom had sung his part in a ravishing manner, received the felicitations of the First Consul and the most gracious thanks of Madame Bonaparte.

What I noticed most in the couplets which were sung on this occasion and which resembled all occasional verses, was that the First Consul was extolled in the same terms that all the poets of the Empire have since employed. All the exaggerations of flattery were exhausted in the time of the Consulate; in the years that followed it was necessary to repeat them. Thus, in the Lyons couplets the First Consul was *the god of victory, the conqueror of the Nile and of Neptune, the saviour of the country, the peacemaker of the world, the arbiter of Europe.* The French soldiers were transformed into *friends and companions of Alcides, etc.* This was to cut the grass from under the feet of future poets.

The Lyons fête terminated by a ball which lasted until daybreak. The First Consul remained two hours, during which time he conversed with the city magistrates.

While the more considerable inhabitants were offering to their guests this magnificent entertainment, the people, in spite of the cold, were devoting themselves to dancing and pleasure in the public squares.

Toward midnight, some very fine fireworks were set off on the Place Bonaparte.

After spending fifteen or eighteen days at Lyons, we resumed the road to Paris. The First Consul and his wife still continued to reside by preference at Malmaison. It was, I think, shortly after the return of the First Consul, that a man not at all well dressed, solicited an audience. He was ushered into the cabinet and asked what he wanted. "General," responded the solicitor, intimidated by his presence, "it was I who had the honor to give you writing lessons at the school of Brienne." "The fine pupil that you made there!" quickly interrupted the First Consul, "I compliment you on it." Then he was the first to laugh at his vivacity, and addressed some good-natured remarks to this honest man, whose timidity had not been lessened by such a compliment. A few days later, the master received from the worst, doubtless, of all his pupils of Brienne (every one knows how badly the Emperor wrote), a pension sufficient for his needs.

Another of the former teachers of the First Consul, M. l'Abbé Dupuis, had been placed by him at Malmaison in the capacity of private librarian. He lived and died there. He was a modest man and had the reputation of being well informed. The First Consul often visited him in his apartment and always showed him every imaginable regard and attention.

CHAPTER IX

Proclamation of the law on public worship — Conversation on this subject — The regulation — The plenipotentiaries for the Concordat — The Abbé Bernier and Cardinal Caprara — The red hat and the red cap — Costume of the First Consul and his colleagues — The first *Te Deum* chanted at Notre-Dame — Different sentiments of the spectators — The Republican calendar — The beard and the white shirt — General Abdallah-Menou — His courage in resisting the Jacobins — His flag — His romantic death — Institution of the order of the Legion of Honor — The First Consul at Ivry — The inscriptions of 1802 and the inscription of 1814 — The mayor of Ivry and the mayor of Evreux — Simplicity of a high functionary — The *cinq-z-enfants* — The First Consul's arrival at Rouen — M. Beugnot and Archbishop Cambacérès — The mayor of Rouen in the carriage of the First Consul — General Soult and General Moncey — The First Consul has a corporal to breakfast at his table — The First Consul at Havre and Honfleur — Goes from Havre to Fécamp — The First Consul's arrival at Dieppe — Return to Saint-Cloud.

THE day of the proclamation made by the First Consul of the law on public worship, he arose early and summoned his attendants to make his toilet. While they were dressing him, I saw M. Joseph Bonaparte and Consul Cambacérès enter his apartment.

"Well," said the First Consul to the latter; "we are going to Mass; what do they think of that in Paris?"

"Many people," responded M. Cambacérès, "propose going to the first representation and hissing the piece, if they do not find it amusing."

"If any one takes a notion to hiss, I will have him turned out of doors by the grenadiers of the consular guard."

"But what if the grenadiers begin to hiss like the others?"

"As to that I have no fears. My 'old moustaches' will go to Notre-Dame here, just as they went to the mosque in Cairo. They will look to see what I am doing, and seeing me behave seriously and decently, they will do the same, saying to themselves: That's the regulation."

"I am afraid," said M. Joseph Bonaparte, "that the general officers may not be so accommodating. I have just left Augereau, who is spitting fire and flame at what he calls your pious affectations. He and several others will not be easy to bring into the bosom of our holy mother, the Church."

"Bah! is Augereau like that? He's a brawler who makes a good deal of racket, and if he has some imbecile little cousin, he will put him in the seminary for me to make a chaplain of him. Apropos," pursued the First Consul, addressing his colleague, "when is your brother going to take possession of his see of Rouen? Do you know he has the finest archbishopric in France there? He will be a cardinal before the year is over; that is a settled affair."

The Second Consul bowed. From that moment

his behavior towards the First Consul was rather that of a courtier than an equal.

The plenipotentiaries who had been appointed to discuss and sign the Concordat were MM. Joseph Bonaparte, Crétet, and the Abbé Bernier. The latter, whom I have sometimes seen at the Tuileries, had been a chief of Chouans, and everything about him showed it. In the same conversation of which I have just related the commencement, the First Consul spoke with his two interlocutors about the conferences on the Concordat. "The Abbé Bernier," said he, "frightened the Italian prelates by the vehemence of his logic. One would have thought he believed himself still conducting the Vendéans to the charge against the *blues*. Nothing was more singular than the contrast of his rude and disputatious manners with the polished formalities and honeyed tone of the prelates. Cardinal Caprara came two days ago with a frightened air, to ask whether it was true that during the war of La Vendée the Abbé Bernier made an altar out of Republican corpses to celebrate the Mass on. I told him that I knew nothing about it, but that it was possible. 'General First Consul,' cried the terrified Cardinal, 'it is not a red hat but a red cap that this man needs!'

"I am very much afraid," went on the First Consul, "that that may stand in the way of the Abbé Bernier's berretta."

These gentlemen quitted the First Consul when

his toilet was finished, and went to prepare themselves for the ceremony. On that day the First Consul wore the consular costume, which was a scarlet coat without lapels, with a large embroidery of golden palms on all the seams. The sabre he had brought from Egypt was suspended at his side by a shoulder belt that was rather narrow, but finely wrought and richly embroidered. He retained his black collar, being unwilling to wear a lace cravat. Otherwise he was like his colleagues, in knee-breeches and slippers. A French hat with waving plumes in the three colors completed this rich apparel.

This first celebration of the divine office at Notre-Dame was a singular spectacle for the Parisians. Many people hastened thither as they would to a theatrical representation. Many also, especially among the military men, made it a subject of raillery rather than of edification. And as to those who, during the Revolution, had done all in their power to overthrow the cult which the First Consul had just re-established, they found it hard to hide their indignation and chagrin. The populace saw nothing in the *Te Deum* which was chanted that day for peace and concord but a new aliment offered to their curiosity. But in the middle class, a great number of pious persons, who had keenly regretted the suppression of the devotional practices in which they had been brought up, were glad of the return of the ancient worship. Moreover, there was not at this time any symptom of superstition or rigorism capable of alarming the enemies of intolerance. The clergy were very careful not to show themselves too exacting. They asked very little, condemned nobody, and the representative of the Holy Father, the Cardinal-Legate, pleased everybody, except perhaps some old priests vexed by his indulgence, the worldly grace of his manners, and the freedom of his conduct. This prelate was in perfect accord with the First Consul, who liked his conversation very much.

It is certain also that, all religious sentiment apart, the fidelity of the people to their ancient customs made them return with pleasure to the repose and the celebration of Sunday. The Republican calendar was no doubt learnedly calculated; but it had been smitten with ridicule in the first place by the replacement of the saints of the ancient calendar by the days of the ass, the pig, the turnip, the onion, etc. . . . Besides, if it was skilfully calculated, it was not at all commodiously divided, and on this head I recall the witticism of a very clever man, and one who, in spite of the disapprobation contained in his words, would yet have desired the establishment of the Republican system everywhere except in the almanac. When the decree of the Convention ordaining the adoption of the Republican calendar was published, he said: "*They may say what they like, but they will have to do with two enemies who will not yield: the beard and the white shirt.*" The fact is that for the working class, and for all classes employed in difficult tasks, there was too long an interval between one décadi and another. I do not know whether this was the effect of a deeply rooted routine; but the populace, accustomed to work for six consecutive days, and to rest on the seventh, found nine days of uninterrupted labor very long. Hence, the suppression of the décadis was universally approved. The decree which appointed Sunday as the day for the publication of the banns of marriage was not so much so, some persons dreading that the former pretensions of the clergy over the civil state might revive.

A few days after the formal re-establishment of the Catholic worship, I saw a general officer arrive at the Tuileries who would perhaps have preferred the establishment of the religion of Mahomet, and the change of Notre-Dame into a mosque. This was the last general-in-chief of the army of Egypt, who, people said, had become a Mussulman at Cairo, the *ci-devant* Baron de Menou. In spite of the latest check he had been subjected to by the English in Egypt, General *Abdallah*-Menou was well received by the First Consul, who soon after appointed him governor-general of Piedmont. General Menou's bravery was equal to every test, and he had displayed the greatest courage elsewhere than on the field of battle, and amidst the most difficult circumstances. After the day of August 10, although he belonged to the Republican party, he had been seen to follow Louis XVI. to the assembly, and had been denounced as a Royalists by the Jacobins. In 1795, the Faubourg Saint-Antoine having risen *en masse*, and advanced towards the Convention, General Menou had surrounded and disarmed the seditious; but he had resisted the atrocious orders of the commissioners of the Convention, who wanted to have the entire quarter burned, in order to punish the inhabitants for their continual insurrections. Some time after, having again failed to comply with the order of the Conventionists to riddle the sections of Paris with grapeshot, he was arraigned before a commission, which would have caused him to lose his head if General Bonaparte, who had replaced him in command of the army of the interior, had not used all his influence to save his life. Such multiplied acts of courage and generosity would suffice, and more than suffice, to excuse in this brave officer the otherwise very legitimate pride with which he boasted of having armed the national guards and substituted for the white flag the tricolor, which he called *my standard*. From the government of Piedmont he passed to that of Venice, and died of love, in 1810, in spite of his sixty years, for an actress whom he had followed from Venice to Reggio.

The institution of the order of the Legion of Honor preceded by a few days the proclamation of the Consulate for life. This proclamation gave rise to a feast which was celebrated the 15th of August. This was the anniversary of the First Consul's birth, and people profited by the occasion to celebrate this anniversary for the first time. On that day the First Consul completed his thirty-third year.

In the following month of October I attended the First Consul in his journey to Normandy. We stopped at Ivry, where the First Consul visited the battle-field. He said on reaching it: "*Honor to the memory of the best Frenchman who ever sat on the throne of France.*" And he ordered the restoration of the column which had been erected in memory of the victory gained by Henri IV.

The reader will perhaps thank me for giving here the inscriptions cut on the four faces of the pyramid.

First inscription.

Napoleon Bonaparte, First Consul, to the memory of Henri IV., victorious over the enemies of the State, on the field of Ivry, March 14, 1590.

Second inscription.

Great men love the glory of those who resemble them.

Third inscription.

In the year IX. of the French Republic, the 7th Brumaire, Napoleon Bonaparte, First Consul, after having passed over this plain, ordered the reconstruction of the monument destined to consecrate the memory of Henri IV. and that of the victory of Ivry.

Fourth inscription.

The misfortunes experienced by France at the epoch of the battle of Ivry, were the result of the appeal made by the different French parties to the Spanish and English nations. Every family, every party which calls foreign powers to its assistance, has merited and will merit to the latest posterity the maledictions of the French people.

All of these inscriptions have been effaced and replaced by the following:

This is the place of the pillar where Henri IV. stood on the day of Ivry, March 14, 1590.

M. Lédier, mayor of Ivry, accompanied the First Consul on this excursion. The First Consul talked with him a long time and seemed well satisfied. The mayor of Evreux did not give him an equally good idea of his talents; hence he rudely interrupted him in the middle of a sort of compliment this worthy magistrate was trying to pay him, by inquiring whether he knew his confrère, the mayor of Ivry. "No, General," replied the mayor. "Well, so much the worse for you; I advise you to make his acquaintance."

It was at Evreux also that an administrator of high rank had the opportunity of amusing Madame Bonaparte and her suite by a piece of naïveté which diverted everybody but the First Consul, because he did not like such silly things when they proceeded from a man of position. M. de Ch—— did the honors of the county town to the wife of the First Consul, and in spite of his great age showed much alacrity and promptness in so doing. Among other questions dictated by her usual benevolence and grace, Madame Bonaparte asked him if he was married, and if he had a family. "O Madame, I should think so," replied M. de Ch—— with a smile and a bow; "I have *cinq-z-enfants.*" "Ah! *mon Dieu!*"

cried Madame Bonaparte, "what a regiment! it is extraordinary. How, Monsieur, *sixteen children? (seize enfants)*." "Yes, Madame, *cinq-z-enfants, cinq-z-enfants*," repeated the administrator, not seeing anything very marvellous in that, and being astonished merely by the astonishment manifested by Madame Bonaparte. In the end some one explained to the latter the error she had been led into by the dangerous liaison of M. de Ch——, adding as seriously as he could: "Deign, Madame, to excuse M. de Ch——; the Revolution interrupted the course of his studies." He was more than sixty years old.

From Evreux we started for Rouen, where we arrived at about three in the afternoon. M. Chaptal, minister of the interior, M. Beugnot, prefect of the department, and M. Cambacérès, Archbishop of Rouen, came to meet the First Consul at a certain distance from the city. The mayor, M. Fontenay, awaited him at the gates, of which he presented him the keys. The First Consul held them for some time in his hands, and then returned them to the mayor, saying in a tone loud enough to be heard by the crowd surrounding his carriage: "Citizens, I could not better confide the keys than to the charge of the worthy magistrate who enjoys my confidence and yours by so many titles." He caused M. Fontenay to get into his carriage, saying that *he wished to honor Rouen in the person of its mayor.*

Madame Bonaparte was in her husband's carriage; General Moncey rode at the right-hand side of it.

In the second carriage were General Soult and two aides-de-camp; in a third, General Bessières and M. de Luçay; in a fourth, General Lauriston. Then came the servants' carriages. Hambart, Hébert, and I were in the first one.

I should try in vain to give an idea of the enthusiasm of the people of Rouen on the arrival of the First Consul. The market porters and boatmen in grand costume were awaiting us on the outside of the city; and when the carriage containing the two august personages was within their reach, these excellent fellows ranged themselves in double file and preceded the carriage in this way as far as the hotel of the prefecture, where the First Consul alighted.

The prefect and the mayor of Rouen, the Archbishop and the general commanding the division, dined with the First Consul, who displayed the most amiable gaiety during the repast, and was most careful to inform himself concerning the condition of manufactures, new discoveries in the arts of making fabrics, and, in short, all that could relate to the prosperity of this essentially industrial city.

In the evening, and nearly all night, an immense crowd surrounded the hotel and filled the gardens of the prefecture, which were illuminated and adorned with allegorical transparencies in praise of the First Consul. Each time that he showed himself on the terrace of the garden, the air resounded with applause and acclamations which seemed to flatter him extremely.

The next morning, after having made the rounds of the city on horseback, and visiting the magnificent places by which it is surrounded, the First Consul heard Mass, which was celebrated at eleven o'clock by the Archbishop in the chapel of the prefecture. An hour later he had to receive the general council of the department, the municipal council, the clergy of Rouen, and the tribunals. He had to listen to a half-dozen discourses, all conceived in nearly the same terms, and to which he replied in a manner calculated to give the orators the highest opinion of their own merits. All these bodies, on quitting the First Consul, were presented to Madame Bonaparte, who received them with her usual grace.

In the evening Madame Bonaparte gave a reception for the wives of the functionaries. The First Consul was present at this reception, a fact availed of in order to present to him several newly amnestied persons, whom he received with benevolence.

For the rest, there were the same illuminations, the same acclamations as on the evening before. All countenances wore a festive look which delighted me, and, in my opinion, contrasted singularly with the horrible wooden houses, the dirty and narrow streets, and the Gothic constructions which then characterized the city of Rouen.

On Monday, November 1, at seven o'clock in the morning, the First Consul mounted a horse, escorted by a detachment of the young men of the city, forming a voluntary guard. He crossed the bridge of boats, and went through the Faubourg Saint-Sever. On returning from this promenade, we found the people awaiting him at the head of the bridge, who conducted him back to the hotel of the prefecture, making the air ring with shouts of joy.

After breakfast, High Mass was sung by Monseigneur the Archbishop, it being the feast of All Saints; then came the learned societies, the heads of the administration, and the judges of the peace, with their discourses. That of the latter contained a remarkable phrase: these good magistrates, in their enthusiasm, asked the First Consul's permission to surname him the *grand judge of the peace of Europe*. As they were leaving the apartment of the First Consul, I noticed the man who had delivered the speech; there were tears in his eyes, and he was proudly repeating the response just made to him. I regret not having remembered his name; he was, I was told, one of the most respectable men in Rouen. His face inspired confidence and wore an expression of frankness that prepossessed one in his favor.

In the evening, the First Consul went to the theatre. The hall, filled to the roof, presented a charming sight. The municipal authorities had caused a superb entertainment to be prepared, which the First Consul found greatly to his taste; he complimented the prefect and the mayor on it several times. After having seen the opening of the ball, and made two or three turns around the hall, he withdrew, surrounded by the staff of the national guard.

A great part of Tuesday was employed by the First Consul in visiting the workshops of the numerous manufactories of the city. The minister of the interior, the prefect, the mayor, the general commanding the division, the inspector-general of the county police, and the staff of the consular guard accompanied him. In one manufactory of the Faubourg Saint-Sever, the minister of the interior presented to him the senior workman, known for having woven the first piece of velvet in France. After complimenting this honorable old man, the First Consul granted him a pension. Other rewards or encouragements were likewise distributed to several persons whose useful inventions recommended them to public gratitude.

On Monday morning early, we started for Elbeuf, where we arrived at ten o'clock, preceded by some sixty young men of the most distinguished families in the city, who, after the example of those of Rouen, aspired to the honor of forming the guard of the First Consul.

The country all around was covered by an innumerable multitude, coming from the surrounding communes. The First Consul alighted at the house of the mayor of Elbeuf, where he breakfasted. Afterwards he visited the city in detail, seeking information everywhere; and learning that one of the principal needs of the citizens was the construction of a road from Elbeuf to a little neighboring town, called Romilly, he gave orders to the minister of the interior to have the work begun at once.

At Elbeuf, as at Rouen, the First Consul was loaded with homage and benedictions. We returned to the latter city at four in the afternoon.

The merchants of Rouen had prepared a fête in the stock exchange. The First Consul and his wife went there after dinner. He remained a long while on the ground-floor of this great building, where magnificent samples of the industries of the department were displayed. He examined all, and had them examined by Madame Bonaparte, who wished to buy several pieces of stuff.

Then the First Consul went up into the first story; there, in a beautiful salon, were assembled a hundred ladies and misses, nearly all pretty, the wives or daughters of the principal merchants of Rouen, who were waiting to pay him their compliments. He sat down in this charming circle, and remained there about a quarter of an hour, going afterwards into another hall, where he listened to the representation of a little "proverb," mingled with couplets, expressive, as one may guess, of the attachment and the gratitude of the people of Rouen.

This "proverb" was followed by a ball.

On Thursday evening, the First Consul announced that he would leave for Havre the next morning at daybreak. I was, in fact, awakened by Hébert at five in the morning, who told me we would start at six o'clock. I had a bad awakening, which made me sick all day: I would have given a good deal to sleep some hours longer. . . . Finally, we had to set off. Before getting into the carriage, the First Consul made a present to Monseigneur the Archbishop of a snuff-box with his portrait. He also gave one to the mayor bearing the inscription: *The French People.*

We stopped at Caudebec for breakfast. The mayor of this town presented to the First Consul a corporal who had made the Italian campaign (his name, I think, was Roussel), and who had received a sabre of honor as the reward of his fine conduct at Marengo. He was at Caudebec on a six months' furlough, and he asked the First Consul's permission to stand sentry at the door of the apartment occupied by the august travellers. This was granted, and when the First Consul and Madame Bonaparte sat down at table, Roussel was called and invited to breakfast with his former general. At Havre and at Dieppe, the First Consul thus invited to his table all those, whether soldiers or sailors, who had obtained guns, sabres, or boarding-axes of honor. The First Consul stopped for half an hour at Bolbec, displaying much attention and interest in examining the industrial products of the arrondissement, complimenting the guards of honor who came to meet him on their fine appearance, thanking the priest for the prayers he addressed to Heaven for him, and leaving in his hands and those of the mayor tokens for the poor of his passage. On the arrival of the First Consul at Havre, the city was illuminated. The First Consul and his numerous cortège marched between two rows of illumination stands, of fiery columns of every sort. The vessels that were in the harbor looked like a forest in flames; they were surcharged with colored lamps to the tops of their masts. On the day of his arrival, the First Consul received only a part of the authorities of the city; he went to bed shortly afterwards, saying that he was sleepy; but by six o'clock next morning he was on horseback, and for more than two hours he was ranging the beach, the hillsides of Ingouville for more than a league, the banks of the Seine as far as the acclivity of Hoc; and he made the exterior round of the citadel. About three o'clock the First Consul began to receive the authorities. He conversed with them, in the greatest detail, about the works which must be accomplished in order that their port, which he always called the port of Paris, should attain the highest degree of prosperity. He did the sub-prefect, the mayor, the two presidents of the tribunals, the commandant of the place, and the chief of the 10th half brigade of light infantry, the honor of inviting them to his table.

In the evening the First Consul went to the theatre, where they played a little piece written for the occasion, about as good as such things ever are, but for which the First Consul, and especially

Madame Bonaparte, were well pleased with the authors. The illuminations were still more brilliant than on the previous evening. I especially remember that the majority of the transparencies were inscribed with these words: 18 *Brumaire, year VIII.*

At seven o'clock on Sunday morning, after having visited the marine arsenal and all the basins, the First Consul embarked on a little yawl, the weather being fine, and remained in the roadstead during several hours. His cortège was composed of a great number of boats filled with fashionable men and women, and with musicians who played the favorite airs of the First Consul. Several more hours were spent in receiving merchants, to whom the First Consul said openly that he had had the greatest pleasure in conferring on the commerce of Havre with the colonies. That evening there was a fête arranged by the mercantile community, at which the First Consul was present for half an hour. On Monday, at five o'clock in the morning, he embarked on a lugger, and went to Honfleur. The weather was somewhat threatening at the time of departure, and several persons had tried to persuade the First Consul not to go on board. Madame Bonaparte, to whose ears this rumor came, ran to her husband and begged him not to start; but he embraced her, laughing and calling her a trembler, and went aboard the boat that was awaiting him. He had scarcely done so when the wind suddenly became more calm and the weather was magnificent. On his return to Havre, the First Consul held a review on the Place de la Citadelle, and visited the artillery establishments. He again received until evening a great number of public functionaries and merchants, and the next day, at six o'clock in the morning, we started for Dieppe.

At the moment when we arrived at Fécamp, the town presented an extremely curious spectacle. All the inhabitants of the neighboring towns and villages accompanied the clergy in chanting a *Te Deum* for the anniversary of the 18th Brumaire. These innumerable voices, rising to Heaven in prayer for him, moved the First Consul deeply. He repeated several times, during breakfast, that he had experienced more emotion from these chants under the vaulted sky, than he had ever done from more brilliant music.

We reached Dieppe at six in the evening; the First Consul did not go to bed until after having received all the felicitations, which were certainly very sincere there, as they were at that time throughout France. At eight o'clock next day he went down to the wharf, where he stayed a long time watching the fishing boats come in, and then visited the Faubourg du Pollet and the works they were commencing in the basins. He admitted to his table the sub-prefect, the mayor, and three sailors of Dieppe, who had obtained boarding-axes of honor for distinguishing themselves at the combat of Boulogne. The First Consul ordered the construction of a sluice in the last wharf, and the continuation of a canal which was to extend to Paris, but of which only a few feet had yet been built. From Dieppe we went to Gisors and to Beauvais; and finally the First Consul and his wife returned to Saint-Cloud, after an absence of fifteen days, during which time active restorations had been in progress in this ancient royal residence, which the First Consul had decided to accept, as I shall presently explain.

CHAPTER X

Influence of the journey to Normandy on the mind of the First Consul — The evolution of the Empire — Memories and history — First ladies and first officers of Madame Bonaparte — Mesdames de Rémusat, de Cramayel, de Luçay, de Lauriston — Mademoiselle d'Arberg and Mademoiselle de Luçay — Prudence at court — MM. de Rémusat, de Cramayel, de Luçay, Didelot — The palace refused, then accepted — Bawbles — The servitors of Marie-Antoinette better treated under the Consulate than since the Restoration — Fire at Saint-Cloud — The watch chamber — The bourgeois bed — How the First Consul went down to his wife's room at night — Duty and conjugal triumph — Excessive severity toward a young woman — Weapons of honor and the troopers — The baptism of blood — The First Consul following the plough — Laborers and councillors of state — The Republican grenadier becomes a laborer — Audience of the First Consul — The author introduced into the General's cabinet — A good reception and a curious conversation.

THE journey of the First Consul in the richest and most enlightened departments of France must have banished from his mind many of the difficulties he might at first have dreaded to encounter in the execution of his schemes. Everywhere he had been received like a monarch; and not he alone, but Madame Bonaparte had been welcomed with all the honors usually reserved for crowned heads. There was not the slightest difference between the homage paid them then, and that with which they were afterward surrounded even under the Empire, when Their Majesties made journeys through their dominions at different epochs. This is why I have entered into some details concerning this one; if they appear too long, or too devoid of novelty to some readers, I beg them to remember that I am not writing merely for those who *have seen* the Empire. The generation which was a witness of so many great things and which was able to see close at hand, and from his beginnings, the greatest man of this century, is already giving place to other generations which cannot and could not judge except on the testimony of that which preceded them. What is familiar to this person, who has examined it with his own eyes, is not so for others who need to have somebody relate to them what they could not have seen. Moreover, details neglected as futile and common by history, which makes a profession of gravity, are perfectly suitable to simple souvenirs, and sometimes enable one to understand and judge an epoch well. It seems to me, for example, that the cordiality of the whole population and of the authorities toward the First Consul and Madame Bonaparte during their journey in Normandy, sufficiently shows that the chief of the State would not have to fear a very great opposition, at least on the part of the nation, when it should please him to change his title and proclaim himself Emperor.

Not long after our return, a decision of the consuls

accorded to Madame Bonaparte four ladies *to assist her in doing the honors of the palace.* They were Mesdames de Rémusat, de Tallouet, de Luçay, and de Lauriston. Under the Empire they became ladies of the palace. Madame de Luçay often occasioned a laugh among the servants by little traits of parsimony; but she was good and obliging. Madame de Rémusat was a woman of the greatest merit, and very sensible. She seemed a trifle haughty, and that was the more noticed because M. de Rémusat was full of good-nature.

In the sequel, there was a lady of honor, Madame de la Rochefoucauld, of whom I shall have occasion to speak later;

A lady of the bed-chamber, Madame de Luçay, who was replaced by Madame de la Villette, so gloriously known afterwards by her devotion to her husband;

Twenty-four ladies of the palace, Frenchwomen, among them Mesdames de Rémusat, de Tallouet, de Lauriston, Ney, d'Arberg, Louise d'Arberg, afterward the Countess de Lobau, de Walsh-Sérent, de Colbert, Lannes, Savary, de Turenne, Octave de Ségur, de Montalivet, de Marescot, de Bouillé, Solar, Lascaris, de Brignolé, de Canisy, de Chevreuse, Victor de Mortemart, de Montmorency, Matignon, and Maret;

Twelve ladies of the palace, Italians;

These ladies were on duty every month, so that one Italian and two Frenchwomen were always together. The Emperor would not, at first, have misses among the ladies of the palace, but he relaxed this regulation for Mademoiselle Louise d'Arberg, since Madame the Countess de Lobau, and Mademoiselle de Luçay, who married Count Philippe de Ségur, author of the fine history of the Russian campaign. These two young ladies proved by their prudent and reserved conduct that it is possible to be discreet, even at court;

Four ladies *d'annonce*, Mesdames Soustras, Ducrest-Villeneuve, Félicité Longroy, and Eglé Marchery;

Two chief lady's-maids, Mesdames Roy and Marco de Saint-Hilaire, who had under their charge the grand wardrobe and the jewel cases;

Four ordinary lady's-maids;

A reader.

In men, the personnel of the household of Her Majesty the Empress was composed in the sequel of:

A first equerry, Senator Harville, fulfilling the functions of chevalier of honor;

A first chamberlain, General of division Nansouty;

A second chamberlain, introducer of ambassadors, M. de Beaumont;

Four ordinary chamberlains, MM. de Courtomer, Degrave, Galard de Béarn, Hector d'Aubusson de La Feuillade;

Four chief equerries, MM. Corbineau, Berckeim, d'Audenarde, and Fouler;

A major-domo-general of Her Majesty's household, M. Hinguerlot;

A private secretary, M. Deschamps;

Two chief valets de chambre, MM. Frère and Douville;

Four ordinary valets de chambre;

Four ushers of the chamber;

Two chief footmen, MM. Lespérance and d'Argens;

Six ordinary footmen;

The kitchen and sanitary officers were those of the Emperor's household. In addition, six of the Emperor's pages were always on duty near the Empress.

The first chaplain was M. Ferdinand de Rohan, former Archbishop of Cambray.

Another decision of the same epoch settled the functions of the prefects of the palace. The four first prefects of the consular palace were MM. de Rémusat, de Cramayel appointed later as introducer of ambassadors and master of ceremonies; de Luçay, and Didelot, since prefect of Cher.

Malmaison no longer sufficed for the First Consul, whose household, like that of Madame Bonaparte, daily became more numerous. A more extensive dwelling had become necessary, and the First Consul decided on Saint-Cloud.

The inhabitants of Saint-Cloud had addressed a petition to the legislative body, asking the First Consul to be so good as to make their château his summer residence, and the Assembly had hastened to transmit it to the First Consul, supporting it, even, by its own entreaties, and by comparisons which it believed flattering. The General formally refused, saying that when he should have acquitted himself of the functions with which the people had charged him, he would consider himself honored by a recompense awarded by the people; but so long as he should be chief of the government, he would never accept anything. In spite of the determined tone of this response, the inhabitants of Saint-Cloud, who had the greatest interest in having their request granted, renewed it when the First Consul was appointed consul for life, and this time he consented to accept it. The expenses for repairing and furnishing it were immense, greatly surpassing the estimates, and yet he was dissatisfied with the furniture and adornments. He complained to M. Charvet, concierge of Malmaison, whom he had appointed concierge of this new palace, and whom he had directed to supervise the distribution of the rooms and to look after the furnishing, that *the apartments prepared for him were like those of a kept woman; that there was nothing in them but baubles, and knick-knacks, and nothing of importance.* On this occasion he again gave a proof of his eagerness to do what was right, without disturbing himself about prejudices which still had much weight. Knowing that there were at Saint-Cloud a great number of the former servitors of Queen Marie-Antoinette, he told M. Charvet to offer them either their former places or pensions; the greater number resumed their places. In 1814 people were much less generous. All the employees were sent off, even those who had served Marie-Antoinette.

The First Consul had not been long installed in Saint-Cloud when this château, once more become a *sovereign residence*, was very nearly a prey to flames. There was a guard-house under the vestibule of the centre of the palace. One night when the soldiers had made too much fire, the stove became so hot that an armchair which was shoved against one of the hot-air holes which warmed the salon took fire, and the flame promptly communicated itself to all the furniture. The officer of the post noticing it immediately notified the concierge, and they ran to the room of General Duroc, whom they awakened. The General rose in all haste, and recommending perfect silence, they organized a chain. He got into the reservoir himself, together with the concierge, to pass the buckets of water to the soldiers, and in two or three hours the fire, which had already devoured all the furniture, was extinct. It was not until the next morning that the First Consul, Josephine, Hortense, in a word, all the inhabitants of the château, were apprised of this accident, and they all testified, the First Consul especially, their gratitude for the care that had been taken not to awaken them. To prevent such accidents, or at least to render them less dangerous in future, the First Consul organized a night guard at Saint-Cloud, and, in the sequel, in all his residences. This guard was called the *watch chamber*.

In the early days of the First Consul's residence in the palace of Saint-Cloud, he slept in the same bed with his wife. Etiquette supervened later on, and in this respect somewhat chilled conjugal tenderness. In effect, the First Consul ended by occupying an apartment rather remote from that of Madame Bonaparte. To go to her he had to pass through a long servants' corridor. The ladies of the palace, the serving women, etc., had rooms on either side of it. When the First Consul wished to pass the night with his wife, he undressed in his own room, whence he issued in a dressing-gown and a bandana handkerchief around his head. I walked in front of him, carrying a flambeau. At the end of this corridor was a staircase of fifteen or sixteen steps which led to Madame Bonaparte's apartment. It was a great joy for her to receive a visit from her husband; the whole house heard of it the next day. I see her still saying to every newcomer, and rubbing her little hands: "*I got up late to-day, but you see it is because Bonaparte came to spend the night with me.*" On that day she would be still more amiable than usual; she repelled nobody, and we could obtain whatever we wanted. For my part, I have often tried the experiment.

One evening when I was conducting the First Consul to one of these conjugal visits, we perceived in the corridor a very well-dressed young man who was coming out of the room of one of Madame Bonaparte's women. He tried to slip away, but the First Consul cried out in a loud voice: "*Who is there? where are you going? what are you doing? what is your game?*" It was simply one of Madame Bonaparte's valets. Stupefied by these hasty interrogations, he replied in a frightened voice that he had been executing a commission for Madame Bonaparte. "All right," returned the First Consul, "but don't let me find you here again." Persuaded that the gallant would profit by the lesson, the General did not seek to learn his name or that of his fair friend.

That reminds me that he was much more severe in regard to another lady's-maid of Madame Bonaparte. She was young and very pretty, and inspired very tender sentiments in two aides-de-camp, MM. R—— and E——. They sighed incessantly at her door, and sent her flowers and *billets doux*. The young girl — at least such was the general opinion of the household — gave them nothing in return. Josephine liked her very much, and yet the First Consul, having noticed the gallantries of these gentlemen, displayed great anger, and had the poor young woman sent away, in spite of her tears and the entreaties of Madame Bonaparte and those of the brave and good Colonel R—— who naïvely swore that the fault was all on his side, that the poor little thing deserved nothing but praise, and had never listened to him. All was unavailing against the resolution of the First Consul, who replied to everything by saying: "I will have no disorders, no scandals in my house."

Whenever the First Consul made a distribution of weapons of honor, there was a banquet at the Tuileries, to which all were admitted indiscriminately, no matter what their grades might be, who had shared in these rewards. There were sometimes two hundred guests at these dinners, which were served in the grand gallery of the château. General Duroc was master of ceremonies, and the First Consul was careful to recommend him to intermingle common soldiers, colonels, generals, etc. It was the former especially that he ordered the domestics to take good care of, and give them plenty to eat and drink. These were the longest repasts that I ever saw given by the Emperor; here he showed a perfect amiability and unconstraint; he made every effort to put his guests at their ease; but with a good many of them he had trouble in doing so. Nothing was funnier than to see these honest troopers holding themselves two feet away from the table, not daring to approach either their napkin or their bread; red to their ears, and their necks stretched towards their general, as if to receive the countersign. The First Consul would make them relate the lofty deed which had earned them the national reward, and sometimes shouted with laughter at their singular narrations. He persuaded them to make a good meal, and sometimes drank to their health; but with some, his encouragements failed to overcome their timidity, and the footmen would take away their plates one after another, without their having touched them. This constraint did not prevent them from being full of joy and enthusiasm on quitting the table. "*Au revoir*, my heroes," the First Consul would say to them, "baptize those new-born babies for me as soon as possible" (pointing with his finger at their sabres of honor). God knows that they did not fail to do so when the opportunity came.

This kindliness of the First Consul toward common soldiers reminds me of an anecdote that happened at Malmaison, and which gives another reply to those accusations of pride and severity that have been made against him.

The First Consul went out very early one morning, dressed in his gray overcoat, and accompanied by General Duroc, to walk in the direction of the machinery of Marly. As they were walking and talking, they saw a laborer who was tracing a furrow and coming towards them. "Say, my good fellow," said the First Consul, stopping, " your furrow is not straight; don't you know your trade?" "At any rate, you can't teach it to me, my fine gentleman; you would find it very hard work to do as well." — "Nonsense!" "You think so? well, try it," replied the honest man, ceding his place to the First Consul. The latter took the handle of the plough, and, urging on the horses, wanted to commence the lesson; but he did not make a single step in a straight line, so awkwardly did he take hold. "Come, come," said the peasant, laying his hand on that of the General to take back his plough, " your work is good for nothing; every one to his trade; you go and take a walk, that is your business." But the First Consul did not continue his walk without paying for the lesson in morals he had just received from

the laborer. General Duroc gave him two or three
louis to reimburse him for the loss of time they had
caused him. The peasant, astonished by this generosity, left his plough to go and tell his adventure,
and on the road met a woman to whom he said that
he certainly thought he had met two big gentlemen
(*gros messieurs*), to judge of them by what he still
had in his hand. The farmer's wife, better advised,
asked him how the two promenaders were dressed,
and from his description divined that it was the First
Consul and one of his friends. The good man was
dumfounded for a time; but the next day he took
a fine resolution, and having arrayed himself in his
best clothes, he presented himself at Malmaison, and
asked to speak to the First Consul to thank him, as
he said, for the fine present he had made him the day
before. I went to inform the First Consul of this
visit, and he ordered me to introduce the laborer.[1]
The latter, while I was absent on this errand, had, to
use his own expression, *taken his courage in both hands*
to prepare himself for this great interview. I found
him standing in the middle of the antechamber (for

---

[1] The author of the *Memorial* cites an anecdote of the Emperor
at Saint-Helena, similar to that I am relating here. His Majesty
professed the highest esteem for the cultivators of the soil, and
took pleasure in consulting them even on matters foreign to their
occupations, but on which their good sense and experience might
suggest to them a sound opinion. He used to say that *he made
known to the peasants the difficulties of his Council of State, and
communicated to the Council of State the observations of the
peasants.*

he had not dared to sit down on the benches, which, although of the simplest, appeared to him magnificent), dreaming of what he was going to say to the First Consul to show his gratitude. I marched before him, he following, putting his feet down on the carpet with the utmost precaution, and, when I opened the door of the cabinet for him, politely urging me to go in first. When the First Consul had nothing secret to say or dictate, he was willing enough to leave the door of his cabinet open. This time he made me a sign not to close it, so that I could see and hear all that passed.

The honest laborer commenced, on entering the cabinet, by saluting the *back* of M. de Bourrienne, who could not see him, occupied as he was in writing at a little table placed in the embrasure of the window. The First Consul looked at him making his salutes, threw himself back in his armchair, one of whose arms he was, as usual, tormenting with a penknife. At last, however, he began to speak in this fashion:

"Well, my good fellow" (the peasant turned round, recognized him and saluted again), "well," pursued the First Consul, "has the harvest been good this year?"

"But, saving your presence, Citizen my General, it has not been so bad as all that."

"To make the earth bring forth," resumed the First Consul, "it must be dug up; isn't that so? Fine gentlemen are good for nothing at that work."

"Without offence to you, General, the hands of the bourgeois are too soft to manage a plough. It needs a solid fist to move those tools."

"That's true," responded the First Consul, smiling. "But big and strong as you are, you ought to be able to handle something besides a plough. A good musket, for example, or else the hilt of a fine sabre."

The laborer drew himself up with an air of pride: "General, in my time I have done like the others. I had been married five years when those b—— of Prussians (pardon, General) entered Landrecies. The requisition came; they gave me a musket and a cartridge-box at the town house, and march! Ah well, we were not equipped like those big fellows I saw just now on entering the court."

He meant the grenadiers of the consular guard.

"Why did you quit the service?" continued the First Consul, who seemed to take great interest in this conversation.

"Faith, General, every one in his turn. There are sabre thrusts enough for all. One hit me here" (the worthy laborer stooped and showed his head, pushing aside the hair), "and after several weeks in the hospital, they gave me leave to return to my wife and my plough."

"Have you any children?"

"I have three, General; two boys and a girl."

"You must make a soldier of your oldest boy. If he behaves himself well, I will take charge of him. Adieu, my good fellow; when you have need of me come back to see me." Thereupon the First Consul rose, asked M. de Bourrienne for some louis, which he added to those the laborer had already received from him, and ordered me to take him away. We were already in the antechamber, when the First Consul called the laborer back to say:

"Were you at Fleurus?"

"Yes, General."

"Could you tell me the name of your general-in-chief?"

"Well, I should think so! It was General Jourdan."

"Good; *au revoir.*" And I led the old soldier of the Republic away, enchanted with his reception.

CHAPTER XI

The envoy of the Bey of Tunis and the Arabian horses — Bad faith of England — Journey to Boulogne — In Flanders and Belgium — Continual jaunts — The author acts as first valet de chambre — Constant's debut as barber to the First Consul — Apprenticeship — Plebeian chins — The eagle glance — The First Consul difficult to shave — Constant persuades him to shave himself — His reasons for doing so — Imprudent confidence of the First Consul — The first lesson — The cuts — Slight reproaches — The First Consul's awkward way of holding his razor — The chiefs and the harangues — Arrival of the First Consul at Boulogne — Preludes to the formation of the camp of Boulogne — Speech of twenty fathers of families — Naval combat gained by Admiral Bruix against the English — The dinner and the victory — The English and the Iron Coast — Projected assault upon the person of the First Consul — Rapidity of the journey — The minister of police — Presents offered by the cities — Works commanded by the First Consul — Munificence — The First Consul a bad driver — Pallor of Cambacérès — The swoon — The Gospel precept — Dreamless sleep — The Ottoman ambassador — The cashmere shawls — The Mussulman at prayers and at the theatre.

AT the beginning of this year (1803) there arrived in Paris an envoy from Tunis, who presented the First Consul, in the name of the Bey, with ten Arabian horses. The Bey was then in dread of the wrath of England, and he was trying to secure France as a powerful ally who would be able to protect him; he could not have done better, for everything announced the rupture of that Peace of Amiens so greatly rejoiced over by all Europe. England kept none of its promises and executed not a single article of the treaty; on his side, the First Consul, revolted by such bad faith, and unwilling to be duped by it, armed publicly, ordered the complement of officers to be filled up and a new levy of one hundred and twenty thousand conscripts. War was officially declared in June; but there had been hostilities before that.

At the end of this month the First Consul made a journey to Boulogne, and visited Picardy, Flanders, and Belgium, to organize the expedition he meditated against the English and to put the northern coasts in a state of defence. Returning to Paris in August, he left it again in November for a second visit to Boulogne. These repeated jaunts were too much for M. Hambart, first valet de chambre, who had long been sick. Hence, when the First Consul had been on the point of setting out on his first tour in the north, M. Hambart had asked his permission not to be of the party, alleging, which was very true, the bad state of his health. "That is the way you are," said the First Consul, "always sick and complaining! And if you stay here, who is going to shave me?" "General," replied M. Hambart, "Constant knows how to shave as well as I do." I was present and occupied at that very moment in dressing the First Consul. He looked at me and said: "Eh! *monsieur le drôle,* since you are so clever, you may make your trial on the spot; we shall see how you will go at it." I knew the mishap of poor Hébert, which I have previously related, and not wishing to experience one like it, I had long been learning to shave. I had paid a barber to teach me his trade, and had even, in my leisure moments, apprenticed myself at his shop, where I had shaved all his customers indiscriminately. The chins of these worthy people had had somewhat to suffer before my hand was light enough for me to dare to bring my razor near the consular chin. But by dint of reiterated experiences on the beards of the vulgar, I had arrived at a degree of address which inspired me with the greatest confidence. Hence, on the First Consul's order, I got ready the hot water and soap-ball, opened the razor boldly, and began the operation. Just as I was about to bring the razor to the First Consul's face, he rose brusquely, turned round, and fixed his two eyes on me with an expression of severity and interrogation which I cannot describe. Seeing that I remained undisturbed, he sat down again, saying with more gentleness: "Continue;" which I did with sufficient address to satisfy him very well. When I had finished he said to me: "Hereafter it is you that shall shave me." And, in fact, from that time, he would have no other barber. Thenceforward my duties became much more active; for every day I was obliged to make my appearance to shave the First Consul, and I can affirm that it was no easy thing to do. During the ceremony of removing his beard he frequently talked, read the papers, moved round on his chair, turned suddenly, and I was obliged to use the greatest precaution to avoid wounding him. Luckily, this misfortune never happened to me. When by chance he did not talk, he remained immovable and stiff as a statue, and one could not make him lower, raise, or bend his head, as would have been necessary in order to accomplish the task more easily. He had also one singular mania, which was to have only one side of his face lathered and shaved at a time. He would never let me pass to the other side until the first was finished. The First Consul found this more convenient.

Later on, when I had become his first valet de chambre, when he deigned to treat me with the greatest kindness, and I had as much freedom of speech with him as his rank permitted, I took the liberty of persuading him to shave himself; for, as I have just said, being unwilling to allow himself to be shaved by anybody but me, he was obliged to wait to have me sent for, with the army especially, where he was not always regular about rising. He refused for a long time to follow my advice, and whenever I repeated it: "Ah ha! Mr. Laziness!" he would say to me, laughing, "wouldn't you be very glad to have me do half your work?" At last I had the good fortune to convince him of the disinterestedness and wisdom of my advice.

The fact is that I wanted very much to persuade him; for, representing to myself what would necessarily happen if an indispensable absence, a malady, or any other motive should keep me at a distance from the First Consul, I could not think without a shudder that his life would be at the mercy of the first comer. For him, I am sure he never thought of this; for, whatever stories have been told about his distrust, it is certain that he never took any precautions against the snares that treachery might lay for him. His confidence on this point verged even on imprudence. Hence all who loved him, and they were all who surrounded him, sought to remedy this lack of precaution by all the vigilance of which they were capable. I need not say that it was above all this very solicitude for the precious life of my master which induced me to insist on the advice I had given him to shave himself.

The first times when he essayed to put my lessons into practice, it was more disquieting than laughable to see the Emperor (he was that then), who did not know how to hold the razor, in spite of the principles I had just laid down, illustrating them by reiterated examples, seize it by the handle and apply it perpendicularly to his cheek without laying it flat. He would make an abrupt slash with it, never failing to cut himself, and then draw back his hand as quickly as possible, exclaiming: "You see very well, you rogue! you are the cause of my cutting myself!" Then I would take the razor and finish the operation.

The next day, the same scene as the day before, but with less bloodshed. Every day increased the Emperor's skill; and he ended, by dint of repeated lessons, in being able to dispense with me. Only he still cut himself occasionally, and then he would begin again to scold me a little; but in a bantering way and kindly. Besides, from the manner in which he went at it, and which he would not change, it was very possible that he would never avoid cutting himself frequently; for he shaved himself from top to bottom, and not from bottom to top like everybody else, and this bad method, which all my efforts could never alter, added to the habitual abruptness of his movements, made it impossible for me not to shudder every time I saw him take his razor.

Madame Bonaparte accompanied the First Consul on the first of these journeys. Like that to Lyons, it was a continual series of fêtes and triumphs.

In expectation of the arrival of the First Consul, the inhabitants of Boulogne had raised triumphal arches all the way from the Montreuil gate to the temporary building erected for him at the camp at the right. Each arch was of foliage, and bore the names of the combats and pitched battles in which he had been victorious. These domes and arcades of verdure and flowers presented an admirable sight. One of them, much higher than the others, rose in the middle of the rue de l'Ecu (the chief street); the élite of the city were assembled around it; more than a hundred young persons adorned with flowers, children, fine old men, and a large number of veterans who had not been detained in camp by military duty, were awaiting the arrival of the First Consul with impatience. As he approached, rejoicing cannons announced to the English, whose fleet was still lying in Boulogne waters, the appearance of Napoleon on the shore where the formidable army he had resolved to throw into England was assembling.

The First Consul, who had been mounted on a little gray horse which had the vivacity of a squirrel, alighted, and, followed by his brilliant staff, he addressed these paternal words to the city authorities: "I come to assure the welfare of France; the sentiments you manifest, your tokens of gratitude, all affect me; I shall never forget my entry into Boulogne, which I have chosen as the centre of reunion for my armies. Citizens, do not be alarmed by this rendezvous; it is that of the defenders of the country, and presently of the conquerors of haughty England." The First Consul continued his march, surrounded by the whole population, who only left him at the door of his *baraque,* where more than thirty generals received him. The firing of cannons, the ringing of bells, and shouts of joy lasted until nightfall.

The next day after our arrival, the First Consul visited the Pont-de-Briques, a little village situated half a league from Boulogne; a farmer read him the following compliment:

"General, we twenty are fathers of families who

offer you a score of big fellows who are and always will be at your orders: take them with you, General, they may aid you serviceably when you go to England. As for us, we are fulfilling another duty; our arms will cultivate the earth so that bread shall not be lacking to the heroes who are to crush the English."

Napoleon smilingly thanked the outspoken countryman, glanced at a small country house built beside the high road, and said, addressing himself to General Berthier: "I will have my headquarters established there." Then he spurred his horse and rode away. A general and several officers remained to execute his order, and the First Consul returned the same night to sleep at Pont-de-Briques.

I was told at Boulogne the details of a naval combat fought a short time before our arrival between the French fleet, commanded by Admiral Bruix, and the English squadron with which Nelson was blocking the port of Boulogne. I will tell them as they were told to me, as I thought the convenient manner in which the French admiral directed the operations of his seamen very curious.

About two hundred vessels, both gunboats and bomb-ketches, flat-boats and pinnaces, formed the line of defence; the coast and the forts were bristling with batteries. Several frigates detached themselves from the enemy's station, and, preceded by two or three brigs, got into battle array in front of the line and within range of the cannon of our flotilla. Then the fight began, and the balls came from every direction. Nelson, who had promised the destruction of the flotilla, reinforced his line of battle by two other ranks of vessels and frigates; thus placed in echelon, they fought with a great superiority of forces. For more than seven hours, the sea, covered with fire and smoke, offered to the whole population of Boulogne the superb and frightful spectacle of a naval combat where more than eighteen hundred cannons were discharged at once. Nelson's genius could do nothing against our sailors and soldiers. Admiral Bruix was in his barrack, which was placed near the coast-telegraph of signals. He fought Nelson from there, drinking with his staff and several ladies of Boulogne whom he had invited to dinner. The guests were chanting the first victories of the First Consul, while the Admiral, without leaving the table, manœuvred the flotilla by means of the signals he ordered. Nelson, impatient to conquer, brought forward all his naval forces, but the wind being against him, he could not keep the promise he had made in London to burn our flotilla. Far from that, several of his vessels were badly damaged, and Admiral Bruix, seeing the English drawing off, shouted victory while pouring champagne for his guests. The French flotilla had not suffered much, while the enemy's squadron had been ruined by the continual firing of our stationary batteries. On that day, the English recognized that it would be impossible for them to approach the coast of Boulogne, which they have since surnamed the Iron Coast (*Côte de Fer*).

When the First Consul quitted Boulogne, he was to go to Abbeville and remain there twenty-four hours. The mayor of that town had neglected nothing to receive him worthily. Abbeville was superb on that day. The most beautiful trees in a neighboring wood had been dug up by their roots to form avenues in all the streets through which the First Consul was to pass. Several inhabitants who owned magnificent gardens, had sent their rarest shrubs to range along his route. Carpets from the manufactory of MM. Hecquet-Dorval were stretched on the ground to be trodden by his horses. An unexpected circumstance suddenly disturbed the fête: a courier, expedited by the minister of police, arrived just as we were approaching the city. The minister warned the First Consul that they meant to assassinate him two leagues from there; the day and hour were indicated.

To frustrate the intended attack against his person, the First Consul passed through the city on a gallop, and, followed by several lancers, went to the place where he was to be attacked; there he made a halt of about half an hour, ate some Abbeville biscuits, and went back again. The assassins were tricked; their preparations had been made for the next day.

The First Consul and Madame Bonaparte continued their journey across Picardy, Flanders, and the Low Countries. War vessels were daily offered him by the different councils-general. They continued to address him and to present him with the keys of cities as if he were exercising royal power. Amiens, Dunkirk, Lille, Bruges, Ghent, Brussels, Liège, Namur, distinguished themselves by the brilliancy of the reception they gave the illustrious travellers. The inhabitants of the city of Antwerp presented the First Consul with six magnificent bay horses. Likewise the First Consul left behind him serviceable marks of his passage. By his orders the works were at once begun for cleaning and improving the port of Amiens. In this city, and in others when it was going on, he visited the exhibition of industrial products, encouraging the manufacturers by his counsels and assisting them by his decrees. At Liège he placed at the disposal of the prefect of the Ourthe a sum of three hundred thousand francs for the repair of the houses burned by the Austrians in this department, during the first wars of the Revolution. Antwerp owed to him its inner port, its basins, and its dockyards. At Brussels, he ordered the junction of the Rhine, the Meuse, and the Scheldt by a canal. He caused a stone bridge to be thrown across the Meuse at Givet, and, at Sedan, the widow Rousseau received from him a sum of sixty thousand francs for the rebuilding of her factory, which had been destroyed by fire. In fine, I could not enumerate all the benefits, public or private, which the First Consul and Madame Bonaparte strewed along their route.

Shortly after our return to Saint-Cloud, the First Consul, being out in a carriage with his wife and M. Cambacérès, took the notion to drive four-in-hand the horses attached to it, which were those that had been given to him by the inhabitants of Antwerp. He mounted on the box, therefore, and took the reins from the hands of César, his coachman, who got up behind. They were just then in the horseshoe alley, which goes by way of the Breteuil pavilion and Ville-d'Avray. It says in the *Memorial of Saint-Helena*, that *the aide-de-camp, having awkwardly crossed the horses, made them run away.* César, who gave me all the details of this lamentable adventure, did not say a word about the aide-de-camp; and, in all conscience, no other awkwardness was required to upset the carriage than that of a coachman as inexperienced as the First Consul. Besides, the horses were young and spirited, and César himself needed all his skill to drive them. Not feeling his hand any longer, they started off at a gallop; and César, seeing the new direction they were taking towards the right, began to shout: *To the left!* with the voice of a stentor. Consul Cambacérès, paler than ever, took very little pains to reassure the frightened Madame Bonaparte, but cried with all his might: "Stop! stop! you are going to smash us!" That might easily have happened; but the First Consul heard nothing, and moreover he was no longer master of his horses. On arriving, or rather on being dragged to the gate, he could not take the middle of the road, but ran against a post and fell out heavily. Fortunately the horses stopped. The First Consul, thrown ten feet and striking on his stomach, fainted and did not come to himself until some one touched him to pick him up. Madame Bonaparte and the Second Consul received only slight contusions, but the good Josephine had suffered horribly from anxiety about her husband. However, though he had been rudely shaken up, he would not be bled, and contented himself with being rubbed with cologne water, his favorite remedy. That night, on going to bed, he talked gayly about his mishap and the extreme fright which his colleague had displayed, and ended by saying: "*We must render to César the things that are César's;* let him keep his whip, and every one stick to his trade." He admitted, however, in spite of his pleasantries, that he had never thought himself so near death, and even that he deemed himself dead for some seconds. I do not remember whether it was on this occasion or on some other that I heard the Emperor say that *death was nothing but a sleep without dreams.*

In October of this year the First Consul received in public audience Haled-Effendi, ambassador of the Ottoman Porte.

The arrival of the Turkish ambassador made a sensation at the Tuileries, because he brought a great quantity of cashmere shawls to the First Consul; people were sure they would be distributed, and each woman flattered herself on being favorably treated.

I think that without his strange costume, and especially without his cashmeres, he would have produced very little effect on persons accustomed to see sovereign princes pay their court to the head of the government both at home and abroad. Even his costume was not more remarkable than that of Roustan, to which we were accustomed, and as to his obeisances, they were hardly more profound than those of the ordinary courtiers of the First Consul. At Paris, they say that the enthusiasm lasted longer. *'Tis so droll to be a Turk!* Some ladies had the honor to see the bearded ambassador eat; he was polite and even gallant with them, and gave them several presents which were much boasted of. His manners were not too Mussulman-like, and he was not afraid to see our pretty Parisians without a veil on their faces. One day, which he spent almost entirely at Saint-Cloud, I saw him making his prayer. It was in the court of honor, on a large parapet bordered by a stone balustrade. The ambassador had carpets stretched alongside the apartments which were afterwards those of the King of Rome, and there he made his genuflections in sight of several members of the household, who, out of discretion, kept themselves behind the shutters. In the evening he was present at the theatre. I think they played *Zaire* or *Mahomet;* he did not understand a word.

CHAPTER XII

Another journey to Boulogne — Visit to the flotilla and review of the troops — The line's jealousy of the guard — The First Consul at the camp — The General's anger with the soldiers — Boredom of the officers and pleasures of the camp — Timidity of the Boulognese women — Jealousy of the husbands — Visits of the women of Paris, Abbeville, Dunkirk, and Amiens to the camp of Boulogne — Soirées at the house of the mistress of Colonel Joseph Bonaparte — Generals Soult, Saint-Hilaire, and Andréossy — The clever woman and the two happy lovers — Curiosity of the First Consul — The First Consul taken for a war commissioner — Commencement of General Bertrand's favor — Regulator Arcambal and the two visitors — The First Consul spying on his brother, who pretends not to recognize him — The First Consul and the innocent games — The First Consul has nothing to give as a forfeit — Note from the First Consul — Naval combat — The First Consul commands a manœuvre and makes a mistake — Error recognized and silence of the General — The First Consul points the cannons and has the bullets reddened — Fight between two Picards — Continual explosion — Dinner to the roar of cannons — English frigate dismasted and brig run down.

IN November of this year, the First Consul returned to Boulogne to visit the flotilla and review some troops which were already assembled there, in the camps destined for the army with which he proposed to descend on England. I have preserved some notes and still more souvenirs of my different sojourns in Boulogne. Never did the Emperor display elsewhere a greater military power.

Never did any one see assembled, on one spot, troops that were finer or readier to march at the slightest sign from their chief. It is not surprising, then, that I have found in my memory of this epoch details which no one, I think, has yet thought of publishing. Nor has any person, if I do not deceive myself, been in a better position to know them than I. As to that, the reader will soon be able to judge for himself.

In the different reviews held by the First Consul, he seemed to wish to excite the enthusiasm of the soldiers and their attachment to his person, by the care with which he seized every occasion to flatter their self-love.

One day, having particularly remarked the excellent appearance of the 36th and 57th regiments of the line and of the 10th light infantry, he made all the chiefs come out of the ranks, from the corporals to the colonels, and going amongst them, he showed his satisfaction by reminding them of the occasions when, under the fire of cannon, he had also made complimentary remarks on these three brave regiments. He complimented the non-commissioned officers on the good training of the soldiers, and the captains and chiefs of battalion on the ensemble and the precision of the manœuvres. In a word, each one had his share of praise.

This flattering distinction did not excite the jealousy of the other army corps; each regiment had received that day its greater or lesser portion of compliments, and when the review was ended, they returned peaceably to their cantonments. But the soldiers of the 36th, 57th, and 10th, very proud of having been favored so signally, went in the afternoon to display their triumph in an out-of-town café frequented by the mounted grenadiers of the guard. They began by quiet drinking, talking about campaigns, cities that had been taken, the First Consul, and finally the morning's review; then some young men of Boulogne, who had mingled with the drinkers, took the notion of singing some very recently composed couplets, in which the bravery and the exploits of the three regiments were lauded to the skies, without a word being said of the rest of the army, not even of the guard; and it was in the favorite café of the guard that these couplets were sung! The latter at first maintained a gloomy silence; but presently, pushed too far, they loudly protested against these verses, which they declared detestable. The quarrel began in a very lively fashion; there was a good deal of shouting, they insulted each other, and then separated, but without too much noise, giving a rendezvous for the next morning at four o'clock, in the environs of Marquise, a little village two leagues from Boulogne. It was very late in the evening when the soldiers left the café.

More than two hundred grenadiers of the guard repaired separately to the place of rendezvous, and found the ground occupied by a nearly equal number of adversaries of the 36th, 57th, and 10th.

Without explanations, without uproar, each took his sabre in his hand, and fought during more than an hour with appalling coolness. One Martin, a grenadier of the guard, a man of gigantic stature, killed with his own hand seven or eight soldiers of the 10th. They would probably all have been massacred if General Saint-Hilaire, apprised too late of this sanguinary quarrel, had not at once sent out a regiment of cavalry which put a stop to the fighting. The grenadiers had lost ten men, and the soldiers of the line thirteen; the wounded on both sides were very many.

The First Consul went to the camp the next morning, had the provocators of this terrible scene brought before him, and said to them in a severe tone: "I know why you fought; several brave men have succumbed in a struggle unworthy of them and of you. You shall be punished. I have ordered that the verses which were the cause of so many misfortunes shall be printed. I intend that in learning your punishment, the Boulognese shall know that you have forfeited the esteem of your brothers in arms."

Meanwhile the troops, and especially the officers, began to be tired of their stay in Boulogne, a city less adapted, perhaps, than any other to render an inactive existence supportable. Nevertheless they did not murmur, for there had never been found room for murmurs where the First Consul was; but they stormed with bated breath at being kept in camp or in the harbor, with England before them and only nine or ten leagues off. Pleasures were rare in Boulogne; the Boulognese women, charming persons in general, dared not give parties in their own houses, lest they should displease their husbands, very jealous men, like all Picards. And yet there was a fine hall in which balls and soirées might easily have been given; but, although they may have wished to, these ladies dared not make use of it; it was necessary that a certain number of fair Parisians, moved by the sad fate of so many brave and handsome officers, should come to Boulogne to beguile the weariness of so long a repose. The example of the Parisians piqued the women of Abbeville, Dunkirk, and Amiens, and Boulogne was presently replenished with male and female strangers who came to do the honors of the city.

Among all these ladies, she who attracted most attention by an excellent tone and plenty of wit and beauty, was one Madame F——, of Dunkirk, an excellent musician, full of gaiety, graces, and youth; it was impossible that Madame F—— should not turn many heads. Colonel Joseph, brother of the First Consul, General Soult, who was afterwards marshal, Generals Saint-Hilaire and Andréossy, and several other great personages were at her feet. Only two succeeded in making themselves acceptable, and of these one was Colonel Joseph, who soon passed in the town for the favored lover of Madame F——. The fair Dunkirker often gave soirées, at which Colonel

Joseph never failed to be present. Among all his rivals, and he certainly had a good many, one alone took umbrage at him; this was Soult, the general-in-chief. This rivalry was not at all prejudicial to the interests of Madame F⸺; like a skilful tactician, she adroitly provoked the jealousy of her two aspirants, by accepting in turn from each of them compliments, bouquets of roses, and better than that occasionally.

The First Consul, informed of his brother's amours, took the whim one evening of going to amuse himself at the little salon of Madame F⸺, which was merely a room on the first story of a joiner's house in the rue des Minimes. So as not to be recognized, he put on citizen's dress, and wore a wig and spectacles. He took General Bertrand into his confidence, who was already in great favor with him, and who also was careful to do all in his power to make himself unrecognizable.

Thus disguised, the First Consul and his companion presented themselves at Madame F⸺'s and asked for the major-domo Arcambal. The strictest incognito was recommended to M. Arcambal by the First Consul, who would not have been recognized for all the world. M. Arcambal promised secrecy. The two visitors were announced as civil commissioners at the army.

They were playing *bouillotte:* the tables were covered with gold, and the game and the punch absorbed the attention of the joyous habitués to such a point that none of them took any heed of the two personages who had just entered. As to the mistress of the house, she had never seen close by either the First Consul or General Bertrand; consequently there was nothing to fear from her. I can well believe that Colonel Joseph recognized his brother, but he gave no sign of it.

The First Consul, avoiding observation as much as possible, watched the looks interchanged between his brother and Madame F——. Convinced of their mutual understanding, he was about to quit the salon of the pretty Dunkirker, when she, who did not fancy seeing the number of her guests diminishing as yet, ran to the pretended commissioners, and graciously detained them, saying that they were going to play little games, and that they must not go without having given forfeits. The First Consul, having consulted General Bertrand by a glance, found it amusing to remain and play at *innocent* games.

In fact, at the end of several minutes, on the request of Madame F——, the players deserted *bouillotte* and ranged themselves in a circle around her. They began by dancing the *boulangère*; then followed the *innocent* games. It came the First Consul's turn to give a forfeit. He was at first much embarrassed, having nothing about him but a scrap of paper on which he had written the names of certain colonels in lead pencil. However, he confided this paper to Madame F——, begging her not to open it. The wish of the First Consul was respected, and the paper remained closed on the knees of the fair lady until the forfeit should be redeemed. This moment arrived, and some one imposed on the great captain the singular penance of playing the *porter*, while Madame F——, with Colonel Joseph, should make the *voyage to Cythera* in the next room. The First Consul acquitted himself with a good grace of the part he had to play; then, after the forfeits had been returned, he signed to General Bertrand to follow him. They went out, and presently the joiner, who lived on the ground-floor, came up to deliver a little note to Madame F——. It contained these words:

"I thank you, Madame, for the amiable welcome you have given me. If you come some day to my *baraque*, I will again play the porter, if you like; but this time I will not leave to others the care of accompanying you in the voyage to Cythera.

"*Signed:*   BONAPARTE."

The charming Dunkirker read the note to herself; but she did not allow the givers of forfeits to remain ignorant that they had received the visit of the First Consul. At the end of an hour they separated, leaving Madame F—— alone to reflect on the visit and the note of the great man.

It was during this same sojourn that there was a terrible combat in the roadstead of Boulogne to protect the entry into the port of a flotilla composed of twenty or thirty vessels, coming from Ostend, Dunkirk, and Nieuport, loaded with munitions for the national fleet.

A magnificent frigate, carrying thirty-six cannon, a cutter and a brig of the first rank were detached from the English fleet in order to intercept the Batavian flotilla; but they were received in a manner that deprived them of all wish to return there.

The port of Boulogne was defended by five forts: the fort de la Crèche, the fort en Bois, the fort Musoir, and the ordnance tower, all provided with an extraordinary abundance of cannons and mortars. The line of broadside which barred the entry was composed of two hundred and fifty gunboats and other vessels; the division of imperial gunboats formed part of them.

Each gunboat carried three twenty-four pound cannons, two bow-chasers, and one stern-chaser. Five hundred pieces of ordnance, then, were playing on the enemy independently of all the batteries of the forts. Each piece fired more than three times a minute.

The fight began at one in the afternoon. The weather was superb. At the first discharge of cannon, the First Consul left the headquarters at the Pont-de-Briques, and went off at a gallop, followed by his staff, to give his orders to Admiral Bruix. Presently, wishing to observe for himself the movements of the defence, and aid in directing them, he jumped into a boat rowed by the marines of the guard, and was followed by the Admiral and several officers.

Thus it was that the First Consul went into the midst of the vessels which formed the line of broadside, through a thousand dangers and a rain of shells, bombs, and bullets. Intending to land at Wimereux after having gone through the line, he turned toward the Croï tower, saying that he must double it. Admiral Bruix, alarmed at the thought of the useless danger they were going to incur, represented the imprudence of this manœuvre to the First Consul. "What shall we gain by doubling this fort? Nothing but bullets. . . . General, by turning it we should arrive just as quickly." The First Consul was not of the Admiral's opinion; he persisted in wishing to double the tower. The Admiral, at the risk of being cashiered, gave contrary orders to the sailors; and the First Consul saw himself obliged to pass behind the fort, very much irritated and addressing reproaches to the Admiral, which very soon ceased; for the yawl had hardly passed when a transport boat which had doubled the Croï tower, was crushed and sunk by three or four shells.

The First Consul held his peace on seeing how right the Admiral had been, and the rest of the way was accomplished without hindrance as far as the little port of Wimereux. On arriving there, he went up the cliff to encourage the cannoneers. He spoke to every one of them, slapped them on the shoulder, and incited them to take good aim. "Courage, my friends," he said to them; "think that you are fighting fellows who will hold out a long time: send them off with the honors of war." While looking at the fine resistance and the majestic manœuvres of the frigate, he asked: "Do you think the captain can be English, my lads? I don't believe it."

The gunners, inflamed by the words of the First Consul, redoubled their ardor and speed. "Keep looking at the frigate, General," cried one of them; "the bowsprit is going to come down." He had spoken truly; the mast of the bowsprit was cut in two by the ball. "Give this fellow twenty francs," said the First Consul, addressing the officers who had followed him.

Beside the batteries of Wimereux was a forge to heat the bullets. The First Consul watched the smiths at work and gave them his advice. "That is not red enough, my lads; we must send them redder than that . . . come, come!" One of the men had known him as a lieutenant of artillery, and said to his comrades: "He understands these little things finely . . . just as he does big ones."

That day, two soldiers without arms, who, stationed on the cliff, were looking at the manœuvres, began to quarrel with each other in a very comical manner. "Look," said one, "do you see the little corporal down there?" "No, I don't see him." — "What, don't you see him in his yawl?" "Ah yes! but he can't be thinking what he is about, that's sure; if he should get a rap now, he would set the whole army crying. Why does he expose himself like that?" — "Heavens! that's his place." "Not at all." — "I say it is." "No, I say." — "Look here, what would you do to-morrow if the little corporal were killed?" "Eh! but I tell you that's his place," etc.; and not having, as it appeared, strong enough arguments on either side, they came to fisticuffs. It took a good deal of trouble to separate them.

The combat had begun at one o'clock in the afternoon; at about ten in the evening the Batavian flotilla entered the port amidst the most horrible firing I ever saw. In this obscurity, the bombs which crossed each other in every direction formed an arch of fire above the harbor and the city. The continual explosion of all this artillery was repeated by the echoes from the cliffs with a frightful noise; and, singularly enough, not a person in the city was afraid. The Boulognese had become accustomed to danger; they were expecting something terrible every day; they had the preparations for attack or defence under their eyes all the time; they had become soldiers by dint of seeing them. On that day they dined to the roar of cannon, but everybody dined; the dinner hour was neither advanced nor retarded. Men went to their business, women occupied themselves with their housekeeping, young girls practised the piano. . . . All beheld with indifference the cannon balls passing over their heads, and the curious, whom a desire to see the combat had attracted to the cliff, seemed scarcely more affected than people usually are on seeing a military piece played at Franconi's.

I still wonder how three vessels could have endured for more than nine hours such a violent shock. At the moment when the flotilla entered the port the English cutter had sunk, the brig had been burned by the red-hot balls; nothing remained but the frigate, with its masts shattered, its sails torn, and yet standing as immovable as a rock. It was so close to the line of broadside that the sailors on either side could recognize and count each other. Behind her, at a reasonable distance, were more than a hundred English sail. At last, after ten o'clock, a signal from the English admiral made the frigate put about, and the firing ceased. The line of broadside was not greatly damaged in this long and terrible fight, because the guns of the frigate carried nearly always into the rigging, and never into the body of the boats. The brig and the cutter did the most harm.

CHAPTER XIII

Return of the First Consul to Paris — Arrival of Prince Camille Borghese — Pauline Bonaparte and her first husband, General Leclerc — The General's love for his wife — Portrait of General Leclerc — Departure of the General for Santo Domingo — The First Consul decrees the departure of his sister also — Revolt of Christophe and Dessalines — Arrival of the General and his wife at the Cape — Courage of Madame Leclerc — Insurrection of the blacks — The remains of the army of Brest, and twelve thousand revolted negroes — Heroic valor of the General-in-Chief, attacked by a fatal disease — Courage of Madame Leclerc — Nobleness and intrepidity — Pauline saving her son — Death of General Leclerc — Marriage of Pauline — Chagrin of Lafon, and response of Mademoiselle Duchesnois — M. Jules de Canouville and the Princess Borghese — The Princess in disgrace with the Emperor — Generosity of the Princess toward her brother — The only friend that remained to him — The diamonds of the Princess in the Emperor's carriage at the battle of Waterloo.

THE First Consul quitted Boulogne to return to Paris, where he wished to be present at the marriage of one of his sisters. Prince Camille Borghese, a descendant of one of the most noble families of Rome, had arrived there to marry Madame Pauline Bonaparte, widow of General Leclerc, who died of yellow fever at Santo Domingo.

I remember having seen this unhappy general, at the house of the First Consul, some time before his departure for the fatal expedition which cost him his life and France the loss of so many brave soldiers and of enormous sums of money. General Leclerc, whose name is now almost forgotten, or even in some sort abandoned to contempt, was a kind and benevolent man. He was passionately enamoured of his wife, whose levity, to say nothing worse, afflicted and plunged him into a profound and habitual melancholy which it was painful to behold. The Princess Pauline (who was far enough from being a princess then) had nevertheless married him freely and from choice; which did not prevent her from tormenting her husband by caprices without end, and telling him a hundred times a day that he was very fortunate in having a sister of the First Consul for his wife. I am convinced that, with his simple tastes and pacific temper, General Leclerc would have liked less brilliancy and more repose much better.

The First Consul had required his sister to accompany the General to Santo Domingo. She was obliged to obey and to quit Paris, where she wielded the sceptre of fashion and eclipsed all other women by her elegance and her coquetry as much as by her incomparable beauty, in order to go and brave a dangerous climate and the ferocious companions of Christophe and Dessalines. At the close of the year 1801, the flag-ship *Océan* had sailed for the Cape, with General Leclerc, his wife, and their son on board.

On arriving at the Cape, the conduct of Madame Leclerc was above all praise. On more than one occasion, but particularly on that which I am going to try to recall, she displayed a courage worthy of her name and the position of her husband. I have these details from an eye-witness, whom I knew in Paris in the service of the Princess Pauline.

The day of the great insurrection of the blacks, in September, 1802, the bands of Christophe and Dessalines, composed of more than twelve thousand negroes exasperated by their hatred against the whites, and their certainty that if they failed no quarter would be given them, came to assault the Cape town, which was defended by only a thousand soldiers. These were the only remnants of that numerous army which had gone out of Brest a year earlier, so brilliant and so full of hope. This handful of heroes, the majority of them weak from fever, commanded by the general-in-chief of the expedition, who was likewise suffering from the malady of which he died, repulsed the repeated attacks of the negroes with unheard-of efforts and heroic valor.

During the combat, in which the fury if not the numbers and force were equal on both sides, Madame Leclerc was with her son, and under the guard of a devoted friend who had only a weak artillery company at his orders, in the house where her husband had established his residence, at the foot of the rocks bordering the coast. The General-in-Chief, fearing lest this residence might be surprised by a part of the enemy, and unable to foresee the result of the struggle he was maintaining at the upper end of the Cape, where the blacks were making their most furious assaults, sent orders to have his wife and son taken on board the French fleet. Pauline would not consent to it. Always true to the pride inspired in her by her name (though there was this time both grandeur and nobility in her pride), she said to the ladies of the city, who had taken shelter with her, and who were entreating her to depart, and telling her horrible things about the treatment to which women were exposed by the negroes: "The rest of you can go. You are not Bonaparte's sisters."

However, the danger increasing every moment, General Leclerc sent an aide-de-camp to the residence, who was enjoined, in case of a new refusal on the part of Pauline, to take her on board in spite of herself. The officer was obliged to execute this order strictly. Madame Leclerc was held by force in an armchair carried by four soldiers. A grenadier marched at her side, with the son of his general in his arms; and during this scene of flight and terror, the child, already worthy of his mother, played with his conductor's plume. Followed by her cortège of women, all trembling and in tears, of whom her courage was the only rampart on this dangerous transit, Pauline was transported in this way as far as the seashore. But just as they were about to put her in the boat, another of her husband's aides brought her news of the defeat of the blacks. "You see," said she as they were returning to the house, "I was right in not wishing to embark." Still she was not yet entirely out of danger. A troop of negroes belonging to the army which had just been so miraculously repulsed, and seeking to effect their retreat among the piers, met the feeble escort of Madame Leclerc. The insurgents seemed to be intending to attack them; they had to be driven off by muskets fired in their very faces. Pauline maintained an imperturbable presence of mind in the midst of this affray.

All these circumstances were of course reported to the First Consul; his self-love was flattered by them, and I think it was to the Prince Borghese that he said one day at his levee: "Pauline was predestined to espouse a Roman; for she is all Roman, from head to foot."

Unhappily this courage, which a man might have envied her, was not accompanied in the Princess Pauline by those less brilliant and more modest virtues which are nevertheless more necessary to a woman and more rightfully expected of her than audacity and indifference to danger.

I do not know whether it is true, as has been written somewhere, that Madame Leclerc had an affection for an actor of the Théâtre Français at the time she was obliged to go to Santo Domingo. Neither can I say whether Mademoiselle Duchesnois did really have the naïveté to exclaim in the presence of a hundred persons, apropos of this departure: "Lafon will never be consoled for it; he is capable of dying on account of it." But what I personally knew of the frailties of this princess would easily incline me to believe this anecdote.

All Paris knew the particular favor with which she honored M. Jules de Canouville,[1] a young and brilliant colonel, of great bravery, perfect figure,

---

[1] M. Bousquet, a celebrated dentist, was summoned to Neuilly (the residence of the Princess Pauline), in order to examine the teeth of Her Imperial Highness. On being introduced into her apartments, he made ready to begin his operation. "Sir," said a charming young man in a dressing gown, lying negligently on a sofa, "take good care, I entreat you, about what you are going to do. I am extremely attached to my Paulette's teeth, and will make you responsible for any accident." "Be easy, my Prince; I can assure Your Imperial Highness that there will not be the least danger." The advice continued all the time that M. Bousquet was occupied in arranging this pretty mouth; at last, having finished what he had to do, he passed into the attendants' hall, where the ladies of the palace, the chamberlains, etc., were assembled, awaiting their time to enter the apartment of the Princess. They made haste to ask M. Bousquet questions. "Her Imperial Highness is very well," said he, "and she ought to be very happy in the tender attachment of her august spouse, which he has just been displaying before me in such a touching manner. His anxiety was extreme, and it was with difficulty that I could reassure him about the consequences of the simplest thing in the world. I shall tell everywhere what I have just witnessed. It is sweet to be able to cite such examples of conjugal tenderness in so elevated a rank. I am really impressed by it." Nobody tried to interrupt the worthy M. Bousquet in the expression of his enthusiasm; the longing to laugh prevented a word from being said; and he went away convinced that nowhere was there to be found a more admirable family life than that of the Prince and Princess Borghese. The former was in Italy, and the handsome young man was M. de Canouville. I have borrowed this curious anecdote from the *Mémoires de Joséphine*, the author of which, who has seen and observed the courts of Navarre and Malmaison with so much truth and good judgment, is, I am told, a woman, and who cannot, in fact, be other than a very intelligent woman, and one better placed than any one else for knowing the private life of Her Majesty the Empress.

and a recklessness which gained him innumerable successes with certain women, although he employed very little discretion with them. The Princess Pauline's liaison with this amiable officer was the most durable that she ever formed. Unfortunately, neither of them was at all reserved, and their mutual affection soon acquired a scandalous publicity. Later, I shall have occasion to relate, in its own place, the adventure which caused the disgrace, banishment, and perhaps the death of Colonel de Canouville; the whole army deplored his death, so premature and above all so cruel, because it was not by an enemy's bullet that he was struck.[1]

Yet, whatever may have been the weakness of the Princess Pauline for her lovers, and although such incredible examples of it may be cited, without departing from truth, her admirable devotion to the person of His Majesty the Emperor, in 1814, should cause her faults to be treated with indulgence.

A hundred times had the heedlessness of her conduct, and especially her failure in attention and respect toward the Empress Marie-Louise, irritated the Emperor against the Princess Borghese. He always ended by forgiving her. Still, at the time of her august brother's fall, she was again in disgrace. On being informed that the island of Elba had been assigned as a prison to the Emperor, she hastened to

---

[1] He was killed by a bullet from a French gun, discharged by some one after an action in which he had displayed the most brilliant courage.

shut herself up there with him, abandoning Rome and Italy, whose most beautiful palaces belonged to her. At the critical period before the battle of Waterloo, His Majesty found the heart of his sister Pauline faithful. Fearing that he might need money, she sent him her richest diamond ornaments, the price of which was enormous. They were found in the carriage of the Emperor, which was taken at Waterloo, and exposed to the curiosity of the inhabitants of London. But the diamonds have been lost, at least to their legitimate owner.

CHAPTER XIV

Arrest of General Moreau — Constant sent as an observer — General Moreau married by Madame Bonaparte — Mademoiselle Hulot — Madame Hulot — Lofty pretensions — Moreau's opposition — His railleries — Intrigues and conspiracies of malcontents — Testimonies of affection given by the First Consul to General Moreau — What the Emperor said and did the day that General Moreau's aides-de-camp were arrested — General Foy's companion in arms — The abduction — Excessive severity toward Colonel Delélée — A child's stratagem — Arbitrary measures — The Emperor's inflexibility — The deputies of Besançon and Marshal M—— — Panic and firmness — Court friends — A formal audience at the Tuileries — Reception of the Bisontins — Courageous response — Reparation — A change of opinions — The old comrades — The chief of staff of the army of Portugal — Premature death — Surveillance exercised over the members of the Emperor's household at each new conspiracy — The keeper of the portfolio — Registers of the concierges — The Emperor's jealousy excited by a suspected name.

THE First Consul was in a state of great agitation on the day of General Moreau's arrest. All the morning, his emissaries and the agents of the police were going and coming. Measures had been taken so that the arrest should be made at the same hour, whether at Gros-Bois, or at the general's residence in the rue du Faubourg Saint-Honoré. The First Consul was anxiously walking up and down in his chamber. He had me called and ordered me to go and station myself in front of the general's Paris house to observe whether the arrest was made, and if there were any tumult, and to come back quickly and report to him. I obeyed, but nothing extraordinary was passing in the house, and I saw nobody but some police spies strolling in the street, and keeping an eye on the door of the dwelling inhabited by the man who had been designated as their prey. My presence might have been noticed, so I departed, and on my way back to the château, I learned that General Moreau had been arrested on the road as he was returning to Paris from Gros-Bois, which he sold a few months later to Marshal Berthier, before starting for the United States. I quickened my pace and ran to announce the tidings of the arrest to the First Consul. He knew it already and made me no reply. He was still pensive and dreamy, as he had been in the morning.

As I have been led to speak of General Moreau, I will recall the fatal circumstances by which he was impelled to tarnish his fame. Madame Bonaparte had married him to Mademoiselle Hulot, her friend, and like herself a creole of the Isle de France. This young person, sweet, amiable, and full of the qualities which make a good wife and mother, loved her husband passionately; she was proud of that glorious name which surrounded her with respect and honors. But, unfortunately, she had the greatest deference for her mother, who was very ambitious, and desired nothing less than to behold her daughter seated on a throne. Her empire over Madame Moreau soon included the general himself, who, ruled by her counsels, became sombre, dreamy, melancholy, and lost forever that tranquillity of mind which had distinguished him. From that time the general's house was open to plots and intrigues; all the malcontents, and there were many of them, met each other there; from that time the general undertook to disapprove all the acts of the First Consul; he opposed the re-establishment of public worship, he called the institution of the Legion of Honor a piece of childish and ridiculous mummery. These grave imprudences, and plenty of others, soon reached, as may readily be believed, the ears of the First Consul, who at first refused to credit them; but how could he remain deaf to insinuations that daily returned with increased force, and were doubtless envenomed by malice?

Now, while the imprudent speeches of the general were contributing to ruin him in the mind of the First Consul, his mother-in-law, with dangerous obstinacy, encouraged him in his opposition, persuaded, as she said, that the future would do justice to the present. She was not aware how truly she spoke. The general rushed headlong into the abyss which opened in front of him. How altogether contrary was his conduct to his character! He had a decided aversion for the English; he detested the Chouans and all that pertained to the old nobility. Besides, a man like General Moreau, after having served his country so gloriously, was not made to carry arms against her. But he was misled, and he misled himself in thinking that he was fit to play a great political rôle. He was ruined by the flattery of a party which raised as many enmities as it could against the First Consul by exciting the jealousy of his former companions in arms.

I have seen more than one token of affection given by the First Consul to General Moreau. During one of the latter's visits to the Tuileries, and while he was conversing with the First Consul, General Carnot came in from Versailles with a pair of very elaborately wrought pistols, presented to the First Consul by the manufactory of Versailles. To take these two beautiful weapons from the hands of General Carnot, to examine them a moment, and then offer them to General Moreau, saying: "Keep them; they could not come more apropos," — all that was done quicker than I can write it. The general could not have been more flattered by this proof of friendship, and he warmly thanked the First Consul.

The name and the trial of General Moreau remind me of the story of a brave officer who found himself compromised in this unhappy affair, and barely extricated himself from it, after several years of disgrace, by dint of the courage with which he ventured to expose himself to the Emperor's wrath. The authenticity of the details I am going to give can be attested, at need, by living persons whom I shall have occasion to name in my recital, and whose testimony no reader would dream of rejecting.

General Moreau's disgrace at first extended to all who were connected with him: the affection and devotion borne him by the army men, whether officers or soldiers, who had served under him, was well known. His aides-de-camp were arrested, even those who were not in Paris.

One of these, Colonel Delélée, had been several months at Besançon on furlough, reposing from his campaigns in the bosom of his family, along with a young wife to whom he had not long been married, but occupying himself very little with political affairs, a good deal with his pleasures, and not at all with conspiracies. The comrade and brother in arms of Colonels Guilleminot, Hugo,[1] and Foy,[2] all three of whom afterward became generals, he spent joyous evenings with them in garrison and agreeable ones at home. All at once Colonel Delélée was arrested, thrown into a post-chaise, and it was only when they were rolling at a gallop on the road to Paris that he learned from the officer of gendarmerie, who accompanied him, that General Moreau had conspired, and that in his capacity as aide-de-camp of the General he was included among the conspirators.

On arriving at Paris, the Colonel was put into close custody, at *La Force*, I think. His wife, justly alarmed, hastened in pursuit of him; but it was not until after a great many days that she obtained

---

[1] The father of M. Victor Hugo, who is himself the godson of Madame Delélée.

[2] The illustrious General Foy.

permission to communicate with the prisoner, and even then she could do so only by signs. She would remain in the court of the prison, while he would show himself for some moments, and pass his hand through the bars of his window.

However, the rigor of these orders was abated for the Colonel's son, a little child of three or four years. His father obtained the favor of embracing him. He came every morning in his mother's arms, and a turnkey would take him to the prisoner. In presence of this troublesome witness the poor little fellow would play his part with all the cunning of a consummate dissimulator. He would pretend to be lame, and complain that there were grains of sand in his shoe that hurt him. The Colonel, turning his back on the jailer, would take the child on his knee to rid him of what troubled him, and find in the shoe a note from his wife, apprising him in very few words of the progress of the legal inquiry, and what he had to hope or fear on his own account.

At last, after several months of captivity, sentence having been passed on the conspirators, Colonel Delélée, against whom no accusation had been brought, was not absolved, as he had a right to expect, but struck off the army rolls, and arbitrarily sent away under surveillance, and forbidden to come within forty leagues of Paris. At first he was also enjoined not to return to Besançon, and it was not until he had been out of prison for a year that he was permitted to live there.

Young and full of courage, the Colonel beheld, from the depths of his retreat, his friends and comrades making their way and gaining name, rank, and glory on the field of battle. He saw himself condemned to inaction and obscurity. He spent his days in following on the maps the triumphant march of those armies in which he felt that he deserved to resume his rank. A thousand requests were addressed by him and by his friends to the chief of the Empire, that he would permit him to go merely as a volunteer, to join his former comrades, were it with a knapsack on his back. His prayers were rejected. The Emperor's will was inflexible, and to every new application he answered: " Let him wait."

The inhabitants of Besançon, who considered Colonel Delélée their compatriot, interested themselves keenly in the misfortune of this brave officer. An occasion presented itself to recommend him anew to the clemency, or rather to the justice, of the Emperor, and they profited by it.

This was, I think, on the return from the campaign of Prussia and Poland. Deputations were coming from all parts of France, charged to congratulate the Emperor on his new victories. Colonel Delélée was unanimously elected a member of the deputation from Doubs, of which the mayor and the prefect of Besançon formed part, and which was presided over by the worthy Marshal M——.

An occasion, then, is at last offered to Colonel Delélée to have the long interdict raised which has weighed upon his head and kept his sword idle! He will speak to the Emperor; he will complain, respectfully but with dignity, of the motiveless disgrace in which he has been detained so long. He will render heartfelt thanks to the generous affection of his fellow-citizens, whose suffrages will, he hopes, plead in his favor with His Majesty.

The Besançon deputies, on their arrival in Paris, have themselves presented to the different ministers. The minister of police takes the president of the deputation aside, and asks him what signifies the presence among the deputies of a man publicly known to be in disgrace, and the sight of whom cannot fail to be disagreeable to the chief of the Empire.

On issuing from this private interview, Marshal M—— enters, pale and terrified, the apartment of Colonel Delélée.

"All is lost, my friend! I see, by the looks of things at the bureau, that they are still ill-disposed toward you. If the Emperor sees you amongst us, he will take that for an express intention to go against his orders, and he will be furious."

"Ah well, what can I do about that?"

"But, to avoid compromising the department, the deputation, to avoid compromising yourself, you might well, perhaps —"

The Marshal hesitates.

"I should do well?" asks the Colonel.

"Perhaps by withdrawing without making any scandal —"

Here the Colonel interrupted the president of the deputation.

"Marshal, permit me to refuse this counsel. I did not come so far in order to recoil, like a child, before the first obstacle. I am tired of a disgrace I have not deserved; still more tired of my idleness. Whether the Emperor is angry or is appeased, he will see me; let him have me shot if he likes, I do not cling to a life such as I have led for the last four years. However, Marshal, I will submit to what shall be decided by my colleagues, the deputies of Besançon."

These latter did not disapprove the Colonel's resolution, and he went with them to the Tuileries on the day of the formal reception of all the deputations of the Empire.

Every hall in the Tuileries was encumbered by a crowd in richly embroidered coats and brilliant uniforms. The military household of the Emperor, his civil family, the generals present in Paris, the diplomatic corps, the ministers and chiefs of the different administrations, the deputies of the departments with their prefects and their mayors, decorated with tri-colored scarfs; all were assembled in innumerable groups, and were awaiting the arrival of His Majesty, talking meanwhile in undertones.

In one of these groups was seen a tall officer, dressed in a very simple uniform and of a fashion which dated several years back. He did not wear either on his neck or on his breast the decoration which at that time no officer of his grade was without. It was Colonel Delclée. The president of the deputation of which he formed part, seemed embarrassed and almost afflicted. The former comrades of the Colonel hardly dared to recognize him. The most adventurous gave him a little nod from a distance, which expressed both anxiety and pity. The most prudent did not look at him at all.

As for him, he remained impassive and resolute.

At last a folding door flew open, and an usher cried:

"The Emperor, gentlemen."

The groups broke up; people ranged themselves in two rows. The Colonel placed himself in the first rank.

His Majesty began his turn around the salon. He addressed remarks to the president of each deputation, and said to every one of them some flattering words. Arriving in front of the deputation of Doubs, the Emperor, after having said a few words to the brave marshal who conducted it, was about to pass on to others, when his eyes fell upon an officer whom he had never seen. He stopped in surprise, and addressed his familiar question to the deputy:

"Who are you?"

"Sire, I am Colonel Delclée, formerly first aide-de-camp of General Moreau."

These words were uttered in a steady voice which resounded through the profound silence commanded by the presence of the sovereign.

The Emperor drew back a step, and fixed both eyes upon the Colonel. The latter did not flinch before this glance, but he bowed slightly.

Marshal M—— was as pale as a dead man.

The Emperor resumed: "What do you come to ask for here?"

"What I have asked for years, Sire; that Your Majesty would deign to tell me of what I am guilty, or else restore me to my rank."

Among those who were near enough to hear these questions and answers, there were not many who could breathe freely.

At last a smile parted the Emperor's tightly closed lips. He lifted a finger to his mouth as he approached the Colonel, and said to him in an almost friendly tone:

"People have complained a little of that; but don't say any more about it."

And he went on his way. He had hardly gone ten steps beyond the group formed by the deputies of Besançon, when he came back, and stopping opposite the Colonel:

"Mr. Minister of War," said His Majesty, "take the name of this officer, and take care to remind me of it. He is tired of doing nothing; we will give him some occupation."

As soon as the audience was over, it was who should get to the Colonel quickest. They surrounded him, they congratulated him, they embraced him, they tore him away from each other. All of his former companions wanted to take him away with them. His hand could not grasp all the hands extended to him. General S——, who only the day before had still further increased the alarms of Marshal M—— by expressing his astonishment that any one should have the audacity to come and brave the Emperor in this way, stretched his arm above the shoulders of those who were pressing around the Colonel, and shaking hands with him in the most cordial way in the world: "Delélée," he cried, "don't forget that I expect you to breakfast to-morrow."

Two days after this court scene, Delélée received his appointment as chief of staff of the army of Portugal, commanded by the Duc d'Abrantès. His equipments were soon ready, and at the moment of departing he had a final audience of the Emperor, who said to him: "Colonel, I know it is needless to urge you to make up for lost time. Before long, I hope, we shall be quite content with each other." On coming out from this last audience, the brave Delélée said that all he lacked now to make him happy was a good occasion to have himself cut to pieces for a man who knew so well how to close the wounds of a long disgrace. Such was the empire that His Majesty exercised over men's minds.

The Colonel had soon crossed the Pyrenees; he went through Spain and was received by Junot with open arms. The army of Portugal had had much to suffer during the two years it had been fighting against the population and against the English with unequal forces. They were badly supplied with provisions, the soldiers ill clothed and not well shod. The new chief of staff did all in his power to remedy this disorder, and the soldiers began to be sensible of his presence, when he fell sick from overwork and fatigue, and died before having, to use the Emperor's expression, *made up for lost time.*

I have said elsewhere that on every conspiracy against the life of the First Consul, all the persons of his household were naturally subjected to close surveillance. Their least proceedings were watched; they were followed when outside the château; their conduct was inspected in its most minute details. At the time when the Pichegru plot was discovered, there was only one keeper of the portfolio, named Landoire, and his place was therefore one of the most difficult, because he could never go away from a little dark corridor on which the door of the cabinet opened, and he ate his meals running, and almost on the sly. Luckily for Landoire, they gave him a second; and on this occasion Augel, one of the palace porters, was designated by the First Consul to go and establish himself at the barrier des Bons-Hommes, during Pichegru's trial, in order to reconnoitre and observe domestics of the house as they came and went about their service, nobody being allowed to leave Paris without permission. Augel's reports pleased the First Consul. He had him summoned, seemed satisfied with his answers and his intelligence, and appointed him as substitute for Landoire in keeping the portfolio. Thus the task of the latter became easier by half. Augel went on the Russian campaign, in 1802, and died on the return, when he was only a few leagues from Paris, in consequence of the fatigues and privations which we shared with the army.

However, it was not merely the servants attached to the household of the First Consul who found themselves subjected to this régime of surveillance. From the time he became Emperor, he established, among the concierges of all the imperial palaces, a register on which people from outside, and strangers who came to visit any one within, were obliged to inscribe their names and that of the persons they came to see. Every evening this register was carried to the grand marshal of the palace, or in his absence to the governor; and the Emperor often consulted it. He once read there a name which, in his capacity as husband, he had his reasons, and perhaps even *reason*, for suspecting. His Majesty had previously ordered the absence of this person; hence, on meeting this unlucky name again on the concierge's book, he was beside himself with rage, believing that *both sides* had dared to disobey his orders. Information was sought for on the spot, and it turned out, very luckily, that the suspected visitor was merely a very insignificant person, whose only fault was that of bearing a name justly compromised.

CHAPTER XV

The awakening of the First Consul, March 21, 1804 — Silence of the First Consul — Josephine's arrival in the chamber of the First Consul — Chagrin of Josephine and pallor of the First Consul — *The wretches have been too quick* — News of the death of the Duc d'Enghien — The First Consul's emotion — Preludes of the Empire — The First Consul Emperor — The Senate at Saint-Cloud — Cambacérès the first to salute the Emperor by the name of *Sire* — The senators present their homage to the Empress — Joy in the château — Everybody promoted — The salon and the antechamber — Embarrassment of all the attendants — The first awakening of the Emperor — The French princes — M. Lucien and Madame Jouberton — The marshals of the Empire — Awkwardness of the first courtiers — The chamberlains and the grand officers — Lessons given by the men of the former court — Contempt of the Emperor for the anniversaries of the Revolution — The Emperor's first fête and the first imperial cortège — The Temple of Mars and the grand master of ceremonies — Cardinal du Belloy and the grand chancellor of the Legion of Honor — The man of the people and the imperial accolade — Departure from Paris for the camp of Boulogne — The only holiday the Emperor gave me — My arrival at Boulogne — Details of my service near the Emperor — M. de Rémusat, MM. Boyer and Yvan — The Emperor's habits — M. de Bourrienne and the tip of the ear — Mania for giving little blows — Vivacity of the Emperor against his equerry — M. de Caulaincourt, grand equerry — Reparation — A generous gratuity.

THE year 1804, which was so glorious for the Emperor, was also, with the exception of 1814 and 1815, that which brought him the most vexations. It does not belong to me to judge of such grave events, nor to examine what part the Emperor took in them, nor who are those who surrounded and counselled him. I ought not and cannot recount anything but what I saw and heard. March 21 of that year, I entered the First Consul's chamber very early. I found him awake, his elbow leaning on his pillow; he looked sombre and fatigued. On seeing me come in, he sat up, passed his hand several times across his forehead, and said: "Constant, I have a headache." Then jerking off the bedclothes, he added: "I have slept badly." He could not have seemed more preoccupied and absorbed; he even had a sad and suffering air which surprised and affected me. While I was dressing him he did not say a word to me, a thing that never happened except when some thought disturbed and tormented him. There was nobody in his chamber with him but Roustan and me. At the moment when, his toilet being finished, I was handing him his snuff-box, handkerchief, and *bonbonnière*, the door suddenly opened and we saw the wife of the First Consul appear in her morning gown, her features drawn and her face covered with tears. This sudden apparition astonished and even alarmed us, that is, Roustan and me, because there was only one extraordinary circumstance which could induce Madame Bonaparte to leave her room in this costume, and before having taken all necessary precautions to disguise the ravages usually hidden by the toilet. She entered, or rather she rushed into the chamber, crying: "The

Duc d'Enghien is dead! Ah! my friend, what have you done?" Then she fell sobbing into the First Consul's arms. He became as pale as death, and said with extraordinary emotion: "*The wretches have been too quick!*" Then he went out, supporting Madame Bonaparte, who could scarcely walk and continued to weep. The news of the Prince's death spread consternation throughout the château. The First Consul remarked this universal grief, and yet he reproached nobody. The fact is that the greatest chagrin which this fatal catastrophe caused to his servitors, who for the most part were attached to him still more by affection than by duty, sprang from the thought that it could not fail to detract from the glory and tranquillity of their master. The First Consul probably knew how to interpret our sentiments. However that may be, this is all I saw and all I heard in private of this deplorable event. I do not pretend to know what passed in the interior of the cabinet. The First Consul's emotion seemed to me sincere and not affected. He remained sad and silent for several days, speaking very little at his toilet and only when necessity required.

During the course of this month and the next one, I noticed the continual goings and comings, and the frequent interviews with the First Consul of different persons who were said to be members of the Council of State, tribunes or senators. For a long time the army and the majority of the citizens, who idolized the hero of Italy and Egypt, had openly manifested their desire to see him wear a title worthy of his renown and the grandeur of France. It was known, moreover, that it was he that did all that was done in the State, and that his pretended colleagues were really his inferiors. People thought it just that he should become supreme chief in name, since he was already so in fact. Since his fall I have often heard His Majesty called by the name of usurper; and the only effect it has ever produced upon me has been to make me laugh with pity. If the Emperor usurped the throne, he had more accomplices than all the tyrants of tragedy and melodrama; for three-fourths of the French people were in the plot. It is known that it was May 18 when the Empire was proclaimed, and that the First Consul (I shall call him the Emperor hereafter) received the Senate at Saint-Cloud, led by Consul Cambacérès, who was arch-chancellor of the Empire a few hours later. It was from his mouth that the Emperor heard himself for the first time saluted by the name of *Sire*. On issuing from this audience, the Senate went to present its homage to the Empress Josephine. The remainder of the day was passed in receptions, presentations, interviews, and felicitations. Everybody in the château was intoxicated with joy, every one produced the effect of having received a sudden promotion. They embraced, they congratulated each other, they mutually communicated their hopes and plans for the future: there was not even the meanest subaltern who was not seized with ambition; in a word, the antechamber, saving the difference of personages, offered the exact repetition of what was passing in the salon.

Nothing could be funnier than the embarrassment of all the attendants when it was a question of how to respond to the interrogations of His Majesty. They began by making mistakes; then they would correct themselves and do worse still; they repeated ten times in a minute, *sire, general, your majesty, citizen, first consul.* Entering the Emperor's chamber next morning as usual, I replied to his customary questions, *What time is it? How is the weather?* "Sire, seven o'clock, fine weather." Having approached his bed, he pulled my ear, struck me on the cheek, and called me *monsieur le drôle;* it was his favorite word for me when he was particularly pleased with my service. His Majesty had sat up and worked far into the night. He looked serious and occupied, but contented. What a difference between this waking and that of the preceding March 21.

That same day His Majesty went to hold his first grand levee at the Tuileries, where all the civil and military authorities were presented. The brothers and sisters of the Emperor were made princes and princesses, with the exception of M. Lucien, who had quarrelled with His Majesty on the occasion of his marriage with Madame Jouberton. Eighteen generals were elevated to the dignity of marshals of the Empire. Everything surrounding Their Majesties put on a semblance of court and of royal power from this first day. A great deal has been said of the awkwardness of their first courtiers, who were very little accustomed to the service imposed on them by their new appointments, and to the ceremonies of etiquette; but this has been exaggerated like everything else. There might well be in the commencement something of that embarrassment which those in the Emperor's private service experienced, as I have said above. Still that lasted only a short time, and the chamberlains and great officers remodelled themselves almost as quickly as we valets de chambre. Moreover, there presented themselves to give them lessons, a swarm of men of the former court, who had obtained from the kindness of the Emperor the favor of being struck from the list of *émigrés*, and who eagerly solicited appointments in the budding imperial court for themselves and their wives.

His Majesty did not like the anniversary fêtes of the Republic; some of them had always seemed to him odious and cruel, and the others ridiculous. I have seen him grow indignant that they should have dared to make an annual fête of the 21st of January, and smile with pity at the remembrance of what he called the *masquerades* of the theophilanthropists, "*who*," said he, "*would have none of Jesus Christ, and made saints of Fénelon and Las-Casas, Catholic prelates.*" M. de Bourrienne says in his *Memoirs*, that "it was not one of the least oddities of Napoleon's policy that he should have kept for the first year of his reign the fête of July 14."

Concerning this passage I will permit myself to call attention to the fact that, if His Majesty profited by the epoch of an annual solemnity to appear in pomp in public, on the other hand he so changed the object of the fête that it would have been difficult to recognize in it the anniversary of the taking of the Bastille and of the first federation. I do not know whether there was a word said of either of these events in the whole ceremony; and to disconcert still more the souvenirs of the Republicans, the Emperor ordered that the fête should not be celebrated until the 15th, because that was a Sunday, and hence there would be no loss of time for the inhabitants of the capital. Besides, there was no question at all of celebrating the conquerors of the Bastille, but solely of a great distribution of crosses of the Legion of Honor.

This was the first time that Their Majesties displayed themselves to the people in all the magnificence of their power. The procession passed through the grand avenue of the Tuileries on its way to the Hôtel des Invalides, whose church, changed during the Revolution into a *Temple of Mars*, had been restored to the Catholic worship by the Emperor, and was to serve for the magnificent ceremonial of this day. It was also the first time that the Emperor used the privilege of passing through the garden of the Tuileries in a carriage. His cortège was superb; that of the Empress Josephine was not less brilliant. The rapt ecstasy of the people was at its height, and cannot be described. By the Emperor's orders, I had mingled with the crowd, so as to observe in what spirit they took part in the fête; I did not hear a murmur; so great, whatever may have been said about it since, was the enthusiasm of all classes for His Majesty. The Emperor and the Empress were received at the door of the Invalides by the governor and by the Count de Ségur, grand master of ceremonies; and at the entrance of the church by Cardinal du Belloy, at the head of a large number of the clergy. After the Mass M. de Lacépède, grand chancellor of the Legion of Honor, pronounced a discourse which was followed by the roll-call of the grand officers of the Legion. Then the Emperor seated himself, put on his hat, and repeated in a loud voice the formula of the oath, at the end of which all the legionaries shouted: *I swear it!* and at once a thousand-times repeated cries of *Long live the Emperor!* resounded through the church and beyond it. A singular circumstance enhanced the interest excited by the ceremony. While the knights of the new order were passing one after another in front of the Emperor who received them, a man of the people, wearing a round jacket, came and stood on the steps of the throne. His Majesty seemed somewhat astonished and paused for an instant. The man was questioned and showed his certificate. At once the Emperor showed eagerness to have him draw near, and gave him the decoration with a brisk accolade. On returning, the cortège followed the same road, passing again through the Tuileries garden.

July 18, three days after this ceremony, the Emperor left Saint-Cloud for the camp of Boulogne. I thought His Majesty would be willing to dispense with my presence for several days; and as it was a number of years since I had seen my family, that I would experience the very natural pleasure of seeing them again, and conversing with my relatives about the singular circumstances in which I had found myself since we parted. I would have felt, I confess, great joy in chatting with them about my present condition and my expectations, and I needed the expansion and the confidence of domestic intimacy to compensate for the constraint and annoyances which my service imposed on me. Therefore I asked permission to go and spend eight days at Perueltz. It was granted without difficulty, and I lost no time in starting. But what was my astonishment when, on the very day after my arrival, I received by courier a letter from Count Rémusat, who commanded me to rejoin the Emperor without delay, adding that His Majesty had need of me, and that I must occupy myself with nothing but getting there promptly! In spite of the disappointment I had experienced on receiving such orders, I nevertheless felt flattered at having become so necessary to the great man who had deigned to admit me to his service. Hence I bade farewell to my family without delay. His Majesty had scarcely arrived in Boulogne when he set off again on an excursion of several days to the departments of the North. I was at Boulogne before he returned, and I hastened to organize the service of His Majesty, who found everything ready on his arrival; which did not prevent his telling me that I had been *absent a long time.*

Since I am on that subject, I will set down here, although it will be to anticipate by years, one or two circumstances which will give the reader a chance to judge for himself of the rigorous assiduity to which I was obliged to restrict myself.

By reason of the fatigues incident to my continual journeys in the train of the Emperor, I had contracted a malady of the bladder from which I suffered horribly. For a long time I armed myself against my pains by patience and dieting: but the anguish having at length become totally insupportable, I requested His Majesty, in 1808, to give me a month to have myself treated. Doctor Boyer had told me that a month was the least time strictly necessary for my cure, and that, without it, my malady would become incurable. My request was granted, and I went to Saint-Cloud, to the family of my wife. M. Yvan, the Emperor's surgeon, came to see me every day. A week had hardly elapsed when he told me that His Majesty thought that I must be pretty well cured, and that he desired that I should resume my service. This desire was equivalent to an order; I felt it, and I returned to the Emperor, who, seeing me pale and suffering, deigned to say a thousand kind things to me, but not a word of a new leave of absence. These two absences are the only ones I took during sixteen years; hence, on my return from Moscow, and during the campaign of France, my illness had attained its extremest phase; and if I quitted the Emperor at Fontainebleau, it was because it was impossible, notwithstanding all my attachment for so good a master, for me to serve him any longer. After this separation which was so painful to me, a year hardly sufficed to cure me, and not entirely even then. But I shall have to speak of this sad epoch later on. I return to the recital of facts which prove that I could, with more justice than some others, have believed myself a great personage, since my humble services seemed to be indispensable to the master of Europe. A good many habitués of the Tuileries would have had more trouble than I should to demonstrate their *utility*. Is there too much vanity in what I have just said? and the chamberlains, will they not have reason to be vexed by it? I can't say about that, and I will go on with my story.

The Emperor clung to his habits; he would, as has been seen, be served by me in preference to any one else; and yet I ought to say that these gentlemen of the chamber were all full of zeal and devotion; but I was the longest in service, and I never quitted him. One day the Emperor asked for some tea in the middle of the day. M. Sénéchal was on duty; he made it and presented it to His Majesty, who found it detestable. I was summoned; the Emperor complained to me that some one wanted to *poison him*. (That was his word when anything tasted bad.) Going back to the pantry, I poured, from the same teapot, a cup which I arranged and carried to His Majesty, with two silver-gilt teaspoons, according to custom, one to taste of it before the Emperor, the other for him. This time he found the tea excellent. He complimented me on it with the benevolent familiarity he sometimes used toward his attendants; and on giving me back the cup, he pulled my ears and said: "Now teach them how to make tea; they know nothing about it."

M. de Bourrienne, whose excellent *Memoirs* I have read with the greatest pleasure, says somewhere that the Emperor in his moments of good humor would pinch his intimates by *the tip of the ear;* I have my own experience that he pinched the whole of it, and often both ears at once; and that with a master hand. It is also said in the same *Memoirs* that he only gave his *little* friendly taps with two fingers; in that M. de Bourrienne is very modest; I can again attest thereupon that His Majesty, although his hand was not large, distributed his favors much more *largely;* but this species of caress, as well as the preceding, was given and received as a mark of special kindliness, and far from any one complaining of it *then*, I have heard more than one dignitary say with pride, like that sergeant of the comedy:

"Master, try it again;
The blow on my cheek is still too warm."

In his private life the Emperor was nearly always gay, amiable, chatting familiarly with his attendants, and questioning them about their family, their affairs, and even their pleasures. His toilet finished, his face suddenly changed; he was grave, thoughtful, he resumed his imperial air. It has been said that he often struck the domestics of his household; that is false. I never but once saw him yield to an impulse of that description; and certainly the circumstances which caused it and the reparation which followed it, may render it, if not excusable, at least easy to understand. This is the fact which I witnessed, and which occurred in the environs of Vienna, the day after the death of Marshal Lannes. The Emperor was profoundly affected; he had not spoken a word during his toilet. He was hardly dressed when he demanded his horse. An unlucky chance would have it that M. Jardin, his groom, was not in the stables at the time when it was saddled, and the stable-man did not put his usual bridle on the horse. His Majesty was barely mounted, when the animal backed, reared, and the rider fell heavily to the ground. M. Jardin came up just as the Emperor rose, irritated, and in this first transport of anger he received a cut of the whip across the face. M. Jardin went away in despair at an ill-usage to which His Majesty had not accustomed him, and a few hours afterward, M. de Caulaincourt, grand equerry, finding himself alone with His Majesty, described to him the chagrin of his head groom. The Emperor expressed keen regret for his vivacity, had M. Jardin summoned, talked to him with a kindness which effaced his injustice, and sent him, a few days later, a gratuity of three thousand francs. I have been told that a similar thing[1] happened to M. Vigogne senior, in Egypt. But even if that were true, ought two such facts in the whole life of the Emperor, coupled with circumstances so well calculated to make even the mildest man act out of character, to suffice to draw upon Napoleon the odious reproach *of beating cruelly the persons who waited on him?*

[1] We arrived at Tentoura the 20th of May. It was very hot that day, which produced a general discouragement. All we had to rest upon were dry and burning sands; on our right was an unfriendly and deserted sea. Our loss in killed and wounded was already considerable since we had quitted Acre. There was nothing cheerful about the future. This truly afflicting state in which the remnant of the army corps which had been called *triumphant* found itself, made an impression upon the General which it was impossible not to feel. We had hardly reached Tentoura when he had his tent set up; he called me and dictated in a preoccupied way an order that everybody should walk, and the horses, mules, and camels be given to the wounded, the sick, and the plague-stricken who had been brought along, and who still showed any signs of life. "*Take that to Berthier.*" The order was sent on the spot. Hardly had I got back to the tent, when Vigogne senior, equerry to the General-in-Chief, entered, and touching his hat, said : "*General, what will you reserve for yourself?*" In the first movement of anger excited by this question, the General-in-Chief struck the equerry a violent blow in the face with his whip, and then he added in a terrible voice: "Everybody is to go on foot, and I the first: don't you know the order? Get out." (*Mémoires de M. de Bourrienne*, tom. 2, chap. 16, p. 252.)

CHAPTER XVI

The Emperor's assiduity at labor — Roustan and the flask of eau-de-vie — The army of Boulogne — The four camps — The Pont-de-Briques — The Emperor's *baraque* — The council-chamber — The eagle guided by the tutelary star — The Emperor's bed-chamber — The bed — The furniture — The telescope room — The portmanteau — Distribution of the rooms — The semaphore — The gigantic mortars — The Emperor launches the first bomb — Marshal Soult's *baraque* — The Emperor sees Dover and its garrison from his chamber — The streets of the camp of the right — A road cut perpendicularly up the cliff — The forgotten engineer — The flotilla — The forts — *Baraque* of Prince Joseph — The grenadier stuck in the mire — Kind action of the Emperor — The bridge of service — The terrible countersign — The sentinels and sailors of the watch — Exclusion of women and foreigners — The spies — Fusillade — The schoolmaster shot — The incendiaries — Terror in the city — Military chant — False alarm — Consternation — Calmness of Madame F —— — The commandant condemned to death, and pardoned by the Emperor.

AT the headquarters of Pont-de-Briques, the Emperor worked as much as in his cabinet at the Tuileries. After his excursions on horseback, his inspections, his visits, his reviews, he took his repast in haste and re-entered his cabinet, where he often worked a great part of the night. He thus led the same sort of life as in Paris. In his turns on horseback Roustan followed him everywhere: the latter always carried with him a little silver flask of eau-de-vie, for the use of His Majesty, who, for that matter, seldom availed himself of it.

The army of Boulogne was composed of about a hundred and fifty thousand infantry and ninety thousand cavalry, divided into four principal camps: the *camp of the right*, the *camp of the left*, the *camp of Wimereux*, and the *camp of Ambleteuse*.

His Majesty the Emperor had his headquarters at Pont-de-Briques, so called, I have been told, because there had been discovered there the brick foundations of an ancient camp of Cæsar! Pont-de-Briques, as I have said before, is half a league or thereabouts from Boulogne, and His Majesty's headquarters was established in the only house of the place that was then habitable. The headquarters was guarded by a mounted post of the imperial guard.

The four camps were on a very high cliff, dominating the sea in such a manner that on a fair day one might see the English coast. In the right camp barracks had been established for the Emperor, Admiral Bruix, Marshal Soult, and M. Decrès, then minister of the navy.

The Emperor's barrack, constructed by the care of M. Sordi, acting as chief engineer of military communications, and whose nephew, M. Lecat de Rue, attached at this period as aide-de-camp to the staff of Marshal Soult, has been so kind as to furnish me with information which is not specially within my competence;—the barrack of the Emperor, I say, was made of planks, like the booths of a fair, but with this difference, that the planks were carefully wrought and painted light gray. In shape it was a long square, having two semicircular pavilions at each extremity. It was surrounded by a circular piazza closed by a wooden lattice, and lighted from without by reflectors four feet apart. The windows were placed at the sides.

The pavilion which looked out to sea was composed of three rooms and a lobby. The principal room served for the council-chamber, and was decorated with silver-gray paper; the ceiling was painted with golden clouds, amidst which could be seen a background of blue sky, an eagle holding the thunder, and guided toward England by a star, the Emperor's tutelary star. In the middle of this chamber was a large oval table covered with a green cloth, without fringe. There was nothing in front of this table but His Majesty's armchair, made of simple native wood, covered with green morocco and stuffed with horse-hair, and which could be taken to pieces. On the table was a boxwood stand for ink and pens. This was the only furniture of the council-chamber, where nobody but the Emperor could sit down, the generals standing before him, and having nothing but the hilt of their swords to lean on during these councils, which sometimes lasted three or four hours.

The council-chamber was entered through a lobby. In this lobby, on the right hand, was His Majesty's bed-chamber, which was closed by a glass door and lighted by a window which opened on the camp of the right, with a view of the sea on the left. Here was the Emperor's iron bedstead, with a large green sarcenet curtain, fastened to the ceiling by a ring of gilded copper. It had two pallets, a hair mattress, two bolsters, one at the head and the other at the foot, and no pillow; and two coverlets, one in white cotton, the other in green sarcenet, wadded and quilted. Two very simple folding chairs stood beside it. The casement was hung with small green sarcenet curtains. This room was papered in rose-color with a lace-work tracery and an Etruscan border.

Opposite the sleeping-room was another chamber parallel to it, in which was a sort of telescope which had cost twelve thousand francs. This instrument was about four feet long by one in diameter. It was mounted on a mahogany support some three feet in height, and the case which served to contain it was shaped almost like a piano. In the same room, on two stools, was a yellow leather casket which contained three complete changes of dress and linen. This was the campaign wardrobe of His Majesty; above it was a square hat, lined with white satin and much worn. The Emperor had a very sensitive head, did not like new hats and kept the same ones a long while.

The main body of the imperial barrack was divided into three rooms: a salon, a vestibule, and a large dining-room which communicated with the kitchens by a lobby parallel to that I have just described. Outside of the barrack, and in the direction of the kitchens, was a little thatched cabin which served as a laundry and scullery.

The barrack of Admiral Bruix was arranged in the same way as the Emperor's, but on a smaller scale. The signal semaphore was beside it, a sort of maritime telegraph for making signals. A little further off was the ordnance tower, a terrible battery composed of six mortars, six howitzers, and twelve twenty-four pounders. These six mortars, the greatest in calibre that had ever been made, were sixteen inches thick, carried forty-five pounds of powder in the chamber, and sent seven-hundred-pound bombs fifteen hundred fathoms into the air and a league and a half out to sea. Each bomb fired cost the State three hundred francs. Lances twelve feet in length were employed in touching off these frightful machines, and the cannoneer protected himself as much as possible by putting his head between his legs and not rising until after the discharge. The Emperor wished to launch the first bomb himself.

Marshal Soult's barrack was on the right of the ordnance tower. It was built like the hut of a savage, covered with thatch down to the ground, lighted from above, and with a door by which one descended into apartments which seemed buried. The principal room was round; there was a large work table in it covered with green cloth and surrounded by small camp-stools.

The last barrack was that of M. Decrès, minister

of the navy, which was built and arranged like that of Marshal Soult.

From his barrack the Emperor could observe all the manœuvres at sea, and the telescope of which I have spoken was so good that Dover castle, with its garrison, was, so to say, under the eyes of His Majesty.

The right camp, established on the cliff, was divided into streets each of which bore the name of some distinguished general. This cliff was bristling with batteries from Boulogne to Ambleteuse, that is to say, for a distance of more than ten leagues.

To go from Boulogne to the right camp, there was but one road, which began in the rue des Vieillards and passed to the cliff between His Majesty's barrack and those of MM. Bruix, Soult, and Decrès. When the Emperor wished to go down on the beach at low tide, he had to make a great detour. One day he complained of it very loudly. M. Bonnefoux, maritime prefect of Boulogne, heard His Majesty's complaints, and addressing himself to M. Sordi, engineer of military communications, he asked if it were not possible to remedy this serious inconvenience. The engineer replied that the thing was feasible; means could be found by which His Majesty could go directly from his barrack to the beach, but that, on account of the excessive elevation of the cliff, it would be necessary to dig the road in a zigzag to avoid the rapidity of the descent. "Make it as you think best," said the Emperor, "but I must go down by it in three days." The skilful engineer set to work; in three days and three nights, a road of stones fastened together by iron clamps was constructed, and the Emperor, charmed by such diligence and talent, set M. Sordi down for the next distribution of crosses. It is not known by what regrettable negligence this skilful man was forgotten.

The harbor of Boulogne contained about seventeen hundred vessels, such as flatboats, gunboats, skiffs, lighters, bomb-ketches, etc. The entrance of the port was defended by an enormous chain and by four forts, two on the right and two on the left.

The Musoir fort, on the left, was armed by three formidable batteries, placed one above the other; the second and third by thirty-six pounders. On the right of this fort was the tow-bridge, and behind this bridge an old tower called the Croï tower, garnished with good and handsome batteries. On the left, about a quarter of a league from fort Musoir, was fort la Crèche, advanced a good way into the sea, built of cut stone, and terrible. On the right of this, finally, was the wooden fort, armed in a prodigious manner, and pierced by a large opening, which was exposed at low tide.

On the cliff at the left of the city, the same height as the other or very near it, was the left camp. Here could be seen the barrack of Prince Joseph, then colonel of the 4th regiment of the line. This barrack was thatched. At the foot of this camp and of the cliff, the Emperor had a basin dug by a part of the troops.

It was in this basin that a young soldier of the guard, up to his knees in mud, was pulling with all his might to disengage his wheelbarrow, which was still more muddy than he; but he could not manage it, and, all covered with sweat, he swore and cursed like an angry grenadier. All of a sudden, as he happened to lift his eyes, he perceived the Emperor, who was passing by the works to go and see his brother Joseph, at the camp of the left. Thereupon he began to look at him with a suppliant air and gestures, singing in an almost sentimental tone: "*Come, come unto my aid.*" His Majesty could not avoid smiling, and he made a sign to the soldier to approach, which the poor devil did, brushing off the mud with much difficulty. "What is your regiment?" "Sire, the first of the guard."—"Since when have you been a soldier?" "Since you have been Emperor, Sire."—"*Diable!* that's not long — Not long enough for me to make you an officer, is it? But conduct yourself well and I'll have you made sergeant-major. After that, if you like, the cross and the epaulettes on the first battle-field. Are you content?" "Yes, Sire." "Major-general," continued the Emperor, turning to General Berthier, "take the name of this young man. Make them give him three hundred francs to clean his pantaloons and have his wheelbarrow mended." And His Majesty went on, amidst the acclamations of the soldiers.

At the inner side of the harbor was a wooden bridge which was called the *pont de service*. The powder magazines were behind it and they contained immense munitions. After nightfall no one entered by this bridge without giving the countersign to the second sentinel, for the first one always allowed people to pass. But he did not allow them to return. If the person coming on the bridge did not know or had forgotten the countersign, he was sent back by the second sentinel, and the first one, placed at the head of the bridge, had express orders to run his bayonet through the imprudent one who had entered this dangerous passage without being able to answer the questions of the sentries. These rigorous precautions were rendered necessary by the proximity of the terrible magazines, which a spark might blow up along with the city, the fleet, and the two camps.

At night the port was closed by the great chain which I have spoken of, and the wharves were protected by sentinels placed fifteen feet apart. Every quarter of an hour they cried: "*Sentinels, take care of yourselves!*" And the marines stationed in the top-sails would respond to this cry by that of: "*All's well*," pronounced in a drawling and melancholy voice. Nothing more monotonous and sad than this continual murmur, this roll of voices all howling in the same tone, and all the more so because those who uttered these cries did all they knew how to make them as alarming as possible.

Women not domiciled in Boulogne were forbidden

to stay there without a special authorization from the minister of police. This measure had been deemed necessary on account of the army. Otherwise, each soldier might fetch a woman to Boulogne; and God knows what disorder that would have entailed. And in general, foreigners were not received into the city without the greatest difficulty.

In spite of all these precautions, spies from the English fleet were daily introduced into the city. No mercy was shown them when they were discovered; and yet emissaries, who landed from no one knew where, came to the theatre in the evenings, and pushed imprudence so far as to write their opinions of the actors and actresses, whom they designated by name, and to paste these writings on the walls of the theatre. They braved the police in this way: One day two little boats covered with tarred canvas were found on the shore, which these gentlemen had probably employed for their excursions.

In June, 1804, eight English were arrested, perfectly well dressed, in white silk stockings, etc. They had sulphur machines about them designed to set the fleet on fire. They were shot at the end of an hour without any other trial.

There were traitors also at Boulogne. A schoolmaster, the secret agent of Lords Keith and Melville, was surprised one morning on the cliff of the camp of the right making telegraphic signals with his arms. Arrested almost at the same moment by the sentries, he wanted to protest his innocence and turn the thing into a joke. But his papers were searched and a correspondence found among them with the English which proved his treason to demonstration. He was brought before the council of war and shot the next day

One evening, between eleven o'clock and midnight, a fire-ship, rigged in the French style, carrying a French flag, and having quite the appearance of a gunboat, advanced toward the line of broadside and passed. By an unpardonable negligence, the chain of the port was not stretched that night. This fire-ship was followed by a second, which blew up and carried with it a shallop. The explosion gave the alarm to the whole fleet: on the instant lights were burning all around, and, thanks to these lights, the beholders, to their inexpressible anxiety, saw the first fire-ship advancing between the jetties. Two or three pieces of wood attached with cables luckily arrested its progress. It exploded with such an uproar that all the windows in the city were broken, and a great number of the inhabitants who, for lack of beds, were sleeping on tables, were thrown to the floor and awakened by the fall without comprehending what had happened. In ten minutes everybody was afoot. They thought the English were in the harbor. Then there was trouble, a tumult, cries to deafen one. Criers preceded by drums were sent around the city, who reassured the inhabitants by telling them that the danger was over.

The next day ballads were made on this nocturnal alarm. They were presently in all mouths. I have preserved one which I am going to set down here, and which is the one the soldiers sang the longest:

> Depuis longtemps la Bretagne
> Pour imiter la *Montagne*,
> Menaçait le continent
> D'un funeste événement.
> Dans les ombres du mystère
> Vingt monstres [1] elle enfanta.
> Pitt s'ecria: "j'en suis père,"
> Et personne n'en douta.
>
> Bientot dans la nuit profonde,
> Melville [2] lance sur l'onde
> Tous ces monstres nouveau-nés,
> Pour Boulogne destinés.
> Lord Keith, en bonne nourrice,
> Dans son sein les tient cachés :
> Le flot lui devient propice,
> Et les enfants sont lâchés.
>
> Le Français, qui toujours veille,
> Vers le bruit prête l'oreille ;
> Mais il ne soupçonnait pas
> Des voisins si scélérats.
> Son etoile tutélaire
> Semble briller a ses yeux :
> Le danger même l'éclaire
> En l'éclairant de ses feux.

---

[1] It was afterwards known that there had been twenty of these fire-ships intended to destroy the fleet.

[2] The English fleet was commanded by Lords Melville and Keith.

Cette infernale famille
S'approche de la flotille :
En expirant elle fait
Beaucoup de bruit, peu d'effet.
Les marques qu'elle a laissées
De sa brillant valeur,
Sont quelques vitres cassées
Et la honte de l'auteur.

Mons. Pitt, sur votre rivage
Vous bravez notre courage,
Bien convaincu que jamais
Vous n'y verrez les Français.
Vous comptez sur la distance,
Vos vaisseaux et vos bourgeois :
Mais les soldats de la France
Vous feront compter deux fois.

Dans nos chaloupes agiles,
Les vents devenus dociles,
Vous retenant dans vos ports,
Nous conduiront a vos bords ;
Vous forçant a l'arme égale
Vous verrez que nos soldats
Ont la *machine infernale*
Placée au bout de leurs bras.[1]

---

[1] Britain for a long time past,
  Imitating the *Mountain*,
  Has threatened the continent
  With a terrible event.
  In the shades of mystery,
  Twenty monsters she brought forth.
  "I'm their father," Pitt exclaimed,
  And no one had a doubt about it.

  Presently in darkness deep,
  Melville launched upon the wave

Another alarm, but of a totally different kind, turned all Boulogne upside down in the autumn of 1804. Toward eight o'clock in the evening, a chimney caught fire on the right of the port. The light of this fire, shining through the masts of the fleet, alarmed the commandant of a post which was on the opposite side. At this epoch all the vessels were loaded with powder and munitions. The poor commandant lost his head; he screamed: "*My lads, the fleet is on fire*," and he had the general alarm beat. This frightful news flew like lightning. In less than half an hour, more than sixty thousand men

> All these monsters newly born,
> For Boulogne intended.
> Lord Keith, as a good nurse,
> Kept them in his bosom hidden:
> The tide became propitious,
> And the infants were let loose.
>
> The Frenchman, who always watches,
> Toward the uproar bends his ear;
> But he does not suspect
> Such rascally neighbors.
> His tutelary star
> Seems shining in his eyes:
> The danger itself enlightens him
> By illumining him with its fires.
>
> This infernal family
> Approaches the flotilla:
> In expiring it makes
> A good deal of noise and small effect.
> The marks it has left
> Of its brilliant valor,
> Are a few broken windows
> And its author's shame.

debouched on the quays; the tocsin was sounded in all the churches, the forts discharged alarm guns; and drummers and trumpeters began running through the streets and making an infernal racket.

The Emperor was at headquarters when this terrible cry: "*The fleet is on fire!*" came to his ears. "It is impossible!" he cried at once. Nevertheless we set off instantly.

What a frightful spectacle I witnessed when we entered the city! Women in tears, holding their infants in their arms and running like mad while uttering shrieks of despair; men abandoning their houses, carrying away their most precious objects, knocking against and bruising each other in the darkness. From all sides one heard cries of: "Look out for yourself! We are going to skip! We are

---

> Mr. Pitt, on your shore,
> You affront our courage,
> Well convinced that never
> Will you see the Frenchmen there.
> You reckon on the distance,
> Your vessels and your citizens:
> But the soldiers of France
> Will make you reckon twice.
>
> In our nimble shallops,
> The winds becoming docile,
> You retaining in your ports,
> Us conducting to your shores,
> Forcing you to equal weapons,
> You will see that our soldiers
> Have the *infernal machine*
> Just at the end of their arms.

all ruined!" and maledictions, blasphemies, and lamentations enough to make your hair stand up.

His Majesty's aides-de-camp and those of General Soult galloped wherever they could pass, stopping the drummers and asking them: "Why do you beat the general? Who ordered you to beat the general?" "We know nothing about it," was the reply; and the drums kept on beating, and the tumult increasing, and the crowd hurled themselves to the gates, struck with a terror which an instant of reflection would have banished. But fear admits of no reflection, unfortunately.

It is true to say, however, that a number of the inhabitants, less timid than the others, remained tranquilly at home, knowing very well that if the fleet were on fire they would not have had time to make an outcry. These did all in their power to reassure the frightened crowd. Madame F——, the very pretty and amiable wife of a clockmaker, was busy in her kitchen preparing supper when a neighbor entered in great alarm and said to her: "Save yourself, Madame, you have not a minute to lose!" "Why, what's the matter?" — "The fleet is afire." "Ah! bah!" — "Fly, Madame, fly! I tell you the fleet is on fire." And the neighbor took Madame F—— by the arm and gave her a strong pull. Madame F—— was just then holding a pan in which there were some apple fritters. "Take care! you are making me spoil my fritters," said she, laughing; and a few words, between jest and earnest, were enough to reassure the poor devil, who ended by deriding himself.

At last the tumult quieted down; a profound calm succeeded to this alarm, no explosion had been heard. Was it a false alarm then? Everybody went back home no longer thinking of fire, but disturbed by another fear. Robbers might well have profited by the absence of the inhabitants to pillage the houses. . . . By good luck, no accident of this kind had occurred.

The next day, the poor commandant who had taken and given the alarm so unseasonably, was brought before the council of war. He had no bad intentions, but the law was formal. He was condemned to death, but his judges recommended him to the clemency of the Emperor, who pardoned him.

CHAPTER XVII

Distribution of crosses of the Legion of Honor at the camp of Boulogne — The helmet of Duguesclin — Prince Joseph, colonel — Boat and horse races — Jealousy of a council of superior officers — Justice rendered by the Emperor — Unlucky fall followed by a triumph — A point-blank petition — The minister of marine falls into the water — The Emperor's gaiety — The epicurean general — A *boulangère* danced by the Emperor and Madame Bertrand — Boulognese women at the ball — The macaroons and the reticules — La Maréchale Soult queen of the ball — The beautiful suppliant — The provision dealer condemned to death — Clemency of the Emperor.

MANY of the brave fellows who composed the army of Boulogne had merited the cross in the last campaigns. His Majesty desired this distribution to be a solemnity which should leave immortal memories. He selected for it the day after his own birthday, August 16, 1804. Nothing more beautiful was ever seen, nor could be seen perhaps.

At six o'clock in the morning, more than eighty thousand men started from the four camps and advanced by divisions, drummers and musicians at the head, toward the level ground of the Hubert mill, situated on the cliff beyond the right camp. In this plain, with its back turned toward the sea, a scaffolding some fifteen feet high had been erected. It was ascended by three stairways, one in the middle and one at either side, all three covered by superb carpets. On this amphitheatre of about forty feet square, were three platforms. The middle one supported the imperial armchair, decorated with flags and trophies. The platform on the left was covered with seats for the brothers of the Emperor and the great dignitaries. That on the right supported a tripod of antique shape on which was a helmet, the helmet of Duguesclin, I think, filled with crosses and ribbons; beside the tripod a seat had been placed for the archchancellor.

At about three hundred feet from the throne, the ground rose in a gentle slope that was nearly round; it was on this slope that the troops arranged themselves in a half-circle. On an eminence at the right of the throne were scattered sixty or eighty tents made of naval ensigns. They were for the ladies of the city, and they produced a charming effect. They were so far from the throne that those who occupied them were obliged to use lorgnettes. Between these tents and the throne was a part of the imperial guard on horseback, ranged in order of battle.

The weather was magnificent; not a cloud was in the sky: the English cruiser had disappeared, and nothing was in sight at sea but the line of broadside superbly hung with flags.

At ten o'clock in the morning, a salvo of artillery announced the departure of the Emperor. His Majesty started from his barrack, surrounded by more than eighty generals and two hundred aides-de-camp; he was followed by his entire household. The Emperor wore the uniform of a colonel-general of foot-guards, and came at a gallop to the foot of the throne, amidst universal acclamations and the most frightful racket that could be made by drums, trumpets, and cannons, beating, sounding, and thundering together.

His Majesty ascended the throne, followed by his brothers and some of the great dignitaries. When he was seated, everybody took his place, and the distribution of crosses began in the following manner: an aide-de-camp of the Emperor called the designated soldiers, who came one by one, halted at the foot of the throne, saluted, and mounted the staircase on the right. They were received by the arch-chancellor, who gave them their brevet. Two pages, stationed between the tripod and the Emperor, took the decoration from the helmet of Duguesclin and handed it to His Majesty, who attached it himself to the hero's breast. As he did so, more than eight hundred drummers beat a roll, and when the decorated soldier came down from the throne by the staircase on the left, passing in front of the Emperor's brilliant staff, fanfares executed by more than twelve hundred musicians signalized the return of the legionary to his company. It is needless to say that the cry of *Long live the Emperor* was repeated twice at each decoration.

The distribution, begun at ten o'clock, terminated about three. Then the aides-de-camp were seen passing through the divisions; a salvo of artillery was heard, and eighty thousand men advanced in serried columns to within twenty-five or thirty feet of the throne. The most profound silence succeeded to the roll of the drums, and the Emperor having given his orders, the troops manœuvred for nearly an hour. Afterward each division defiled in front of the throne on the way back to camp, each chief lowering the point of his sword as he passed by.

Prince Joseph, who had newly been made colonel of the 4th regiment of the line, was observed to salute his brother as he passed in a manner more graceful than military. The Emperor repressed by a contraction of the eyebrows the somewhat critical remarks which his former companions seemed inclined to permit themselves on the subject. Save for this slight movement, His Majesty's countenance had never been more radiant.

At the moment when the troops were defiling, the wind, which had been blowing violently for two or three hours, became terrible. An orderly officer came running up to tell the Emperor that four or five gunboats had run aground. The Emperor at once left the plain at a gallop, followed by several marshals, and went to station himself on the beach. The crew of the gunboats were saved, and the Emperor returned to Pont-de-Briques.

This great army could not regain its cantonments before eight in the evening. The next day, the left camp gave a military fête, at which the Emperor was present. From morning, boats mounted on wheels went full sail through the streets of the camp, impelled by a favorable wind. Officers amused themselves by chasing them at a gallop, and seldom caught up to them. These exercises lasted for an hour or two; but, the wind changing, the boats capsized, amidst shouts of laughter.

Next came a horse-race. The prize was twelve hundred francs. A lieutenant of dragoons, much esteemed in his company, asked the favor of competing. But the haughty council of superior officers refused to admit him, on the pretext that his rank was not high enough, but in reality because he was considered a horseman of prodigious skill. Stung to the quick by this unjust refusal, the lieutenant of dragoons addressed himself to the Emperor, who permitted him to run with the others, after having made inquiries the result of which apprised him that this brave officer was the sole support of a numerous family, and that his conduct was irreproachable.

At a given signal the riders started. The lieutenant was not slow in passing the others; he was about to touch the goal, when, by an unlucky accident, a poodle-dog stupidly ran between his horse's legs, and it fell. An aide-de-camp who was directly behind him was proclaimed victor. The lieutenant picked himself up as well as he could, and was about to withdraw very disconsolately, yet somewhat consoled by the marks of interest displayed by the spectators, when the Emperor had him called and said:

"You deserve the prize and you shall have it. . . . I make you a captain." And turning to the grand marshal of the palace: "Have them pay twelve hundred francs to Captain N——" (the name escapes me). And everybody began shouting: *Long live the Emperor!* and congratulating the new captain on his fortunate fall.

In the evening there were fireworks that could be seen from the coast of England. Thirty thousand soldiers executed manœuvres with rockets in their muskets. These rockets rose to an incredible height. The bouquet, which represented the arms of the Empire, was so fine that during five minutes Boulogne, the surrounding country, and the whole coast was as bright as day.

Some days after these fêtes, as the Emperor was passing from one camp to the other, a sailor, who was on the watch for him that he might present a petition, found himself caught in a torrent of rain, and fearing that his paper might be spoilt, he sheltered himself behind an isolated barrack on the beach where ropes were kept. He had been waiting there a long time, drenched to the skin, when he saw the Emperor coming down from the left camp at full gallop. Just as His Majesty, still galloping, was about to pass the barrack, my brave sailor, who was lying in wait for him, sprang from his hiding-place and threw himself in front of the Emperor, holding out his petition in the attitude of a fencing-master making a lunge. The Emperor's horse sprang aside and came to a full stop, frightened by this sudden apparition. His Majesty, astonished for a moment, cast a dissatisfied glance at the seaman, and went on his way, without taking the petition which was presented in such a bizarre fashion.

It was on that day, I think, that the minister of the navy, M. Decrès, had the ill-luck to tumble into the water, to the great amusement of His Majesty. In order to permit His Majesty to go from the quay to a gunboat, a single plank had been thrown between the two. His Majesty passed, or rather jumped across this light bridge, and was received on board in the arms of a seaman of the guard. M. Decrès, much fatter and less nimble than the Emperor, walked cautiously on to the plank, which it alarmed him to find bending beneath his feet. When he reached the middle, the weight of his body broke the plank, and the minister of marine fell into the water between the quay and the boat. His Majesty turned round at the noise made by M. Decrès in falling, and bending over the side of the boat: "What!" said he, "is it our minister of marine who has fallen? How can it possibly be he?" And the Emperor laughed heartily while speaking thus. Meanwhile, two or three sailors were employed in getting M. Decrès out of his scrape. He was hoisted into the boat with a good deal of difficulty, as may be believed, the water pouring from his nose, mouth, and ears, and very much ashamed of his mishap, which the pleasantries of His Majesty made still more afflicting.

Toward the end of our stay, the generals gave a grand ball to the ladies of the city. The ball was magnificent; the Emperor was present at it. For this purpose a hall had been constructed in carpentry and joiner's work. It was decorated in perfectly good taste with garlands, flags, and trophies. General Bertrand was appointed master of ceremonies by his colleagues, and General Bisson took charge of the buffet. This employment perfectly suited General Bisson, the greatest gastronomer in the camp, whose enormous paunch sometimes embarrassed him in marching. He required no less than from six to eight bottles with his dinner, which he never took alone; for it was a torment to him not to chatter while eating. He usually invited his aides-de-camp, whom, doubtless through love of mischief, he always selected from among the thinnest and frailest officers in the army. The buffet was worthy of him who had it in charge.

The orchestra was composed of the bands of twenty regiments, who played by turns. Only, at the commencement of the ball, they executed a triumphal march all together, while the aides-de-camp, dressed in the most gallant manner in the world, were receiving the ladies invited and giving them bouquets.

To be admitted to this ball it was necessary to have at least the rank of commandant. It is impossible to form an idea of the beauty of the sight presented by this multitude of uniforms, all vying with each other in brilliancy. The fifty or sixty generals who gave the ball had sent to Paris for costumes embroidered with inconceivable richness. The group which formed around His Majesty when he entered, glittered with gold and diamonds. The Emperor remained an hour at this entertainment and danced the *boulangère* with Madame Bertrand; he wore the uniform of colonel-general of the mounted guard.

Madame la Maréchale Soult was the queen of the ball. She wore a black velvet robe, strewn with those diamonds known as Rhine pebbles.

In the middle of the night a splendid supper was served, the preparations for which had been superintended by General Bisson. And to say that is to imply that nothing was lacking.

The ladies of Boulogne, who had never been present at anything of the sort before, were amazed. When supper-time came, some of them took the notion of filling their reticules with sweets and dainties; I think they would like to have carried off the hall, the musicians, and the dancers. For more than a month the ball was the only subject of their conversations.

At this epoch, or very near it, as His Majesty was promenading on horseback in the environs of his barrack, a pretty girl of fifteen or sixteen, dressed in white, and all in tears, threw herself on her knees in front of him. The Emperor at once dismounted and ran to pick her up, asking kindly what he could do for her. The poor child had come to ask mercy for her father, a provision dealer, condemned to the galleys for serious frauds. His Majesty could not resist such youth and charms: he pardoned him.

CHAPTER XVIII

Popularity of the Emperor at Boulogne — His fatal obstinacy — Firmness of Admiral Bruix — The Emperor's whip and the Admiral's sword — Unjust exile — Tempest and shipwreck — The Emperor's courage — The corpses and the little hat — Infallible means to stifle murmurs — The drummer saved on his drum — Dialogue between two sailors — False embarkation — Proclamation — Column of the Boulogne camp — Departure of the Emperor — Accounts to settle — Difficulties made by the Emperor about paying for his barrack — A creditor's flatteries — The engineer's bill paid in rix-dollars and frederics.

IN Boulogne, as in every other place, the Emperor knew how to endear himself to all by his moderation, his justice, and the generous grace with which he recognized the slightest service. All the inhabitants of Boulogne, all the peasants of the neighborhood, would have let themselves be killed for him. His slightest peculiarities were the subject of their conversation. And yet his conduct one day excited complaints; he was unjust. He was universally blamed: his injustice had caused so many disasters. I am going to give a faithful report of this sad event of which I did not witness any part.

One morning on mounting his horse, the Emperor announced that he would hold a review of the naval forces, and gave orders to have the vessels forming the line of blockade leave their positions, as he intended to review them in open sea. He set out with Roustan for his usual ride, and expressed the desire that all should be ready on his return, the hour of which he designated. Everybody knew that the Emperor's desire was his will; some one went during his absence to transmit it to Admiral Bruix, who responded with imperturbable coolness that he was very sorry, but that the review would not take place that day. Consequently not a vessel stirred.

On returning from his ride, the Emperor inquired if all was ready; he was told what the Admiral had replied. He had this reply twice repeated to him. He was unaccustomed to the tone of it, and stamping violently, he sent for the Admiral, who presented himself at once.

He did not come quickly enough to suit the Emperor, however, and he met him half-way from his barrack. The staff were following His Majesty, and ranged themselves silently around him. His eyes shot lightning.

"Mr. Admiral," said the Emperor in an agitated voice, "why have you not executed my orders?"

"Sire," replied Admiral Bruix with respectful firmness, "there is a horrible tempest brewing. . . . Your Majesty can see it as well as I can; do you wish to expose the lives of so many brave fellows without necessity?" As a matter of fact, the heaviness of the atmosphere and the dull rumbling in the distance justified the fears of the Admiral but too well. "Sir," replied the Emperor, more and more irritated, "I gave orders; once more, why have you not executed them? The consequences concern me alone. Obey!"—"Sire, I will not obey."—"Sir, you are insolent!" And the Emperor, who still held his whip in his hand, advanced toward the Admiral with a threatening gesture. Admiral Bruix drew back a step, and laid his hand on the hilt of his sword. "Sire," he said, turning pale, "take care!" The Emperor, motionless for a time, his hand raised, fixed his eyes on the Admiral, who, on his side, maintained his terrible attitude. At last, the Emperor threw his whip on the ground. M. Bruix let go of the hilt of his sword, and with uncovered head awaited the result of this horrible scene.

"Mr. Rear-admiral Magon," said the Emperor, "you will have the movement I ordered executed on the instant. As to you, sir," continued he, bringing back his glance to Admiral Bruix, "you will leave Boulogne within twenty-four hours, and retire to Holland. Go." His Majesty withdrew at once. Some officers, but not very many, shook the hand the Admiral held out to them in parting.

Meanwhile Rear-admiral Magon caused the fleet to perform the fatal manœuvre required by the Emperor. Hardly were the first steps taken when the sea became frightful to behold. The heavily clouded sky was furrowed with lightnings, the thunder roared every instant, and the wind broke up all the lines. At last occurred what the Admiral had foreseen, and the most fearful tempest dispersed the vessels in such a manner as to render their situation desperate. The Emperor, with down-bent head and crossed arms, was walking the beach when terrible cries were suddenly heard. More than twenty gunboats crowded with soldiers and sailors had just been cast ashore, and the unfortunates whom they had carried were struggling against furious waves, crying for aid that no one dared to give them. Profoundly touched by this spectacle, his heart torn by the lamentations of the immense crowd drawn by the tempest to the cliffs and the shore, the Emperor, who saw his generals and officers shivering with horror around him, resolved to set the example of devotion, and in spite of every effort made to detain him, he threw himself into a life-boat, saying: "Let me alone! let me alone! some one must get them out." His boat filled with water in an instant. The waves passed and repassed above it, and the Emperor was drenched. A billow still stronger than the others narrowly missed carrying His Majesty overboard, and his hat was thrown into the water. Electrified by such courage, officers, soldiers, sailors, and citizens flew to the rescue, some in boats and some by swimming. But, alas! but a small number of the unfortunates who had composed the crew of the gunboats could be saved, and the next day the sea threw back on the beach more than two hundred corpses, along with the hat of the victor of Marengo.

This sad morrow was a day of desolation for

Boulogne and for the camp. There was no one who did not hasten to the shore, searching anxiously among the corpses heaped up by the waves. The Emperor groaned over so many disasters which interiorly he doubtless could not fail to attribute to his own obstinacy. Agents provided with gold went by his orders through the city and the camp, to prevent the murmurs that were all ready to break out.

That day, I saw a drummer belonging to the crew of the shipwrecked shallops come back on his drum, as if it had been a raft. The poor devil had his thigh broken. He had remained more than twelve hours in this horrible situation.

To finish up with the camp of Boulogne, I will relate here what did not in reality happen until the month of August, 1805, after the return of the Emperor from his journey and his coronation in Italy.

Soldiers and sailors were burning with impatience to embark for England, but the desired moment did not arrive. Every evening they said to each other: To-morrow there will be a good wind, it will be foggy, and we shall start; and they fell asleep in that hope. Day would break with sun or rain.

One evening, however, when the favorable wind was blowing, I heard two sailors, chatting together on the wharf, indulging in conjectures about the future: "The Emperor would do well to start to-morrow," said one; "he will never have better weather, there will surely be a fog." "Bah!" said the other, "he does not even think of it; it is more than a fortnight since the fleet has budged. They don't want to start so soon." "And yet all the munitions are on board; everything could be unmoored in a jiffy." They came to place the night-sentinels, and the conversation of the two old sea-dogs stopped there. But I soon had reason to recognize that their experience had not deceived them. In fact, toward three o'clock in the morning a light fog overspread the sea, which was a little rough; the wind of the previous day sprang up again. At daybreak, the fog thickened so as to hide the fleet from the English. The most profound silence reigned everywhere. Not a single unfriendly sail had been signalled during the night, and, as the sailors had said, everything favored the descent.

At five o'clock in the morning signals came from the semaphore. In a twinkling, all the seamen were stirring. The harbor resounded with shouts of joy; the order to depart had been received! While the sails were being hoisted, the general was beaten in the four camps. The whole army was called to arms and came down precipitately into the city, hardly believing what they had just heard. "We are going to start, then," said all these valiant fellows; "we are going to say two words to those —— of English!" And the pleasure that moved them expressed itself in acclamations which were silenced by a rolling of the drums. The embarkation took place in profound silence, and in an orderly manner which I should vainly try to describe. In seven hours two hundred thousand soldiers were aboard the fleet; and, when a little after midday this fine army was about to start out, amid the farewells and good wishes of the entire city assembled on the wharves and on the cliffs, at the moment when all the soldiers, standing with uncovered heads, were detaching themselves from French soil to the cry of *Long live the Emperor!* a message arrived from the imperial barrack which disembarked the troops and sent them back to camp. A telegraphic despatch received that very moment by His Majesty obliged him to give another direction to his troops.

The soldiers returned sadly to their quarters; some of them testified loudly, and in a very energetic manner, the disappointment caused them by this species of mystification. They had always regarded the success of the enterprise against England as a thing completely certain, and to see themselves arrested at the instant of departure was in their eyes the greatest misfortune that could happen.

When all was in order, the Emperor repaired to the right camp, and there he made a proclamation in presence of the troops which was carried to the other camps, and posted everywhere. This was about the tenor of it:

"Brave soldiers of the camp of Boulogne!

"You will not go to England. English gold has seduced the Emperor of Austria, who has just declared war on France. His army has broken the line it was to keep; Bavaria is invaded. Soldiers! new laurels await you beyond the Rhine; let us speed to conquer from the enemy we have conquered already."

This proclamation was received with universal transports. All frowns vanished. It mattered little to these intrepid men whether they were led to Austria or to England. They were thirsting to fight, war was proclaimed; all their desires were satisfied.

Thus vanished all those grand schemes for a descent on England, ripened so long, so wisely planned. It is not doubtful now that, with time and perseverance, the enterprise would have been crowned with the greatest success. But it was not to be.

Several regiments remained at Boulogne; and while their brethren were overthrowing the Austrians, they erected a column on the beach destined long to recall the souvenir of Napoleon and his immortal army.

Directly after the proclamation of which I have just spoken, His Majesty gave orders to make all ready for his approaching departure. The grand marshal of the palace was directed to examine and pay all the expenses incurred by the Emperor, or which he had caused to be incurred during his different sojourns; not without being recommended, as usual, to take good care not to overpay, or pay too dear. I think I have said already that His Majesty was extremely economical in all that concerned him personally, and that he was afraid of spending twenty francs without some very useful end in view.

Among many other accounts to be regulated, the grand marshal of the palace found that of M. Sordi, engineer of military communications, who had been directed by him to undertake the interior and exterior decorations of His Majesty's barrack. The bill amounted to fifty thousand francs. The grand marshal uttered cries of horror at this alarming total; he would not settle M. Sordi's bill, and dismissed him, saying that he could not authorize the payment without first having taken the Emperor's orders.

The engineer withdrew, after assuring the grand marshal that he had not overcharged for any article, and that he had followed his instructions literally. He added that in this state of things, he could not possibly make the least reduction. The next day M. Sordi received orders to present himself before the Emperor.

The Emperor was in his barrack, the subject of the discussion. He had under his eyes, not the account of the engineer, but a map on which he was following the future march of his army. M. Sordi came and was introduced by General Cafarelli. The half-opened door permitted the General, and me also, to hear the conversation about to begin. "Sir," said His Majesty, "you have spent a great deal too much money in decorating this wretched barrack: yes, certainly, a great deal too much. . . . Fifty thousand francs! do you think of that, sir? but that is frightful. I will not have you paid." The engineer, dumfounded by this brusque rush into the subject, did not at first know what to reply. Happily the Emperor, by casting his eyes once more at the unrolled map, gave him time to collect himself. He responded: "Sire, the gold clouds which formed the ceiling of this room [all this took place in the council-chamber], and which surround the guiding star of Your Majesty, did in fact cost twenty thousand francs. But if I had consulted the heart of your subjects, the imperial eagle which is again about to crush the enemies of France and of your throne would have spread its wings in the midst of the rarest diamonds." "That is all very well," replied the Emperor, laughing; "it is very well, but I will not pay you at present, and since you tell me that this eagle which cost so dear ought to crush the Austrians, wait till it does so, and I will pay your bill with the rix-dollars of the Emperor of Germany and the gold frederics of the King of Prussia." And His Majesty, resuming his compass, began to make his army move over the map.

As a matter of fact, the engineer's account was not settled until after the battle of Austerlitz, and then, as the Emperor had said, in rix-dollars and frederics.

CHAPTER XIX

Journey in Belgium — Furlough of twenty-four hours — The inhabitants of Alost — Their cordiality towards Constant — The valet fêted on the master's account — Kindness of the Emperor — Journal of Madame —— on a journey to Aix-la-Chapelle — History of this journal — NARRATION DE MADAME —— M. d'Aubusson, chamberlain — Ceremony of the oath — Josephine's grace — An old acquaintance — Josephine's aversion to etiquette — Madame de La Rochefoucauld — The faubourg Saint-Germain — A chamberlain's key instead of a colonel's commission — Formation of the imperial households — Members of the old court at the new one — The opposition party in the noble faubourg — Madame de La Rochefoucauld, Madame de Balby, and Madame de Bouilley — Shameful beggars — Distribution of crosses of honor — Napoleon complains of being badly lodged in the Tuileries — Bad humor — The Museum seen by torchlight — A perilous passage — Napoleon before the statue of Alexander — Grandeur and littleness — A saying of the Princess Dolgorouki — The Emperor at Boulogne and the Empress at Aix-la-Chapelle — The Empress fails in etiquette and is rebuked by her grand equerry — The malachite and the wife of the mayor of Rheims — Picard's troupe and his pieces — The diligence and the rue Saint-Denis — Court dresses and rags — Household and circle of the Empress — Madame de Sémonville — Madame de Spare — Madame Macdonald — Confidence of the Empress — Her character that of a child — Her intelligence — Her education — Her manners — Her candor and self-distrust — The Emperor's reserve with the Empress — His superstition — Prediction made to Josephine — M. de Talleyrand — Motive of his hatred for Josephine — The dinner at the house of Barras — M. de Talleyrand urges a divorce — Madame de Staël and M. de Narbonne — Indifference of the Emperor as to whether he were liked by those who surrounded him — The thermometer of court friendships — Profound reverences and profound insipidity — Ceremony in the church of Aix — Arrival of the Emperor — Vexations — Espionage — The young general and the old military man — False reports — The Emperor's jealousy — Josephine justified — Napoleon wholly occupied with etiquette — Grand reception of the constituted authorities — *Pretended* charlatanism of the Emperor — The Emperor talking of the arts and of love — Was the Emperor witty — Adulation of the clergy — The grand relics — M. de Pradt the Emperor's first chaplain — Alexander and the bushel of millet — Talma — Did M. de Pradt believe in God? — The Emperor's whist — The Duc d'Aremberg, the blind player — The author takes a hand at the Emperor's table without knowing the game — An axiom of the great Corneille — Disgrace of M. de Sémonville — M. de Montholon — Madame la Duchesse de Montebello — Napoleon's sally against women — The English muslins — The Emperor's *first sweetheart* — The Emperor represented as insolent, disdainful, and vulgar — Constant's observation on this criticism — The manners of Murat unlike those of the Emperor — The Emperor haughty and contemptuous of the human species.

TOWARD the end of November, the Emperor set out from Boulogne to make an excursion into Belgium, and to rejoin the Empress, who had gone to Aix-la-Chapelle. Everywhere along his route he was received not merely with the honors reserved for crowned heads, but in addition with acclamations intended for his person rather than his power. I shall say nothing of the numerous fêtes given him during his journey, nor of the noteworthy things that occurred. These details can be found everywhere, and I wish to speak only of what is personal to me, or at least of what is not known to each and all. Let it suffice me then to say that we passed through Arras, Valenciennes, Mons, Bruxelles, etc., in triumph as it were. At the gate of each city, the municipal council presented the Emperor with the wine of honor and the keys of the place. We remained several days at Lacken, and being only five leagues from Alost, a little town where I had relatives, I asked His Majesty's permission to leave him for twenty-four hours; which he granted, but with difficulty. Alost, like the rest of Belgium at this period, professed the greatest attachment for the Emperor. I scarcely had a moment to myself. I was staying at the house of one of my friends, M. D——, whose family had long been in one of the chief employments of the Belgian government. I think the whole town came there to visit me; but I was not vain enough to attribute to myself all the honor of this cordiality. They wanted to know even the least details that related to the great man near whom I was placed. I was extraordinarily fêted on this account, and my twenty-four hours passed too quickly. On my return, His Majesty deigned to put a thousand questions about the town of Alost and its inhabitants, what they thought of his government and his person. I could answer him without flattery that he was adored. He seemed pleased, and talked kindly to me about my family and my petty interests. We left Lacken the next day and passed through Alost. If I could have foreseen that the day before, I might have stayed there several hours longer. However, the Emperor had made so much difficulty about granting a single day, that I should probably not have dared venture on more, even if I had known that the household was to pass through the town.

The Emperor liked Laeken; he had considerable repairs and embellishments made there, and through his efforts this palace became a charming place of abode.

This journey of Their Majesties lasted nearly three months. We did not return to Paris, or rather to Saint-Cloud, until some time in October. At Cologne and Coblentz the Emperor had received the visit of several German princes and princesses; but, as I could only know by hearsay what passed in these interviews, I had determined not to speak of them, when there fell into my hands a manuscript in which the author enters into all the details of which I could have no cognizance. This is how I found myself possessor of this curious journal.

It seems that one of the ladies of Her Majesty the Empress Josephine noted down daily everything interesting that happened in the interior of the palace and the imperial family. These souvenirs, among which occur many unflattering portraits, were brought to the Emperor's notice probably, as it was supposed at the time, by the indiscretion and unfaithfulness of a chambermaid.

Their Majesties were very severely, and to my mind very unjustly treated in the Memoirs of Madame ———. Hence the Emperor flew into a violent rage, and Madame ——— received her dismissal. The day when His Majesty read these manuscripts in his bedroom at Saint-Cloud, his secretary, who was accustomed to carry all papers into His Majesty's cabinet, doubtless forgot a rather small paper book, which I found on the floor, near the Emperor's bath-tub. This paper book was nothing less than the *Account of the Journey of the Empress to Aix-la-Chapelle*, a relation which apparently formed part of the Memoirs of Madame ——. As we were just starting for Paris, and moreover as papers negligently forgotten and not missed did not seem to be of great importance, I threw them into the upper part of an *armoire* of a cabinet which was seldom opened, and concerned myself no further about them. It seems that nobody thought more of them than I did; for it was not until two years afterward that, in searching every corner of the bedchamber in search of some mislaid object, my eyes fell upon the dusty manuscript of Madame ——. The Emperor's thoughts were very remote at that time from the petty vexations of 1805, and I did not feel myself guilty of a great indiscretion in taking the manuscript home with me, and I hope nobody will be displeased at finding it annexed to my Memoirs. At the same time I protest here, in advance, against any interpretation which would tend to make me jointly responsible for the opinions of Madame ——. She belonged to the number of those persons who, belonging to the old régime, either individually or through their family ties, had thought they could accept or even solicit appointments in the Emperor's household, without renouncing their prejudices or their hatred for him. This hatred has led the author of the *Journey* into more than one unjust exaggeration concerning whatever relates to Their Majesties, and I have replied in several notes to things that to me seem inexact in her criticisms. In what refers to the German princes and some other personages, Madame —— impresses me as having been ingeniously truthful, although a little too jeering.

DIARY OF THE JOURNEY TO MAYENCE

Paris, July 1, 1804. — I took my oath to-day at Saint-Cloud, as lady of the Empress's palace, at the same time when M. d'Aubusson took his as chamberlain. Madame de La Rochefoucauld was the only person who witnessed this ceremony, which took place in the blue salon in a rather gay manner. Josephine was very gracious about it; she had formerly met M. d'Aubusson in society, and she seemed to find it very pleasant to renew acquaintance with him by receiving his oath as Empress. She speaks of her elevation very frankly, very becomingly. She said to us with delightful artlessness that it was very unpleasant to her to remain seated when women who were formally her equals, or even her superiors, entered her apartments; that she was required to conform to this etiquette, but that she found it quite impossible. Madame de La Rochefoucauld, who had to be entreated for a long time before she would accept the place of lady of honor, and who yielded only through affection for Josephine, has given herself infinite pains to bring the whole faubourg Saint-Germain to this court. It was she who persuaded M. d'Aubusson. He had wished to enter the service as a colonel; he was rather surprised to receive an appointment as chamberlain instead of a regiment. All Paris occupies itself with the formation of the households of the Emperor and the Empress; every day one hears of some family of the old court which is going to form part of this one. The embarrassment with which people accost persons of their acquaintance is curious enough: uncertain whether they have received appointments, one does not like to boast of his own; but on learning theirs, one is enchanted; it is one weapon more for the sheaf they would like to form in opposition to the malicious pleasantries of the faubourg Saint-Germain.

July 8, 1804. — Madame de La Rochefoucauld related a rather amusing adventure this morning. She had just made a call on Madame de Balby. The latter, enchanted to find a chance to throw a stone into her garden, said to her: "Madame de Bouilley has just gone away; I told her that people in society were mentioning her as a lady of the palace; but she denied it in a way that proved to me that they were in the wrong." Madame de La Rochefoucauld had with her at that very moment the letter in which Madame de Bouilley asks for this place; she replied: "I do not know why Madame de Bouilley denies it, for here is her application and her appointment."

July 14, 1804. — What a fatiguing day! We were assembled at the château at eleven o'clock, to accompany the Empress to the church of the Invalides, to witness a distribution of the decorations of the Legion of Honor.

Seated in a tribune opposite the Emperor's throne, we saw him receive nineteen hundred chevaliers. This ceremony was interrupted for an instant by the arrival of a man of the people, wearing a simple jacket, who presented himself on the steps of the throne. Napoleon paused in surprise: some one questioned the man, who showed his brevet, and he received the accolade and his decoration. The cortège followed the same road on returning, passing through the grand alley of the Tuileries. It was the first time that Bonaparte has entered the garden in a carriage. On re-entering the apartments of the Empress, he approached the window; some children who were on the terrace, seeing him, shouted: *Long live the Emperor!* He drew back with very perceptible ill-humor, saying: "I am the worst-lodged sovereign in Europe; no one has ever thought of allowing the public to come so near his palace." I must confess that if I had arrived at the Tuileries in the way that Napoleon has, I should have thought it more suitable not to seem to find myself ill-lodged.

I do not know whether it was because this little spurt of ill-humor lasted; but, on entering the circle which we formed, he approached Madame de La Vallette, and kicking the bottom of her dress, he said:

"Fie! Madame, what a dress! what trimming! It is in the very worst taste!" Madame de La Vallette seemed a little disconcerted.

In the evening we went up to the balcony of the middle pavilion to hear the concert that was given in the garden. After some moments, the Emperor took a whim to see the statues of the Louvre by torchlight. M. Denon, who was there, received his orders; the footmen carried torches; we crossed the grand gallery, and went down into the halls of the antiques. In passing through them, Napoleon paused a long time before a bust of Alexander; there was a sort of affectation in his calling our attention to the fact that necessarily this head was bad, that it was too large, Alexander being much smaller than himself. He dwelt greatly on those words: *much smaller.* I was at a little distance, but I had heard him; having come nearer, he absolutely repeated the phrase; he seemed charmed to inform us that he was larger than Alexander. Ah! how small he seemed to me at that moment!

July 15, 1804. — This evening I was at a house where the Princess Dolgorouki came on leaving the drawing-room at the Tuileries. Some one asked her what she thought about it. "It is certainly a great power," she responded, "but it is not a court."

Paris, July —, 1804. — The Emperor starts to-morrow to go and see the flat-boats at Boulogne, and the Empress for Aix-la-Chapelle, where she will take the waters. I must accompany her.

Rheims, July —, 1804.— This morning, before leaving Saint-Cloud, the Empress crossed two halls to give an order to a person occupying a rather subaltern position in her household. M. d'Harville, her grand equerry, came up in a fright to represent to her that Her Majesty would totally compromise the dignity of the throne, and that she ought to give her orders through his lips. "Eh! sir," said Josephine, gayly, "this etiquette is perfect for princesses born on the throne and accustomed to the restraint which it imposes; but I, who have had the good luck to live so many years as a private person, think it well to give my orders sometimes without an interpreter." The grand equerry bowed, and we set out.

Sedan, July 30, 1804.— This morning I found Josephine very busily reading a large sheet of manuscript, and I was not a little surprised to see that she was learning her lesson. Whenever she travels, everything is fixed, foreseen in advance. It is known in what place she must be harangued by such or such an authority; here she must respond in such a manner; there in such another. All is regulated, even to the presents she must make. But it sometimes happens that her memory fails her; and then, if her response is not as suitable as that which had been prepared, it is at least always made with such courtesy and kindness that people are always satisfied.

Liège, August 1, 1804.— I feared that we should

never get here. The Emperor, without informing himself as to whether a projected road through the forest of Ardennes had been completed, had traced ours on the map; the relays were arranged according to his orders, and we were twenty times in danger of having our carriages smashed. In several places they were kept up with ropes. No one ever imagined making women travel like dragoon officers.

Aix-la-Chapelle, August 7, 1804. — The Empress has established herself here in the house of one M. de Jacoby, lately purchased by the Emperor. It had been spoken of as a very agreeable habitation, and we were surprised on finding a wretched little house. The prefect wished to have Josephine come at once and install herself at the prefecture; but such is her perfect submission to Bonaparte's wishes that she would not do so without his orders. He is bent on favorizing the inhabitants of the reunited departments, desiring to attach them to France. It was this motive that induced him to buy M. de Jacoby's house and pay four times its value for it.

Aix-la-Chapelle, August —, 1804, — This morning, on reading the *Publicist* newspaper, Josephine was rather disagreeably surprised at seeing, in the account of her journey, that some one had reported and printed her adieux to the wife of the mayor of Rheims, with whom she had lodged while in that city. It often happens that one carelessly says something which lacks common sense, without noticing it; but, if one encounters the same phrase in print, then reflection makes one appreciate just what it amounts to. I own that there is no need of it to judge of this one. On leaving Rheims, the Empress gave the mayor's wife a medallion of malachite, and said as she embraced her: "*'Tis the color of hope.*" The fact is that hope had not the least thing to do in this case; it was a mere piece of stupidity. I was there; I heard and I remarked it; but I took good care not to remember it this morning. Josephine was in despair; she was certain, and that in perfectly good faith, that she had not said such a thing: it would have been cruel to contradict her. The private secretary proposed that she should deny using it in the journal; she thought of it for a moment; but whether she suddenly remembered it, or was afraid of doing something which Bonaparte might disapprove, she contented herself with writing to him that she had not uttered this stupidity; that her first impulse had been to contradict it, but she had been unwilling to do anything without his orders. A courier was despatched to Boulogne.[1]

Aix-la-Chapelle, August 11, 1804. — Our life here is tiresome and monotonous. With the exception of a daily ride, which we take in an open carriage through the environs of the city, the remainder of the day is precisely like yesterday. Picard's troupe has come

---

[1] The Emperor's decision was that the journalist must be reprimanded; and from that time they were forbidden ever to publish any response of either the Emperor or the Empress without having first seen it in the *Moniteur.* — *Editor's note.*

here and will remain as long as the Empress does. Every evening we go and yawn at the theatre; Picard's repertory is unimaginably fatiguing in the long run. To be sure it is clever, and has some very good comic scenes; but the subjects are always selected from the lowest ranks of life, one never emerges from the stage-coach or the rue Saint-Denis. For a day it is possible to be amused with the novelty of this tone; but one is presently fatigued at finding one's self so far from home.

August 11, 1804. — Not having gone to the theatre this evening, and some one having spoken of a plan of Paris in relief, the Empress wished to see it. The evening being very fine, why, she asked, should we not walk there? This was a novelty, and every one was in haste to start. M. d'Harville, who is always the chevalier of etiquette, was in despair. He intended to hazard his opinion, but we were already too far away. The fact is that he was quite right, as the sequel of this frolic has proved. The streets being almost empty in the evenings, we met hardly anybody in going; but while we were examining this plan, the rumor of our excursion got around; and when we came out, there were candles in all the windows, and the whole populace on our route. We must have formed a sufficiently amusing cortège; those gentlemen, with their hats under their arms and swords at their sides, who gave us their hands and aided us to pass through the crowd which pressed around us, and whose tatters presented a rather startling contrast with our feathers, our diamonds, and our long dresses. At last we reached the hotel of the prefecture; the Empress felt then that she had acted thoughtlessly, and she frankly acknowledged it.

August 13, 1804. — It was said this evening that the Emperor would soon arrive here: that will impart a little movement and variety to our habitual circle, which is perfectly monotonous. It is composed of Madame de La Rochefoucauld, a woman of very amiable disposition; four ladies of the palace, the grand equerry, two chamberlains, the chief equerry; M. Deschamps, the private secretary; the prefect and his family; two or three generals who have married German women, real caricatures. I must add one very amiable woman, Madame de Sémonville, wife of the French ambassador to Holland; by her first marriage she was Madame de Montholon. She has had two sons and two daughters: one is Madame de Spare; the other, who married General Joubert, became the wife of General Macdonald by a second marriage. This young and lovely woman is dying; she came here to take the waters; her mother, Madame de Sémonville, accompanied and takes care of her. I fear that it will be in vain. Hence we enjoy very little of Madame de Sémonville's society; she seldom leaves her daughter.

Aix-la-Chapelle, August 14, 1804. — I remained alone quite a long time with Josephine this morning;

she talked to me with a confidence which would have flattered me very much, if I had not seen daily that this *abandon* is natural and necessary to her. The estimate I have formed of her character is perhaps premature, since I have known her so short a time; however, I do not believe I am mistaken. She is exactly like a ten-year-old child. She has the good nature and the levity of one; she is quickly moved; weeps and then is consoled in a moment. One might say of her intelligence what Molière said of a man's probity, "that he had just enough to prevent his being hanged." She has precisely what is needed to keep one from being a simpleton. Ignorant, like the generality of creoles, she has learned nothing or almost nothing except through conversation; but having passed her life in good society, she has acquired very good manners, grace, and that jargon which in society sometimes takes the place of wit. Social events are a canvas which she embroiders and arranges, and which supplies materials for her conversation. She has at least quarter of an hour of wit a day. What I find charming in her is that diffidence which, in her position, is a great merit. If she finds intelligence and judgment in any of the persons who surround her, she consults them with a candor and artlessness which are wholly delightful. Her temper is perfectly even and sweet; it is impossible not to love her. I fear that this need of opening her heart, of communicating all her ideas, all that passes between her and the Emperor, must deprive her of much of his confidence. She complains of not possessing it; she told me this morning that never in all the years she has spent with him, has she seen in him a single moment of unreserve; that if, at some moments, he shows a little confidence, it is only to excite that of the person to whom he is talking; but that he never reveals his entire thought. She says that he is very superstitious; that one day being with the army in Italy, he broke in his pocket the glass which covered her portrait and that he was in despair, convinced that it was a warning of her death; he had no repose until after the return of the courier whom he sent to reassure himself.[1]

This conversation led Josephine to speak to me about the singular prediction which was made to her just as she was leaving Martinique. A sort of gypsy said to her: "You are going to France to be married; your marriage will not be happy; your husband will die in a tragic manner; you will incur great dangers yourself at that period; but you will come out triumphantly from them; you are destined to the most glorious condition, and without being a queen, you will be more than a queen." She added that being very young then, she paid very little attention to this prediction; that she only remembered it at the time when M. de Beauharnais was guillotined;

---

[1] At this epoch the Emperor was still in love with Josephine.— *Note of Madame* ——.

that she spoke of it then to several ladies who like herself were imprisoned in the days of the Terror; but that at present she saw it accomplished in every point. It is a very singular chance which has brought about the coincidence between this prediction and her destiny.

August 15. — This morning, while driving, Josephine continued the conversation begun yesterday. I was alone with her in the carriage; she talked to me about M. de Talleyrand; she claims that he hates her, and without any motive but the injuries he has done her. Alas! it is too true that he who has offended never pardons. These words are written large in the history of the human heart. The offended person may forget it, but conscience never fails to remember. During Bonaparte's sojourn in Egypt, at a time when every one regarded him as ruined, M. de Talleyrand, who was always at the feet of power, had been in various circumstances very impolite to Madame Bonaparte. One day, especially, he was dining with her at the house of Barras; Madame Tallien was present; it is claimed that this woman, who was celebrated for her beauty, exercised at this time a great empire over Barras. M. de Talleyrand, placed near her and Madame Bonaparte, showed so much grace in the attentions with which he surrounded Madame Tallien, and so little politeness toward Madame Bonaparte, that the latter, who knew him to be the perfection of courtiers, concluded that General Bonaparte must be known to be dead for him to treat her so badly; because if he had thought he could ever return to France, he would have been afraid he might avenge the slights put upon his wife in his absence. This idea, uniting with wounded self-love, made her leave the table in tears. M. de Talleyrand, who has not forgotten this circumstance, and who fears lest Josephine may one day have the power and the wish to revenge herself for it, did all that lay in his power during the last three months that elapsed before the creation of the Empire, to induce Napoleon to divorce her, in order that he might marry the Princess Wilhelmine of Baden; he urged, with all possible skill, the support he would gain in the courts of Russia and Bavaria, with whom he would become allied by this marriage; and the need of consolidating his Empire by the hope of having children. The Emperor wavered a little; but he finally resisted, and Josephine has no more anxiety on that account.[1]

Although she has not much intelligence, she is not lacking in a certain sort of cleverness; she has known how to profit by the superstitious weakness of the Emperor, and she sometimes says to him: "*They talk of thy star, but it is mine that influences thine; it was to me that a lofty destiny was predicted.*" This idea has probably contributed more than people think to the overthrow of M. de Talley-

---

[1] The sequel proved that she deceived herself. — *Note of Madame ——.*

rand's schemes, and to tighten the bonds he wished to break.[1]

Josephine has just told me a rather piquant anecdote. Madame de Staël wrote to Count Louis de Narbonne not long since. As she was sending her letter by a man whom she believed trusty, she expressed her whole mind; she was particularly sprightly concerning persons who have accepted places at court since the creation of the Empire. She added that she hoped that she would never be chagrined, in reading the journal, by seeing his name beside theirs. The man entrusted with this letter carried it to Fouché. The latter (after paying for this rascally transaction) read it, copied it, and having closed it up again with care, said to the man: "Fulfil your commission; get M. de Narbonne's answer, and bring it to me;" which he did not fail to do. The Count replied in the same tone. They say that we were not spared in this response. I forgive him with all my heart; I am tempted to laugh myself at the bizarre ensemble that we present. This court is a veritable harlequin's dress; but if the costume has all the requisite motleys, harlequin has not all the graces of his state;[2] his awkwardness is in

---

[1] If Napoleon searches into the past for the causes of his downfall, it will be difficult, if he retains this superstitious weakness, for him not to remark that, since his divorce, events, which he had governed so long, have all turned against him. — *Note of Madame* ——.

[2] It is a crime of a new species not to have *all the graces of the state* of a harlequin. The manners of the Emperor were simple

singular contrast with the great nobles by whom he is surrounded. I am sorry that one can set over against the Count's pleasantries his assiduity in the circles of Cambacérès and of all the ministers. Josephine claims that this letter, of which Napoleon is reminded by each obeisance of M. de Narbonne (and he makes a good many of them), deprives them of all their grace, and that he will never obtain anything.[1]

August 16. — I perceive, by the redoublement of politeness in the persons who surround the Empress, how much I am daily losing in their esteem. At court, it is in this way that one must measure the degree of attachment one inspires. For some days I had been astonished to find that I had become the object of general attention; to tell the truth I did not know to what to attribute it, and in my innocence I might perhaps have laid it to my own merits. Who knows just how far self-love might have misled me? M. de ——, the most affected, the most insipid of all courtiers, past, present, and to come, under-

---

and natural, but without awkwardness. Doubtless they did contrast with the obsequious and courtier-like forms of the *great nobles* who surrounded him; for he was the only one who held himself straight and erect, while these gentlemen bowed to the ground. — *Note by the editor.*

[1] Some time after this epoch, Count de Narbonne was appointed to the embassy of Vienna and became one of those who were best treated by Bonaparte. What did he care about the attachment, the devotion of those whom he employed? He knew that he would never obtain them; but he liked the flattery of the old courtiers, because it was more adroit than that of the new ones. — *Note by Madame* ——.

took to enlighten my inexperience; he called on me this morning, ten times more reverentially than usual. He said to me that everybody had remarked Josephine's kindness toward me, our long conversations together, the attention with which she offered me every day at breakfast the dishes she found in front of her; that, for his part, he had been particularly pleased on remarking these distinctions; but that they had become a subject of jealousy to many persons. I laughed at the importance which he attached to all that, and I privately promised myself no longer to put to my own credit attentions which I owe only to the whim of the sovereign.

August 16. — To-day we have had a grand ceremony in the church, for the distribution of several decorations of the Legion of Honor. They had been sent to General Lorges, who desired that Josephine should give them herself. The clergy came to receive her at the door of the church. A throne was prepared for her in the choir, and everything had a solemn appearance. General Lorges made a speech, but he is more brave than eloquent; he knows how to fight better than he knows how to speak in public. He said to us in this discourse that he thought himself happy in seeing beauty on the throne and virtue beside it. If this is not his exact phrase, it is at least his thought. We could all feel aggrieved at this compliment, since to one he accorded virtue without beauty, and to the others beauty without virtue, but we all laughed a good deal over it when we came out. The Empress told us that she was very well content to have virtue for her lot, and asked to which one of us that of beauty had been awarded. Self-love stood ready to persuade each one that she had been intended, and we mutually took the credit of this compliment.

Aix-la-Chapelle, August 18, 1804. — Everything is in commotion in the palace; Bonaparte arrives to-morrow. It is extraordinary that in a situation like his, one should not be loved.[1] That would be so easy when one has only to will to make people happy in order to do so. But it seems that he does not often have this will; for from the first footman to the first officer of the crown, each one experiences a sort of terror at his approach. The court will become more brilliant; the ambassadors, not having been newly accredited since the metamorphosis of the consul into an emperor, will all arrive to present their letters. We shall remain here several days longer. We shall go to Cologne and Coblentz, and remain some days in each city, and

---

[1] There is a great error here, to say the least. The Emperor did know how to make himself loved, and, in fact, he was loved by all who were in his service. I believe I have furnished more than one proof of this in my Memoirs. Of all his old servants, I dare affirm there is not one who will contradict me on this point. That the Emperor may not have been loved by his courtiers is possible. With such power as his, one makes still more ingrates than happy people; and the gratitude of courtiers is proverbial. But ought one to bring that as a reproach against His Majesty? — *Note by Constant.*

from there to Mayence, where all the princes who are to form the Rhine confederation will assemble.

August 19, 1804. — He has arrived, and espionage along with him; the vexations which ordinarily form his cortège have already banished all gaiety from our little circle. His return has apprised us that among a dozen persons who were appointed to accompany Josephine here, there is one who was entrusted with the part of spy. Napoleon knew on arriving that on such a day we had made an excursion, that on such another day we had breakfasted with Madame de Sémonville, in a wood in the environs of Aix-la-Chapelle. The informer (whom we know) thought she would make her recital more meritorious by attributing to General Lorges, who is young and has very agreeable manners, the fault of a poor old military man who, probably, having been a soldier longer than an officer, did not know that one should not sit down before the Empress, on the same sofa. Josephine was too kind to show him that he had done an unsuitable thing; she was afraid of humiliating him. This proof of her goodness of heart had been transformed into a guilty condescension in favor of a young man for whom she must have a great deal of indulgence and kindness, since he could feel himself so perfectly at ease with her. This was the conclusion it was intended that the Emperor should draw. Luckily, this circumstance, so unlikely to be remarked, had been so, and it was not difficult for Josephine to prove who was the guilty person: his age, his lack of experience of society, have effaced all the black with which this action had been painted. How can one help being astonished[1] that a man who has passed his life in camps, who has been nurtured and brought up by the Republic, should attach importance to these trifles! Ah! the love of power is doubtless natural to man; a child does, for the plaything which he disputes with his comrade, what sovereigns do, at a more advanced age, for the provinces they wish to wrest from each other. But how far it is from that noble pride which wishes to dominate its equals, to this code of etiquette which forms at present the dearest occupation of Napoleon! I was wondering this evening, as I looked at all these men standing up, and not daring to move a step outside the circle they formed, why it is that the powerful of all times and of all countries have attached the idea of respect to constrained attitudes. I think they find the sight of all these men bent incessantly in their presence sweet, because it is a continual reminder of their power over them.

August 20, 1804. — This morning Napoleon received all the constituted authorities of the city. They issued from this audience confounded, astonished to the last degree. "What a man!" said the

---

[1] *How can one help being astonished* that it seems *astonishing* to Madame —— that the Emperor loved his honor and his wife well enough to be jealous of both? The *Republic* and the *love of power* had nothing to do with it. — *Note by Constant.*

mayor to me, "what a prodigy! what a universal genius! How is it that he knows this department, so distant from the capital, better than we do? Not a detail escapes him; he knows everything; he is acquainted with all the products of our industry." I smiled; I was greatly tempted to inform this honest man, who was going to retail his admiration throughout the city, that it would bear a good deal of abatement; that this perfect acquaintance which Napoleon displayed to them is a piece of charlatanism with which he subjugates the vulgar. He has had thoroughly exact statistics drawn up of France and its reunited departments. When he travels, he takes with him the manuscript books which relate to the countries he is to visit;[1] these he learns by heart an hour before the audience; then he appears, talks about everything with the air of a man whose mind embraces all the vast country that he governs, and leaves these good people rapt in admiration. An hour afterward, he no longer knows a word of what excited this admiration.

The prefect, M. Méchin, came to this audience with a certain assurance (rather common with him),

---

[1] What matters it whether the Emperor made himself conversant with what related to the country he was to travel through *an hour* or a year before his audience? The only question is whether he did make himself so conversant. And if he learned it *by heart*, how could he have forgotten it by the end of an hour? He remembered it so well that he generously marked his passage by benefits and improvements which attest his perfect knowledge of localities. — *Note by Constant.*

not suspecting the ordeal he was about to undergo. Napoleon, who had just learned his lesson, asked him several questions to which he did not know how to answer; he was troubled, embarrassed. "Monsieur," said the Emperor to him, "when a man does not know a department better than this, he is unworthy to administer it." And he removed him from office. Such was the result of to-day's audience.

Aix-la-Chapelle, August 21. — I am often tempted to inform Napoleon, who asks so many questions about the usages of the old court, that grace and urbanity prevailed there; that in it women dared to converse with princes. Here, we are precisely like little girls who are going to be examined in catechism. Napoleon is very much offended if any one ventures to address a remark to him.[1] Half lying down on a sofa, he alone supplies the conversation; for nobody replies to him except by a *yes* or a *no, sire*, pronounced very timidly. He usually talks about the arts, such as music and painting; he frequently takes love for the subject of conversation, and God knows how he talks about it.[2] It does not belong to a woman to judge a general; hence, I shall not pre-

---

[1] It was no more customary in the old court than in the new one for any one to address a remark to the sovereign without being interrogated. — *Note by the editor.*

[2] The letters written from Italy by General Bonaparte to his wife, and published for the first time in the *Memoirs of a Contemporary*, the admirable novel entitled *Giulio*, in the *Memoirs of M. de Bourrienne*, make it plain enough whether the Emperor did or did not know how to talk of love. — *Note by the editor.*

sume to speak of his military feats; but the spirit of the salon [1] is our province, and concerning that it is permissible to say that he has none at all.

August 22, 1804. — It must be that this need of adulating power is very general, since not even priests are exempt from it. This morning we were shown what are called the grand relics: they were sent as a present to Charlemagne by the Empress Irene, and have been preserved since that time in an iron press contrived in a wall. This press is opened every seven years, to show the relics to the people, a circumstance which attracts a very considerable multitude from all the surrounding region. Each time that the relics are replaced in the press, the door is walled up, and not opened again for seven years. Josephine had a wish to see them, and although the seven years had not elapsed, the wall was demolished. Among these relics, a little silver-gilt casket attracted particular attention. The priests who showed us this treasure piqued our curiosity by saying that the most ancient tradition attached a great happiness to the possibility of opening this coffer, but that so far nobody had been able to do it. Josephine, whose curiosity was keenly excited, took it in her fingers and it opened almost at once. There were no ex-

---

[1] Whoever has been near the Emperor and been able to hear his conversations, sparkling with wit and originality, with the most eminent men of his court, particularly with M. de Fontanes, will be justly surprised at reading in Madame ———'s Diary that Napoleon had no wit. — *Note by the editor.*

ternal traces of a lock, but there must have been some secret for opening the interior spring. I am persuaded that the priests who showed us the relics knew the secret, and that they contrived this little pleasure for the Empress. However it may be, this circumstance has been regarded as *very extraordinary;* they have laid great stress on it to Josephine, who, although sufficiently amused by this surprise, does not attach more importance to it than it deserves. For the rest, curiosity has not been very well satisfied; for nothing was found in the box but a few little scraps of stuff which may be regarded as relics if one chooses, but the authenticity of which is not certified.

I have come back home saddened by this employment of my morning. I do not like to encounter courtiers or ambitious men among the clergy; I cannot even understand how there can be any. I find something so noble, so elevated in their prerogatives, that my imagination likes to disengage them from all our weaknesses. Detached from all the passions which disturb and rule humanity, placed as intermediaries between man and the Divinity, they are entrusted with the sweet employment of consoling the unfortunate, and of showing them, athwart the storms of life, a harbor where at last they will find repose. Can the world offer a dignity equal to this privilege which is reserved to them, of penetrating into the asylum of misfortune; of soothing there the anguish of the dying and again surrounding him with hope; of taking from death that which is most appalling in it, — the dread of nothingness? No, a priest cannot barter these beautiful prerogatives for money, or for what the world calls honors.

August 23, 1804.— On opening my journal, my eyes fastened on the page I wrote yesterday; I could not help smiling as I compared what I said of the simplicity, the sanctity, the dignity of the priesthood, with the conversation I heard this evening between M. de Pradt, the Emperor's first chaplain, and a general. They both wore the same decoration, — the cross of honor. I wondered how the man of God, the minister of peace, had merited the same recompense as the warrior charged with sending death to the enemies of his country. Their sovereigns ought to recall the lesson taught by Alexander on the distinction between recompenses: a man very adroitly darted some grains of millet through a needle in his presence; he ordered that a bushel of millet should be given him, wishing to proportion the recompense to the utility of the talent. This art of rewarding with discernment is not very common at present. We see Talma better paid than a general. He has more than sixty thousand francs, both from the theatre and from Bonaparte. I leave the comedian and return to M. de Pradt. While listening to his brilliant, philosophic conversation this evening, I was reminded of the piquant question once addressed to him by a very witty man who found himself in his company at a dinner of twenty-five persons, and who asked him: "Monseigneur, do you believe in God?"

August 24. — The Emperor plays whist nearly every evening with Josephine and Madame de La Rochefoucauld; the fourth person is chosen from persons who come to the drawing-room. This evening the Duc d'Aremberg was to be the fourth; the Emperor found it rather stimulating to play with a blind man. I was about to sit down at the tiresome loto table, when the first chamberlain came to tell me that Napoleon had designated me for his whist. I replied that I had but one difficulty, which was that I had never learned the game. M. de Rémusat went to carry my response, to which the Emperor, who does not know what an impossibility is, said: "*It is all the same.*" This was an order; I complied with it. Madame de La Rochefoucauld, whose place I occupied, gave me some advice; and besides, excepting the Duc d'Aremberg, who has the memory of a blind man, and who never forgets a single card named to him, I played pretty nearly as well as the Empress and the Emperor. The game was not long. The Duc d'Aremberg usually has a man beside him who arranges his cards; his play is designated to him by means of a little board adapted to the table; by passing his hand over this board, he knows his cards by the pegs in relief which are placed by the man whom he calls his marker. He plays very well and even with astonishing quickness, if one thinks of all the labor required to make him know his cards.

But, not daring to have himself accompanied to the palace by his marker, who is a sort of valet de chambre, the man's place was taken by the Duchesse d'Aremberg, and his play was very much retarded; hence the Emperor, who likes to play quickly, and whose curiosity was satisfied, left the table after the first rubber.

August 25. — Corneille was right when he said:

He who can do what he wills, wills more than he ought.

This line contains a moral axiom of great verity. M. de Sémonville is a victim offered to-day by politics in holocaust to the Dutch. This action is revoltingly unjust; M. de Talleyrand had required of M. de Sémonville some measure which displeased the Hollanders. Bonaparte, who wants to keep on good terms with them, would not avow that his ambassador had only acted in accordance with the orders of M. de Talleyrand, because he would then have to sacrifice him, and (although he detests him), as he thinks him more useful than M. de Sémonville, he sacrifices the latter. Perhaps they think they can excuse this action by telling us that the ideas of justice, considered in connection with a private person, are not applicable to sovereigns; I think, on the contrary, that as their actions belong to posterity, which will judge them apart from the prestige which dazzles us, they ought always to take morality and justice for their guides.

Yesterday, at the reception of ambassadors, when

Bonaparte was near M. de Sémonville, he turned his back, being unwilling to speak to him; and when the latter asked the single favor of being allowed to explain himself in an audience, it was refused him. They knew all he would say; he was justified in advance; but that is precisely why he was not received. They could not say to him: "You were right; M. de Talleyrand was wrong, and yet it is you who will pay for him;" as this is what the Emperor had decided on in his superior wisdom, he will neither see nor listen to him. Is it true, then, that the abuse of power is always linked with power, as the effect is to the cause?

Aix-la-Chapelle, August 26. — I saw M. de Sémonville this morning: he told me that M. de Talleyrand, in talking with him yesterday, tried very adroitly to persuade him that he ought to give orders at the Hague to have all his papers burned. "Take care," he said to him, "the Emperor is a petty Nero.[1] He will perhaps send[2] to seize your papers, and that may be very disagreeable. Madame de Spare, your stepdaughter, is at the Hague; write and tell her to burn everything promptly; it is more essen-

---

[1] These words were heard by the Duc de Bassano, who was leaning on the chimneypiece near which MM. de Talleyrand and Sémonville were talking. There is no doubt that they were repeated by him to Napoleon. — *Note by Madame* ——.

[2] M. de Talleyrand was too shrewd a courtier to use such language before such witnesses; but if he had in fact done so M. the Duc de Bassano was incapable of repeating them to the Emperor. — *Note by the editor.*

tial than you may think." This counsel, given in a friendly and interested tone, might have been followed by a dolt; but M. de Talleyrand was dealing with a man as shrewd as himself. M. de Sémonville perfectly recognized his object, which was to destroy all the documents that would justify him. Instead of writing to Madame de Spare to burn his papers, he had just despatched one of his stepsons, M. de Montholon, in search of them. He will wait until he is supplied with all his proofs; but I doubt much that they will produce any other effect than that of making Bonaparte very cross if he ever consents to look at them, which I do not believe he will.[1]

This evening I was placed beside Madame Lannes[2] in the salon.

This was the first time that I had seen her; she has arrived from Portugal with her husband, who was ambassador there. I found her charming. The Emperor, in going around the drawing-room, said to her in that extraordinary tone he uses with all women: "*They say you lived on fine terms with the Prince-regent of Portugal.*" Madame Lannes replied

---

[1] M. de Sémonville lost his embassy, and was honorably *annulled* by the Senate. In recalling these facts, which are exact, one must be astonished that M. de Montholon, one of the two stepsons of M. de Sémonville, should in the sequel have attached himself to the destiny of Napoleon. When the explanation of this strange conduct is sought for, it may be found in M. de Montholon's marriage, which was not approved by his family, and set them at variance.

[2] Afterwards the Duchess de Montebello.

very suitably that the Prince had always treated her husband and herself with much kindness. She returned to my side, saying to me: "I do not know what fatality always places me under the Emperor's eyes when he is in a bad humor; because I do not think he means to say disagreeable things to me; and yet that often happens." The poor woman almost had tears in her eyes. This unbefitting sarcasm was all the more out of place because her conduct is generally eulogized; but, this evening, Napoleon was unchained against all women; he told us we "had no patriotism, no national spirit; that we ought to blush to wear muslins; that English-women set us an example by wearing nothing but stuffs of their own country; that this craze for English muslins is all the more extraordinary since we have in France linen-cambrics which could replace them and would make much prettier dresses; that for his part he should always love that stuff preferably to any other, because, in his youth, his first sweetheart had a frock of it." At that expression, first sweetheart, I could hardly avoid laughing, all the more because my eyes met those of Madame de La Rochefoucauld, who was dying with desire to do the same. It is extraordinary that Bonaparte should have such common manners.[1] When he wishes to be

---

[1] Again the manners of the Emperor! But that day he was *unchained against women*, which explains Madame ——'s ill-temper with him. We need not say that there is more than exaggeration in describing as *insolence* the brusquerie with which the

dignified, he is insolent and disdainful; and if he has a moment of gaiety, he becomes the most vulgar of men. His brother-in-law Murat, born in a class far beneath his own, and who received no manner of education, has formed himself in the school of society in an astonishing manner. I was at Dijon several years ago, at the time when he went to review an army corps which had been assembled there. I dined with him at the house of General Canclaux, who was in command at Dijon; and then he had altogether the appearance of a soldier in an officer's uniform. I saw him again recently, and I was astonished to find his manners very polished, and even rather agreeable. But Napoleon is too proud ever to acquire anything in point of manners; he has too much respect for himself ever to think of self-examination, and too much contempt for the human species to think for a single moment that any one can be better than he.

Emperor might sometimes be reproached, in common with Frederick II. and other great men, and to see nothing but *the most vulgar gaiety* in his moments of affability. — *Note by the editor.*

CHAPTER XX

THE DIARY CONTINUED.

The Duke and Duchess of Bavaria — Their children — Prince Pius — The little body and the big ribbons — Princess Elisabeth — The Emperor offended by hearing her talk at table — Departure from Aix-la-Chapelle and arrival at Cologne — The steeples, the churches, and the convents — Work and sleep of the Emperor — His use of coffee — The Emperor at the toilet of the Empress — The jewel-case disarranged by the Emperor — Mysteries of the toilet — The Emperor much occupied with the toilet of the ladies of his court — Five toilets a day — The Emperor's antipathy for sensible women — Women considered by him as part of his furniture — The Emperor and the Queen of Prussia — Departure from Cologne and sojourn at Bonn — The house and gardens of M. de Belderbuch — Nocturnal meditation on the bank of the Rhine — Hymns of the German pilgrims — M. de Chaban, prefect of Coblentz — Voyage on the Rhine — Picturesque sites — Storm and tempest on the Rhine — Arrival at Bingen — Delay — Double entrance at Mayence — Discontent attributed to Napoleon — Stormy tête-à-tête — Tears of the Empress — Presentation of the Princess of Baden — Family quarrel on the subject of Prince Eugène — Firmness of the Empress — The Emperor a slave to etiquette — M. de Caulaincourt and the Princess of Baden — Outburst of the Emperor against Kant — The Princess and the Hereditary Prince of Hesse-Darmstadt and his wife the Princess Wilhelmine of Baden — Josephine's curiosity — Portrait of the Princess Wilhelmine — Josephine's little triumph — The yacht of the Prince of Nassau-Weilbourg — Breakfast on a Rhine island — Ravages of war — The Emperor grants the petition of a poor woman — Beneficent action of Josephine — Definition of happiness given by the Emperor — Excursion of the author and

Madame de La Rochefoucauld to Frankfort—The grand Mayence ball — Unreasonableness of the Emperor — Josephine obliged to go to the ball although ill — The princesses of Nassau — The author's humiliation on seeing the Emperor ignore court usages — Breakfast with the Prince of Nassau — Severity of the Emperor toward Madame Lorges — German taste and French taste — Departure from Mayence — Monotony of harangues.

AIX-LA-CHAPELLE, August 28. — The Duke and Duchess Leopold of Bavaria, Prince Pius, their son, and Princess Elisabeth, their daughter,[1] have arrived here to pay their court; they have just taken possession of Dusseldorf, which fell to them by way of indemnity. The Duchess must have been a very beautiful woman; she has a fine figure and a very noble air. Prince Pius, her son, is just at that most disadvantageous age, between childhood and youth. The Emperor has laughed a good deal at his little legs, which have all they can do to support his small body, overladen with orders and grand cordons. They make a droll little caricature of him. The Princess Elisabeth is not pretty, but I think that if she were better dressed she would be well-shaped. She is very polite and very talkative, a thing which scandalizes Napoleon. At dinner she was placed between him and Eugène de Beauharnais: accustomed to her father's little court, and to that of the Elector of Bavaria, she is simple enough not to be at all intimidated in speaking to Bonaparte. He finds it most extraordinary that she does

---

[1] Since Princess of Neufchatel and Wagram.

not wait until she is asked a question, as all the persons do by whom he is surrounded. Hence, I remarked at table that he paid very little attention to her, as if he wished to punish her for not being afraid of him; but Eugène, whose manners are so good, and who sat on the other side of the Princess, was what he always is, perfectly polite.

Cologne, August 31. — We have left Aix-la-Chapelle, and the day before yesterday we arrived at Cologne, a city which has a very gloomy appearance. As we were entering some one called my attention to its three hundred and sixty-five steeples, which shows what an enormous number of convents and churches were here before the French took possession. I hope we shall stay here only a few days. One thing that I had already remarked at Aix-la-Chapelle, but more particularly here, is the errors every one entertains on the subject of Napoleon. It is a common notion that he seldom sleeps, and that he works incessantly; but I see that if he rises early to put the regiments through their manœuvres, he takes good care to go to bed much earlier in the evening. Yesterday, for example, he was on horseback by five o'clock in the morning; in the evening he retired to his apartment before nine; and Josephine told us that it was to go to bed. They pretend also that he makes an immoderate use of coffee, to shake off sleep; he takes a cup after his breakfast, and as much at dinner. But this is the way with the public: if a man, placed in fortunate circumstances, performs great things, we lay it all to the account of his genius. We are unwilling to owe anything to the power of chance: that admission is repugnant to human self-love. Our imagination creates a phantom, and surrounds it with a brilliant aureole;[1] but if we are permitted to see it at closer quarters, all this prestige with which we adorned it when at a distance disappears; once more we find the man with all his weaknesses, all his littleness, and we wax indignant at the worship we have rendered him.

Cologne, September 1. — This morning I was chatting with Josephine while her hair was being dressed. The Emperor came in, and upset the whole jewel-case to make her try on different ornaments. It was good to see Madame Saint-Hilaire, the first femme de chambre, who has charge of the jewels, at the instant when Bonaparte was disarranging them. She was formerly femme de chambre to Madame Adelaide, and would like to establish the same etiquette in the department of the toilet to which she was accustomed in the old court; but that is not easy. A sufficiently large number of femmes de chambre have been appointed, who were each to be on duty three months at a time. Josephine, who is arriving at that age when one has need of all the art and all the mysteries of the toilet, was

---

[1] I do not see why the Emperor should lose his *brilliant aureole* for sometimes going to bed early and using coffee with moderation. — *Note by Constant.*

much annoyed at having all these spectators; she begged to retain only her former women; and, with the exception of Madame Saint-Hilaire, all those who had been appointed were converted into *dames d'annonce*. Their only function is to announce the Emperor when he comes to see the Empress; consequently they are in the interior of the apartments.

This mania for meddling with the toilet of women is very extraordinary in a man entrusted (I mean to say all but) with the destinies of the world. It is so well known that Herbaut, Josephine's valet de chambre, remarked to me the first time that he dressed my hair, that I placed my diadem at one side, and that the Emperor wished to have them all worn absolutely straight. I laughed at his observation, and assured him that I dressed to please myself, and consulted no taste but my own. He was very much astonished, and assured me that all these ladies were careful to conform to that of Napoleon. He occupies himself with these details to such a degree that on one day of great ceremony, Josephine having put on a dress of pink and silver which he did not like, he threw his inkstand at her with violence, to force her to change it. Here we do nothing else: at ten in the morning we dress for breakfast; at noon we make another toilet to go to the presentations; often these are renewed at different hours, and the dress must always be adapted to the sort of persons who are presented: so that it sometimes happens that we change our toilet three times in the course of the morning, making a fourth for dinner, and a fifth for a ball. This continual occupation is a perfect torment to me.

Cologne, September 2. — The Emperor has a very pronounced antipathy for what are called sensible women; he limits our destination to ornamenting a salon. So much so that I think he finds no great difference between a fine vase of flowers and a pretty woman. When he busies himself about their toilet, it is on account of the luxury he wishes to establish in all his furniture; he finds fault with or approves a dress just as he would do with the covering of an armchair; a woman at his court is only one more piece of stage furniture in his salon. Josephine says banteringly that there are at least five or six days in the year on which women might have some influence over him, but that, these few days excepted, they count for nothing (or almost nothing) with him. This evening the conversation turned upon the Queen of Prussia; he cannot endure her, and he does not conceal it. Sovereigns are exactly like lovers; if they quarrel, they say horrible things about each other. They ought to remember when they are at war that they will end by making peace, and that in this case, although they restore the fortresses they have taken, they cannot efface the insulting things they have said. I believe that this method, so fashionable at present, of filling the journals with reciprocal invectives, arises in great part from the character of Napoleon and the newness of his dynasty; for, in reading history, I discover that there was formerly a tone of moderation between princes making war with each other which no longer exists at present.

Bonn, September 5. — We left Cologne this morning. For a long time I have not passed so agreeable an evening as to-day. The Empress has been entertained by M. de Belderbuch, who has a charming house. The garden, which was illuminated, extends to the bank of the Rhine, which is very wide at this place. Musicians had been placed in a boat on the stream. While they were setting off fireworks after supper, I slipped away alone to the bottom of the garden, as far as the shore. I needed to escape for a few moments from the constraint that weighs on me so heavily. The air was pure and calm; little by little people quitted the garden. Nothing was to be heard but sweet harmonious music; but presently even that ceased; the most profound silence was interrupted only by the sound of the waves breaking on the stones near which I was leaning. The moon, which was reflected in the stream, came to replace the lanterns which were going out in the garden, and to spread the harmony of its gentle radiance over the beautiful scene before my eyes. Absorbed in profound reflection, I did not perceive that the hours were gliding by, until some religious hymns which became audible in the extreme distance awakened my attention. I cannot well describe their effect upon me in that instant; they might have been taken for a concert of celestial spirits, these hymns which the winds were bringing me from the other bank of the Rhine. But the pleasure I found in listening to these sounds, aerial as it were, was interrupted. Some persons who, disturbed by my long absence, were looking for me in the garden, came up just at that moment; they told me that at this time of the year it is very common in Germany for the people of several villages to assemble for the purpose of visiting different saints venerated in the region, and that these pilgrims frequently march during the night to avoid the heat, sometimes singing hymns with that harmony almost natural to Germans. Thus were explained the religious hymns I had just listened to.

Coblentz, September 8. — Here we are lodged at the prefecture. The simplicity, I might almost say the poverty of the furniture, does great honor to the prefect, M. de Chaban. The Emperor expressed surprise at this destitution; the prefect replied: "This region is so poor, and there are so many unfortunates, that I should be ashamed to ask the city for an increase for the sake of luxuries. I have everything that is necessary." These *necessaries* are several old armchairs, an old bed, and some tables. This simplicity is admirable. He occupies himself with nothing but the care of the poor. One delights in meeting such a being, who unites much intelligence to so many virtues. The Emperor, who is always surrounded by artistic luxury, was inclined to be displeased on arriving at being lodged in this fashion; his dry and arid soul cannot appreciate all M. de Chaban's worth;[1] but yet he knows how well his paternal administration is adapted to make the French liked in this country.

Coblentz, September 9. — I think I shall have to accuse myself of a little duplicity to-day; because one can have no compromise with conscience; it is not deceived by expressions. The Emperor promised Josephine this morning that, if he did not restore to my husband the unsold property of which I desire the restitution, he would at any rate make it up to him by an appointment. After dinner, when the time came for coffee, the Empress was urging me to thank Napoleon. When he drew near us, asking what we were doing, "She is telling me," replied Josephine, "that she dares not thank you for what you promised me this morning for her." "Why not?" said the Emperor. "Do I frighten you?" "But, Sire," I returned, "it is not extraordinary that the idea of what Your Majesty has done should attach to your person, and consequently make it imposing." I was telling the truth: it is the death of the Duc d'Enghien, and that of so many other victims, which, for me, attaches to his person, and

---

[1] The Emperor was economical and incessantly preached economy. — *Note by Constant.*

always shows him to me stained with their blood. And yet (see the perversity!), I was not sorry that he was deceived by my response, which he understood as a compliment which made him smile. Ah! I fear that example is beginning to corrupt me. It is high time for me to go back and cultivate my fields!

Coblentz, September 10. — It seems that Napoleon had last night a violent attack of the nervous malady or epilepsy to which he is subject. He had been very much indisposed for a long time before Josephine, who occupied the same room, dared to summon assistance; but finally, his suffering being prolonged, she determined to have a light. Roustan, who always lies outside the Emperor's door, was sleeping so profoundly that she could not waken him. The apartment of the prefect is so far removed from luxury that it does not even contain matters of mere convenience. There was no bell; the valets de chambre were far away, and Josephine, only half-dressed, was obliged to set ajar the door of the aide-de-camp on duty in order to get a light. General Rapp, somewhat astonished by this nocturnal visit, gave her one; and, after several hours of anguish, the attack was assuaged. Napoleon had forbidden Josephine to say a single word about his indisposition. Hence she imposed secrecy on all to whom she recounted it this morning. But how can one expect that others will keep a secret that we cannot keep ourselves? And have we a right to impose on others a discretion in which we are lacking? The Emperor was pale enough this evening, depressed enough; but nobody ventured to ask him how he was. They knew they would incur disgrace by seeming to think that His Majesty could be subject to any human infirmity.[1]

Coblentz, September 11. — I stayed for a moment in the salon of the aides-de-camp: Generals Cafarelli, Rapp, and Lauriston were there; they were talking of the extreme favor which M. de Caulaincourt enjoys. " We don't envy it," said these gentlemen ; " we would not have bought it at the same price." This sentiment is doubtless common to many people ; but, in the position of these gentlemen, I thought there was some merit in expressing it so frankly.[2]

---

[1] The Emperor was never subject to attacks of epilepsy. That is another of the stories they have retailed about him. It will be seen, in the portrait I have drawn of the Emperor, what might have given rise to it. — *Note by Constant.*

[2] It is a matter of public notoriety at present that the Duc de Vicenza, so unworthily calumniated during so many years by enemies who skilfully profited by the silence imposed on him by his position near the Emperor, neither took nor could take any part in the catastrophe of the Duc d'Enghien. It is proved that at the moment when General Ordener, who *alone* was commissioned to arrest the unhappy Prince, acquitted himself of this fatal mission, M. de Caulaincourt was thirty leagues from Ettenheim, charged, for his own part, to arrest the Baroness de Reich and several *émigrés* who were keeping up a correspondence against the head of the French government, and that M. de Caulaincourt became less rigorous before repassing the frontier with them. It is proved that M. de Caulaincourt had no knowledge of the mission confided to General Ordener until everybody else knew it, and after this mission was accomplished ; finally, it is proved that M. de Caulain-

Coblentz, September 12. — The Prince of Nassau-Weilbourg has come here to pay his court. He has proposed to Josephine to send her two yachts in which to ascend the Rhine as far as Mayence; which she has accepted. We start to-morrow, and the Emperor will follow the new road which has been opened on the banks of the Rhine.

Bingen, September 13. — Our voyage has been very agreeable all day, and that nothing might be lacking to it, we can even join to it the description of a tempest which was very nearly fatal to us, and which delayed our arrival here until midnight. The banks of the Rhine, from Coblentz to Bingen, are very picturesque; the greater part of the way they bristle with rocks and very lofty mountains, on which may be seen a large number of old castles. It is astonishing that places which seem so wild could have been inhabited by human creatures. Our attention was called to a tower which rises in the middle of the Rhine. The Palatine princesses were formerly obliged to come and inhabit this tower when about to become mothers. I do not know what could have been the motive of this custom, for the tower seems uninhabitable. It is called the Castle of the Mouse

---

court was at Lunéville the day and hour of the sanguinary execution of the Duc d'Enghien. M. de Bourrienne has already rectified in his Memoirs the error of which the Duc de Vicenza has too long been the victim. We likewise make it a duty to protest here against every passage in the journal of Madame ——, which could be construed injuriously against the memory of one of the most honorable men of the Empire. — *Note by the editor.*

(*le château de la Souris*) and, in fact, I think no other species of animal would make it their abode. As we were passing Rhinsels and Bacareuch, some of the inhabitants came in boats, accompanied by bands, to offer us fruits. On reaching Bingen, the Rhine contracts very greatly between the mountains, and rolls its floods with fearful rapidity, which they tell me is not always free from danger. The sky, which had been very clear and serene all day, became overcast by clouds at evening, and we were surprised by a frightful storm said some, a very fine one, according to others; for, in this world, nearly everything is called by a new name, depending on the impression of him who speaks of it. I shall say, then, that a very fine storm came to light up our navigation. Josephine and some other ladies, who were somewhat frightened, shut themselves up in the little cabin of the yacht, but I wanted to enjoy a spectacle which was new to me. The lightning flashes, which rapidly succeeded each other, allowed us to see the other yacht, containing the women and the suite of the Empress, which was following us. Its large white sails, shaken by a violent wind, stood out against the dark clouds which obscured the sky. The noise of the waves and of the thunder which made itself gently heard in the high mountains between which the Rhine is straitened at this spot, added a certain solemnity to the scene. Gradually the storm lulled and we arrived at Bingen at midnight.

Mayence, September 14. — The banks of the Rhine, from Bingen to Mayence, are much less picturesque than those we saw yesterday. The country is more open. We arrived at three o'clock. We were expected at eleven; but Josephine, fatigued the previous evening by the storm which had delayed her arrival at Bingen, was not well, and could not leave as soon as had been expected. Moreover, the relays of horses which had been placed on the banks of the Rhine to work up the yachts, having been badly managed, we could not arrive sooner.

This circumstance, which seemed indifferent enough, was not so to Bonaparte. As luck would have it, the courier who announced him arrived precisely at the instant when the Empress's two yachts were sighted. The entire population of Mayence had been on the wharf since eleven o'clock. Young girls dressed in white, and carrying baskets of flowers, were stationed on both sides of a little bridge which had been prepared for the disembarkation. General Lorges, commanding the division, the mayor, and the prefect were there to receive Josephine, when the courier who preceded the Emperor announced his arrival. General Lorges, followed merely by an aide-de-camp, went on horseback to receive him. On entering Mayence, Napoleon was disagreeably surprised to find all the houses closed, not a single person on his passage, not a solitary cry of *Long live the Emperor!* He seemed to be entering a tomb. It was simple enough that all the people who had gone to the wharf at eleven o'clock, should not have left it the very moment the yachts were perceived. The arrival of the Empress, who was to listen to a speech, presented a more agreeable sight than the carriage in which Napoleon was shut up. It is not astonishing, then, that they should have remained on the bank of the Rhine. It seems that the Emperor was keenly wounded by this preference. Josephine's carriages arrived in the court of the palace at the same time with his own. Napoleon, in passing in front of us, made a slight inclination of the head with an ill-humored air; but as that often happens, we paid little attention to it, and went to our respective apartments. This evening, the Emperor and Empress dining alone, we were waiting in Madame de La Rochefoucauld's apartment for the signal usually given at seven o'clock for us to go down into the salon; but seven, eight, nine o'clock struck, and no one came for us. We were joking about the long tête-à-tête of Their Majesties, when the summons came. On entering the salon, we were surprised to find no one there. In a short time, Bonaparte issued from Josephine's chamber; he crossed the salon, greeting us again with his little ill-humored nod, and retired to his apartment, which he did not leave again that evening.

The Empress remaining in her room, Madame de La Rochefoucauld entered it and found her weeping bitterly. Napoleon had made a frightful scene which had lasted until now. It was her fault that the horses had had difficulty in working up the Rhine; it was her fault that they started so late from Bingen; in his unjust anger I do not know but what he laid to her charge the storm which had incommoded him. According to him, she had arranged and prepared everything so as to arrive at the same hour as he did. He accused her of liking to manœuvre for suffrages; in a word, he had given her the most violent, the most unreasonable, the most unmerited scene that can be imagined. Ah! that old adage which says that there are no heroes for valets de chambre, is truer than people think. We do not see him so close by as his valet does, and yet what littleness we daily discover in him![1]

Mayence, September 16. — This morning the presentations of the princes of Baden and that of the elector archchancellor[2] were to take place. After the presentation, these princes were to ask permission of the Empress to name to her some of the officers of their household, and a nephew of the archchancellor.

While receiving Napoleon's instructions on the etiquette of this presentation, Josephine asked what was to be done about her son; because it was suitable that he should be presented to the princes.

---

[1] I was the Emperor's valet de chambre for fifteen years, and I am not of the opinion of the author of the journal. — *Note by Constant.*

[2] Since Grand Duke of Frankfort.

Bonaparte, who had not thought of this, and who is always vexed when he is taken unawares on any subject whatever, responded crossly that her son would not be presented; that he saw no necessity for it. Very kind, very easy, very feeble even in nearly all circumstances, Josephine is extremely courageous and firm in all that concerns her children. She represented to the Emperor that for both herself and him it would be incongruous that the son of the Empress should be made of no account; that she had never asked anything for herself; and she had the courage to add that she had not cried to be a princess;[1] but that as her son was to dine with her in company with the princes, he ought to be presented to them; also that under the old régime, if M. de Beauharnais (although not presented at the court of France) had travelled in Germany, he would have been admitted everywhere. These last words inflamed Napoleon's anger to an excessive degree. He said to her that she was always citing *her impertinent old régime* (that is the expression he used); and that, after all, her son could not dine with her that evening.[2]

---

[1] This was in allusion to the sisters of Bonaparte, who had not been thought of when the Empire was first created, and who came the next day to torment their brother for the titles they desired, thus occasioning many pleasantries on the subject.

[2] This ridiculous scene shows to what an extent Bonaparte was the slave of etiquette and miserable trivialities, since on such an occasion he could allow himself to be so far carried away by anger as to say things to Josephine that were very hard on both herself

He went out after these words, leaving Josephine very little inclined to appear in the salon for the presentation. During the half hour she spent there, while awaiting the princes, she was constantly wiping her eyes, which were still swollen with tears when they appeared. While she was having this scene with the Emperor, M. de Talleyrand, who was entitled by his position to designate the great officers of the crown who were to go and meet the princes at the door of their carriages, and who never neglects a chance to vex Josephine, said to her son that he was appointed to receive the princes. Eugène, who has a perfect sense of decorum, and who thought it ridiculous that the son of the Empress should be mixed up with the cortège of the princes who were to be presented to her, replied with that dignified simplicity which characterizes him, that he would be there if it were demonstrated to him that he ought to be. He came to tell his mother of this little specimen of M. de Talleyrand's malevolence, and it was agreed between them that he should not accompany the princes, but should enter the salon a little before six o'clock, when Josephine would be there to present him. It all went off very well; Bonaparte did not enter the salon until after six, just as they were about sitting

---

and her son. Yet he loved Prince Eugène as much as he was capable of loving, and shortly after he gave a proof of it, as every one knows.

down to table; he did not inquire whether the presentation had taken place; his anger had cooled down.

When there are princes to dinner, the lady of honor must be there with one or two ladies of the palace. I was designated for to-day. The princes of Nassau-Weilbourg, d'Issembourg, and Nassau-Usingen came to the drawing-room this evening, which was very brilliant.

Mayence, September 17. — Madame de La Rochefoucauld and I remarked a very extraordinary thing this evening, namely, the eager cordiality of M. de Caulaincourt toward the princes of Baden.[1] He thought it incumbent on him to do them the honors of the salon. When I knew that these princes were to be here, I was very curious to observe their first interview with him. I supposed that, not having seen them since he abducted the Duc d'Enghien from their dominions, and this abduction having had such fatal consequences, he would, by keeping himself at a distance, and not recalling by the sight of him the bitter affront he had offered them, silently prove by his countenance that when he executed this order he was far from foreseeing its horrible results. But I was very much deceived; he went up to them with a gaiety which seemed very natural. As soon as the princes arrived, he was at their side; he took absolute possession of them; it seemed as if the

---

[1] See above the editor's note on the Duc de Vicenza.

acquaintance he had made with them in so dismal a manner ought to entitle him to their good will. This conduct confounds me. One must be devoid of tact, of the slightest sentiment of what is befitting, in order to act thus. The father, who is already old, timid, as people are at that age, always trembling lest he should see the almighty hand of the Emperor erase him from the list of sovereigns, displayed almost no external sign on beholding M. de Caulaincourt; the countenance of his grandson,[1] the hereditary prince, who has as yet no character, and, I believe, very little intelligence, was no better an indication of what was going on within; but with regard to Prince Louis,[2] I noticed that whenever M. de Caulaincourt approached them, he drew back behind his father and his nephew, and that as far as possible he avoided speaking with him; but this reserve detracted nothing from M. de Caulaincourt's ease. When I say ease, I mean relatively; for no one has less than he. He might be mistaken for a Prussian rather than a French officer; even his phrases have a German turn; for in speaking to the Emperor or the Empress, he never fails to say *yes*, or *no*, *Your Majesty*. It is extraordinary that M. de Caulain-

---

[1] Afterwards Grand Duke of Baden.

[2] We have demonstrated above that the princes of Baden had nothing to testify *exteriorly* to M. de Caulaincourt, and that the latter's *ease* could astonish nobody but a person already prejudiced against him by too much confidence in an imputation materially false. — *Note by the editor.*

court, whose parents were at court, should not know its usages better.[1]

September 18. — I think the Emperor greatly resembles the man who, bored by the arguments which a wise person adduced in proof of his opinion, exclaimed: "*Hey! sir, I don't want people to prove things to me.*" He was greatly tempted to say as much this evening. The prince archchancellor, who is specially gifted with that analytical spirit which decomposes an idea to its utmost principle, discussed with him a metaphysical question of Kant; but the Emperor settled the question by saying that Kant was obscure, and that he did not like him; then he rudely left the prince, who came and sat down near me. For an observer, there was a very amusing combat going on between the determination of the prince courtier to admire everything in the Emperor and the little dissatisfaction at having been cut short in the midst of his discussion on his dear philosopher; for he is a great partisan of Kant. He remarked to me, as a general thesis, that people often disparage works of pure reasoning, solely on account of the trouble they must take to comprehend them; that people consider nothing well thought but what they can

---

[1] **Every one to his trade.** It was in camps that M. de Caulaincourt made his apprenticeship as a courtier, hence he might well have been less inured to it than were his parents, *who belonged to the old court*. For the rest, we have often heard quite different things said, and we have been able to judge for ourselves of the manners of the Duc de Vicenza. — *Note by the editor.*

understand without trouble, but that it is with a profound idea as it is with water, the depth of which destroys its limpidity; that nothing is easier, with the help of intermediary ideas, than to elevate minds (even the most mediocre) to the loftiest conceptions; that nothing is required for this but to perfect analysis and to decompose a question; and that, if the foundation of it is true, it can always be reduced to a single point. I profited by his little annoyance with the Emperor (an annoyance he would not have owned to for all the world), and found great pleasure in chatting with him.

Mayence, September 19. — The Princess of Hesse-Darmstadt, her son the hereditary prince, and the young Princess Wilhelmine of Baden, whom he has just married, will arrive to-morrow. Josephine cannot conceal her lively curiosity to see this young woman. M. de Talleyrand used to speak of her to the Emperor as the prettiest person in Europe, when he was lately urging him to be divorced. This evening I heard Josephine asking her brother, the hereditary prince, a multitude of questions about his sister. One can see that, although reassured about the divorce, she would be annoyed if the sight of her could occasion the Emperor any regrets.

September 20. — At last we have seen this much vaunted princess! and never was there such a general surprise. One cannot imagine how any charm could be discovered in her. She is of, I will not say a height, but a length beyond measure. There is not the least proportion in her figure, which is much too thin, and utterly wanting in grace. Her eyes are small, her face long and without expression. Her skin is very white, with little color. It is possible that, in some years, when she is formed, she may be a good enough looking woman, but at present she is not at all attractive. I was charmed that Josephine should have had this little triumph, which she has so well enjoyed. Never, perhaps, has she displayed such grace as she put into this reception. As a general thing, one is so benevolent, so gracious, when one is happy. One could see that she was delighted to find the Princess so little agreeable, and so different from what Napoleon had been told. The princess-mother must have been charming; she has the most sprightly and agreeable countenance. She has much vivacity and wit. She entirely governs her little dominions and her husband. Her son, the hereditary prince, is very tall and handsome; but I think that when one has said that, one has said all.

September 21. — The Prince of Nassau-Weilbourg having left his yacht here at Josephine's orders for all the time that she remains, we made use of it this morning to go and breakfast on an island of the Rhine, near Mayence, where the elector's country seat, the *Favorite*, used to be. No trace of it remains; it has been demolished. This island, as well as the environs of Mayence, offers a very sad picture of the results of war. Not a tree is to be seen. When we arrived, we found the breakfast ready. While we were at

table, the Emperor perceived a poor woman who, not
daring to advance, was looking from a distance at
this spectacle so new to her; he sent her word to
come near. When she was close to the table, he had
her asked in German (for she did not understand
French) if she had ever dreamed that she was rich,
and if so, what she had believed herself to possess.
The poor woman found it difficult to understand this
question, and still more so to answer it. At last,
she said that she thought a person who had five hundred florins would be the richest person in the world.
"Her dream is a little dear," said the Emperor, "but
no matter, it must be realized." At once these gentlemen took all the money they had with them, and
this sum was counted out to her. The astonishment
and joy of this woman was the most touching thing;
her hands let fall the gold pieces which they could
not contain; all eyes were moistened with tears of
emotion on beholding the surprise and happiness of
the poor creature. I was looking at the Emperor at
this moment; I thought he must be so happy! No,
his physiognomy expressed nothing, absolutely nothing . . . but a little ill-humor. "I have asked the
same thing twice before," said he, "but their dreams
were more moderate; this good woman is ambitious."
At that moment he had no other sensation than that
of regret that she had asked so much. How wretched
this man is! Of what use is his immense power to
him, if he cannot enjoy the happiness he might dif-
fuse? . . . After breakfast we scattered around the

island for a walk. The Empress, accompanied only by me and two other persons, met a young woman who was suckling her infant. Her situation was not fortunate. Josephine had nothing about her but five twenty-franc pieces; she gave these to the woman without display, without ostentation, and a tear of pity fell on the infant, which she had taken in her arms, and which was caressing her with its little hands, as if it felt the good she had just been doing to its mother, and wished to thank her. On our return to Mayence, the Emperor chatted a good deal, or rather, he talked, because he never chats. I shall never forget while I live the singular definition he gave us of happiness and unhappiness. "There is neither happiness nor unhappiness in the world," said he; "the only difference is that the life of a happy man is a picture with a silver background and some black stars, and the life of an unhappy man is a black background with some silver stars." If any one else comprehends this definition, I do not; and I have not the resource of applying the precept of the archchancellor, who claims that the most obscure metaphysical question (providing it rests upon a true idea) may always be understood by the aid of analysis. Here, I decompose, I analyze and I find . . . zero.

Mayence, September 22, 1804. — Yesterday, the two princesses of Hesse-Darmstadt, who were to leave Mayence to-day, were at dinner. In the evening they went to the theatre. These ladies had no shawls, and Josephine, fearing lest they should be cold, sent for two to lend them. This morning, on going away, the princess mother wrote a very witty, very amiable note to the Empress, to say that they would keep the shawls as a souvenir. The billet was very neatly worded, but I thought I saw that it did not console Josephine for the loss of her two shawls, which she thought the two most beautiful of all her white shawls. She would have liked it better if these women had chosen others.

Mayence, September 24. — Yesterday, on quitting the salon, Madame de La Rochefoucauld and I set off for Frankfort.[1]

We hoped that this rapid excursion might remain unknown to the Emperor. We spent the morning in visiting the city and buying some English goods which Josephine had asked us to fetch her; for she was in our confidence. We left Frankfort at three in the afternoon, with the intention of arriving in Mayence at six. Having been designated for dinner yesterday, I did not expect to be so again to-day, and I thought I should have all the time needed to rest myself, dress, and appear in the salon at eight o'clock. As to Madame de La Rochefoucauld, her health is so poor that she counted on excusing herself this evening on the ground of being indisposed. But all this

---

[1] At this epoch when the Rhine confederation was formed, Frankfort did not as yet form part of it, and Bonaparte was very ill-disposed toward this city, which was the general depot for English goods.

arrangement was brought to naught, at least so far as I was concerned. On arriving, I found a billet from the first chamberlain, which designated me for the dinner. It wanted ten minutes of six; at five minutes past six I was at table. I had tried to make up for the precipitation of my toilet by selecting a very beautiful dress. I was felicitating myself, while eating my soup, on having arrived soon enough not to betray the secret of our journey, when the Emperor, with a rather sarcastic smile, said to me that my dress was very fine, and asked whether I had brought it back from Frankfort. There was no way of denying our trip; it was necessary to laugh and make a joke of the affair, so that the Emperor should not be angry, and that is what I did. He asked if we had brought much English merchandise; but as nothing seems to have annoyed him to-day, he was only half displeased.

Mayence, September 25. — The city of Mayence gave a grand ball to the Empress to-day; but, being very much indisposed, it seemed impossible for her to attend it; she was in her bed at five o'clock, perspiring profusely with fever. Napoleon came into her room and told her she must get up and go to this ball. Josephine having explained to him that she was suffering, and the danger of throwing off her coverings, as she had an eruption on her skin, Bonaparte took her by the arm, pulled her out of bed, and forced her to dress. Madame de La Rochefoucauld, who witnessed this brutal action, told me of it with tears in her eyes; Josephine, with her touching sweetness and submission, dressed herself, and appeared at the ball for half an hour.

Mayence, September 26. — I suffered incredibly on hearing Napoleon call the princesses of Nassau, who were at the drawing-room, *mesdemoiselles*. However little attraction this court may have for me, it is none the less true that I form part of it at present; and, as a Frenchwoman, I feel humiliated that the sovereign in whose suite I find myself should be so little accustomed to the usages of courts. How can he be ignorant that princes, among themselves, give each other their respective titles, without thereby derogating from their authority? But Bonaparte would think he was compromising his own entirely if he did so. He never fails to say *Mr. Elector* to the prince archchancellor, and *mademoiselle* to all the princesses; I have seen more than one slightly ironical smile at it.

Mayence, September 27. — The Empress crossed the Rhine this morning, to pay a visit to the Prince and Princess of Nassau, at the château of Biberich, near Mayence. The troops of the Prince were under arms, all the officers of his little court in full dress. A very elegant breakfast was served in a hall from which the Rhine could be seen for a great distance, affording a magnificent view. It is a grand and superb habitation. On returning to Mayence, the troops of the Prince accompanied the Empress as far as the bank of the Rhine.

Mayence, September 28. — Napoleon said to-day, before forty persons, to Madame Lorges, whose husband commands the division: "Ah! Madame, what a horrible dress you have on! it is exactly like an old curtain. That's German taste, surely!" (Madame Lorges is German.) I do not know whether the dress is in German taste, but what I do know is that this compliment was not in French taste.

Mayence, September 29. — This evening, as I was chatting with two persons in a corner of the salon, I do not know how the conversation led me to mention that Emperor of China who asked Confucius how people talked about him and his government. "Nobody talks," the philosopher told him; "every one keeps silence." "That is what I want," replied the Emperor. Napoleon, who was not far from me, chatting with Prince d'Issembourg, turned round quickly. If I live a thousand years, I shall never forget the threatening glance he darted at me. I did not disturb myself about it; I continued my conversation, and added that this Emperor of China resembled a good many others, who are like the little owls, which scream when a light is brought to their nest. I do not know whether Napoleon seized the meaning of this last phrase, but he probably felt that he had made a mistake in seeming to make a personal application of this story about the Chinese Emperor; for his countenance resumed that immobility, that total lack of expression which he knows how to give himself at will.

Mayence, October 1, 1804. — We left Mayence yesterday, in order to return to Paris, where we shall be in a few days. The authorities of all the countries we pass through give themselves incredible pains to compose harangues; but, in truth, it is lost labor, for I notice that they are all alike. From that of the mayor of a petty German village to that of the president of the Senate, they might all be translated by that fable in which the fox says to the lion:

> "You honor them, my lord,
> Too much in crunching them."

CHAPTER XXI

Portrait of the Emperor — Fleury and Michelot in the rôle of Frederick the Great — Constant's Memoirs consulted by authors and artists — Bonaparte on returning from Egypt — His portrait by M. Horace Vernet — Bonaparte's forehead — His hair — Color and expression of his eyes — His mouth, lips, and teeth — Form of his nose — His entire figure — His extreme meagreness — Circumference and form of his head — Necessity of wadding and breaking-in his hats — Form of his ears — Excessive delicacy — The Emperor's figure — His neck — His shoulders — His chest — His leg and foot — His feet — Beauty of his hand and his coquetry about it — His habit of gnawing his nails a little — His stoutness came with the Empire — The Emperor's complexion — Singular *tic* — Remarkable peculiarity about the Emperor's heart — Length of his dinner — Wise precaution of Prince Eugène — The Emperor's breakfast — His manner of eating — Accommodating guests — The Emperor's favorite dishes — *Poulet à la Marengo* — Use of coffee — Vulgar error on this point — Conjugal attention of both empresses — Use of wine — Anecdote concerning Marshal Augereau — Josephine and Constant the Emperor's sick-nurses — The Emperor *a bad invalid* — Tenderness, cares, and courage of Josephine — The Emperor's maladies — Tenacity of a disease acquired at the siege of Toulon — *Colonel* Bonaparte and the rammer — The Emperor's wounds — The bayonet thrust and the ball of the Tyrolese rifleman — Repugnance for medicines — Precaution recommended by Doctor Corvisart — The Emperor's hour for rising — His familiarity with Constant — Conversations with Doctors Corvisart and Ivan — Tea on rising — The Emperor's bath — Reading the journals — First task with the secretary — Winter and summer dressing-gowns — Night and bathing caps — The ceremony of shaving — Ablution, frictions, toilet, etc. — Costume — Napoleon born to have valets de chambre — The toilet of etiquette not re-established — The

Emperor's hour for going to bed — His expeditious manner of undressing — How he called Constant — The warming-pan — The night lamp — The Empress Josephine his favorite reader — The perfume burners — Napoleon very sensitive to cold — His passion for the bath — Night work — Beverages of the Emperor during the night — Excessive economy of the Emperor in his family — Constant's New Year's gifts — Ear-pinching — Imperial caresses and familiarities — Prince de Neufchâtel.

NOTHING is to be contemned in what relates to great men. Posterity shows itself eager to know their manner of life in its most minute circumstances, their inclinations, their slightest habits. Whenever I happened to go to the theatre, either in my brief moments of leisure, or in the suite of His Majesty, I remarked how much the spectators liked to see some great historical person represented on the stage with his costume, his gestures, his attitudes, and even his infirmities and his defects, such as they have been transmitted in the descriptions of his contemporaries. I have myself always taken the greatest pleasure in seeing these living portraits of celebrated men. I remember very well that I never enjoyed the theatre so much as on the day when I saw played for the first time that charming piece, the *Two Pages*. Fleury, who took the part of Frederick the Great, rendered so perfectly the slow gait, the abrupt speech, the brusque movements, and even the shortsightedness of that monarch, that from the time when he came on the stage, the whole theatre resounded with applause. According to the opinion of people who were qualified to judge, it was the most perfect and most faithful imitation. For me, I could not say whether the resemblance was exact, but I felt that necessarily it must be. Michelot, whom I have since seen in the same part, has given me no less pleasure than his predecessor. No doubt these two clever actors must have drawn from good sources in order to know and reproduce in this way the manners of their model. I confess that I experience some pride in thinking that these Memoirs may impart to their readers something similar to the pleasure I have here essayed to describe; and that, in a doubtless remote future, yet one which cannot fail to arrive, the artist who shall seek to revivify and present before spectators the greatest man of the age, will be obliged, if he desires to be a faithful imitator, to rule himself in accordance with the portrait which I, better than any one else, can delineate from nature. I think, moreover, that no one has done it as yet, at least with so much detail.

On his return from Egypt, the Emperor was very meagre and very yellow, his complexion coppery, his eyes sunken, his shape perfect although rather slender then. I think the portrait made by M. Horace Vernet in his picture, *Une revue du premier consul sur la place du Carrousel*, is very like him. His forehead was very high and open; he had not much hair, especially on the temples, but it was very fine and soft. It was of a chestnut color, and his eyes were a beautiful blue, which depicted in an incredible manner the different emotions which agitated him, sometimes extremely soft and caressing, and again severe and hard. His mouth was very beautiful, the lips smooth and somewhat contracted, especially in ill-humor. His teeth, without being very regular, were very white and very good; he never complained of them. His nose, Grecian in form, was irreproachable, and his sense of smell exceedingly keen. In fine, the ensemble of his face was regularly handsome. Nevertheless, at this epoch his extreme meagreness prevented his beauty of feature from being discerned, and gave his whole physiognomy a somewhat disagreeable effect. It would have been necessary to go over his features one by one and then recombine them in order to comprehend the perfect regularity and beauty of all. His head was large, being twenty-two inches in circumference; it was a little longer than it was wide, and consequently a trifle flattened on the temples; it was extremely sensitive, so that I had to wad his hats, and I took care to wear them several days in my own room, so as to break them in. His ears were small, perfectly shaped, and well placed. The Emperor's feet were also extremely sensitive; I had his shoes worn by a wardrobe boy named Joseph, whose foot was just like that of the Emperor.

His figure was five feet two inches three lines in height; his neck was rather short, his shoulders thrown back, his chest large and very slightly hairy, and his thigh and leg well moulded; his foot was small, with regular toes, and completely exempt from corns and callosities. His arms were well made and well attached; his hands admirable, and his nails did not disfigure them; hence he was very careful of them, as indeed of his entire person, but without being finical. He often bit his nails, but lightly; this was a sign of impatience or preoccupation.

Later he put on a good deal of flesh, but without losing the beauty of his figure; on the contrary, he looked better under the Empire than under the Consulate; his skin became very white and his color animated.

In his moments, or rather in his long hours of work and meditation, the Emperor had a particular *tic* which seemed to be a nervous movement, and which he retained throughout his life; it consisted in a frequent and rapid elevation of the right shoulder, which persons who did not know this habit sometimes construed into a gesture of discontent and disapprobation, and began anxiously to wonder how and in what they could have displeased him. He never thought of it for his own part, and kept on repeating the same movement without being aware of it.

A very remarkable peculiarity is that the Emperor never felt his heart beat. He has often said so both to M. Corvisart and to me, and more than once he had us pass our hands over his breast, so that we could make trial of this singular exception; we never felt any pulsation.

The Emperor ate very fast; he scarcely remained

a dozen minutes at table. When he had finished dining, he rose and went into the family sitting-room; but the Empress Josephine remained, and signalled the guests to do likewise; sometimes, however, she followed His Majesty, and then the ladies of the palace doubtless indemnified themselves in their apartments, where they were served with whatever they desired.

One day when Prince Eugène rose from the table immediately after the Emperor, the latter turned and said: "But you have not had time to dine, Eugène?" "Pardon me," replied the Prince, "I dined beforehand." The other guests probably thought it was not a useless precaution. It was before the Consulate that things took place in this way; for afterwards the Emperor, even while he was only first consul, dined tête-à-tête with the Empress, unless he invited some member of his household to his table, sometimes one and sometimes another, and all received this favor with joy. He had already a court at this epoch.

Most frequently, the Emperor breakfasted alone, on a round mahogany stand, and without a napkin. This repast, still shorter than the other, lasted from eight to ten minutes.

I shall say presently what disastrous effects this bad habit of eating quickly often produced upon the Emperor's health. In addition to this habit and even as a first result of his haste, the Emperor by no means ate in a cleanly manner. He preferred to use his fingers instead of a fork, or even a spoon; we were careful to put the dish he liked best within his reach. He drew it to him, in the fashion I have just described, dipping his bread in the sauce and and the gravy, — which did not prevent the dish from circulating; any one ate of it who could, and there were few guests who could not. I have even seen some who seemed to consider this singular act of courage as a means of making their court. I am willing to believe also that in several their admiration for His Majesty silenced all repugnance, just as one does not scruple to eat from the plate and drink from the glass of a person one loves, even were it not wholly immaculate as to cleanliness; which one does not see, because passion is blind.

The dish the Emperor liked best was that species of chicken fricassee which has been called *poulet à la Marengo* on account of this preference of the conqueror of Italy. He also liked to eat beans, lentils, roast breast of mutton, and roast chicken. The simplest dishes were those he preferred; but he was not easy to please in the quality of his bread. It is not true that the Emperor made, as has been affirmed, an immoderate use of coffee. He took merely half a cup after his breakfast and another after his dinner. Still it sometimes happened, when he was preoccupied, that he took two cups in succession without noticing it. But coffee, drunk in such a quantity, disturbed and prevented the Emperor from sleeping. Often, too, he would chance to take it cold, or without sugar, or with too much. To remedy these inconveniences, the Empress Josephine took charge of pouring the Emperor his coffee, and the Empress Marie-Louise likewise adopted this custom. When the Emperor rose from table and passed into the little salon, a page followed him, carrying a silver-gilt tray on which were a coffee-pot, a sugar-bowl, and a cup. Her Majesty the Empress poured the coffee herself, sugared it, swallowed a few drops to taste it, and offered it to the Emperor.

The Emperor drank nothing but Chambertin, and rarely pure. He did not like wine much, and was no judge of it. That reminds me that one day at the camp of Boulogne, having invited several officers to his table, His Majesty sent some of his wine to Marshal Augereau, and asked him with a certain air of satisfaction how he found it. The Marshal tasted it for awhile, clacking his tongue against the roof of his mouth, and ended by saying: "*There is some that is better,*" in not the most insinuating tone. The Emperor, although he had expected a different reply, smiled, like the rest of the guests, at the Marshal's frankness.

Everybody must have heard that His Majesty took the greatest precautions against being poisoned. That is a story to be put along with that of the ball-and-poniard-proof cuirass. On the contrary, the Emperor pushed his confidence much too far: his breakfast was brought every day into an antechamber open to all to whom he had accorded a private audience, and they were sometimes waiting there for hours together. His Majesty's breakfast also waited for a long time; the dishes were kept as warm as possible until he came out of his cabinet to sit down at table. Their Majesties' dinner was carried from the kitchen to the upper apartments in covered baskets; but it would not have been difficult to slip poison into them; nevertheless no attempt of the kind ever occurred to the minds of the servants, whose devotion and fidelity to the Emperor, even that of the lowest of them, surpassed all I could say about it.

The habit of eating precipitately often occasioned the Emperor violent pains in the stomach, which nearly always ended in vomiting. One day, one of the valets on duty came in a great hurry to notify me that the Emperor was urgently calling for me; that his dinner had disagreed with him and he was suffering very much. I ran to His Majesty's chamber and found him stretched at full length on the carpet; it was his habit when he felt indisposed. The Empress Josephine was sitting beside him, with his head upon her lap. He whined and stormed by turns, for the Emperor supported this sort of pain worse than the thousand more serious accidents incident to camp life; and the hero of Arcola, whose life had been risked in a hundred battles, and elsewhere than in combats, without his courage being taken unawares, showed himself more than effeminate for a trifling hurt, a *bobo*. Her Majesty the Empress was consoling and encouraging him as best she could; courageous herself when suffering from headaches so violent as to amount to real illness, she would willingly, had that been possible, have assumed her husband's malady, the sight of which perhaps made her suffer more than he did. "Constant," she said as soon as I entered, "come quickly, the Emperor needs you; make him some tea and do not leave him until he is better." His Majesty had hardly taken three cups when his pain diminished; he still kept his head on the knees of the Empress, who caressed his forehead with her white, plump hand, and also rubbed his chest. "Do you feel better? Will you lie down a little? I will stay by your bed with Constant." Was not this tenderness very touching? especially in so lofty a rank? The nature of my duties often gave me opportunities of enjoying this picture of happy family life.

While I am on the subject of the Emperor's maladies, I will say a few words of his most serious one, if we except that which caused his death.

At the siege of Toulon, in 1793, when the Emperor was still only a colonel of artillery, a gunner was killed at his piece. Colonel Bonaparte seized the rammer and fired several discharges himself. The unfortunate artillery-man had, or rather had had, an itch of the most malignant description, and the Emperor was infected by it. It was years before he could be cured, and the doctors thought that this badly treated malady was the cause of the extreme meagreness and the bilious hue which he long retained. At the Tuileries he used sulphur baths, and for some time wore a blister. Until then he had always refused, saying that he had no time to nurse himself. M. Corvisart had strongly insisted on a cautery. But the Emperor, who was bent on preserving the shape of his arm intact, declined this remedy.

It was at the same siege that he had been promoted from the rank of chief of battalion to that of colonel, at the close of a brilliant affair against the English, in which he had received a bayonet thrust in his right thigh, the scar of which he often showed me. The wound he received in the foot at the battle of Ratisbonne left no trace, and yet when the Emperor got it the whole army was alarmed.

We were about twelve hundred feet from Ratisbonne, when the Emperor, seeing the Austrians flying in all directions, thought the affair was ended. His canteen breakfast had been made ready in the place the Emperor had designated. He was walking toward this spot, when, turning to Marshal Berthier, he exclaimed: "I am wounded." The blow had been so forcible that the Emperor had fallen into a sitting posture; he had, in fact, just received a ball in the heel. The calibre of this ball showed that it had been fired by a Tyrolese rifleman, whose weapon usually carries as far as we were from the city. It may readily be believed that such an event soon spread trouble and alarm throughout the staff. An aide-de-camp came to look for me, and when I arrived, I found M. Ivan engaged in cutting off

His Majesty's boot, and I assisted in dressing the wound.

Although the pain was still very keen, the Emperor would not even wait to have his boot put on again, but to give the enemy his change and reassure the army, he mounted a horse and set off at a gallop, with all his staff, and went through all the lines. On that day, as one may imagine, nobody breakfasted, and everybody went to Ratisbonne for dinner.

His Majesty had an invincible repugnance for all medicaments, and when he took any, which very seldom happened, it was some broth of chicken or of chicory, and salts of tartar. M. Corvisart had advised him to reject any drink which had an acrid and disagreeable taste; I think it was through fear that some one might try to poison him.

No matter at what hour the Emperor might have gone to bed, I entered his chamber between seven and eight o'clock in the morning. I have said already that his first questions invariably related to the time and the weather. Sometimes he complained to me of looking badly. When that was true, I agreed to it, as I said no when I did not think so. In this case he would pull my ears, call me laughingly a great stupid, ask for a mirror, and often own that he had wanted to deceive me, and that he was very well. He took his newspapers, asked the names of those who were in the waiting-room, said whom he would see, and chatted with one or another. When M. Corvisart came, he entered without waiting for an order. The Emperor liked to tease him by talking about medicine, saying that it was only a conjectural art, that doctors were charlatans, and giving proofs of this, especially from his own experience. The doctor never gave in when he believed himself in the right.

During these conversations the Emperor was shaving himself, for I had at last succeeded in inducing him to take this matter solely into his own hands. He often forgot that he had shaved only one side. I apprised him of it; he would laugh and finish his work. M. Ivan, ordinary surgeon, had, like M. Corvisart, his full share of criticisms and hard sayings against his art. These discussions were most amusing; the Emperor at such times was very gay and talkative, and I think that when he had no convenient example to cite in support of his arguments, he did not scruple to invent one. Nor did these gentlemen believe themselves always on their parole. One day, His Majesty, following his singular habit, took the notion to pull the ears of one of his physicians (M. Hallé, I think). The physician drew back quickly, exclaiming: "Sire, you hurt me!" Perhaps the remark was seasoned with a spice of ill-humor, and perhaps also the doctor was right. However that might be, his ears were never in danger from that day.

Sometimes, before my duties began, His Majesty would question me on what I had done the day before. He would ask if I had dined in the city, and with whom, if they had received me well, and what we had for dinner. Sometimes, too, he wanted to know what such or such a part of my clothes cost me. I would tell him, and then the Emperor would exclaim at the price, and say that, when he was a sub-lieutenant, everything was a good deal cheaper, and that he had often dined at Rose's, a restaurant keeper of that day, and that he dined there very well for forty sous. Several times he talked to me about my family, of my sister, who was a nun before the Revolution, and who had been forced to leave her convent. One day he asked me if she had a pension, and how much it was. I told him, and added that it was not sufficient for her needs, and that I gave her a pension myself, and to my mother also. His Majesty told me to address myself to the Duc de Bassano, that he might make his report on the subject, as he wished to benefit my family. I did not profit by this good intention of His Majesty; for at that time I was so happy as to be able to aid my relatives. I did not think of the future, which it seemed to me could change nothing in my lot, and I scrupled at putting my family, so to say, at the expense of the State. I own that I have since been more than once disposed to repent of this excess of delicacy, the example of which I have seen few persons, whether above or below my position, willing either to give or take.

On rising, the Emperor usually took a cup of tea or of orange-water; if he took a bath, it was immediately on leaving his bed, and while in it he had his despatches and journals read to him by a secretary (by M. de Bourrienne until 1804); when he did not take a bath, he sat down by the fire for the same purpose, unless he read his papers himself, as he often did. He dictated to his secretary his responses and the observations suggested to him by what he saw in the journals. As fast as he ran through them, he threw them on the floor in a disorderly heap. The secretary afterwards gathered them up, put them in order, and carried them into the private cabinet.

Before making his toilet, His Majesty put on in summer a pair of white piqué trousers and a white dressing-gown of the same material; in winter these were replaced by others of a soft woollen goods called *molleton*. On his head he wore a bandana handkerchief, knotted over the forehead, the two ends of which fell down to his neck behind. The Emperor himself put on this elegant coiffure in the evening. When he left the bath, another bandana was handed him, because that he had on was always wet, as he was constantly turning in the water. The bath over or the despatches read, he began his toilet. I shaved him before I had taught him to shave himself. When the Emperor first acquired this habit, he availed himself, like everybody else, of a mirror attached to the window; but he came so near it, and besmeared himself so recklessly with soap, that the glass, the window panes, the curtains, and his own dress were covered with it. To remedy this inconvenience, a council of attendants was summoned, and it was resolved that Roustan should hold the mirror for His Majesty. When the Emperor had shaved one side, he turned the other to the light and made Roustan go from left to right or from right to left, according to the side on which he had begun. The toilet-table was transferred in like manner. His shaving over, the Emperor washed his face and hands, and carefully attended to his nails; afterwards I took off his flannel waistcoat and his shirt, and rubbed the whole chest with an extremely soft silk brush. I rubbed him afterwards with Cologne water, a great deal of which he consumed in this manner; for he was brushed and arranged in this way every day. It was in the Orient that he had acquired this hygienic habit, which he found very good, and which is, in fact, excellent. All these preparatives being terminated, I put a pair of light flannel or cashmere socks on his feet, and over them white silk stockings (he never wore any others), drawers of very fine linen or twilled cotton, and sometimes of white cashmere with soft riding-boots, and sometimes tights of the same stuff and color, with little English boots which reached to the middle of his calf. They were provided with small silver spurs, not more than six lines long. All his boots were spurred in this way. Then I put on his flannel waistcoat and his shirt, a very fine muslin cravat, and above it a black silk stock; finally a short vest of white piqué, and either a riding-coat or that of a grenadier, but more frequently the former. His toilet finished, his handkerchief, his snuffbox, and a little shell box filled with licorice flavored with aniseed and cut very fine, were handed to him. It is plain, from all this, that the Emperor had himself dressed from head to foot; he never put a hand to anything, but let himself be treated like a child, and during this process he occupied himself with his affairs.

I forgot to say that for his teeth he used a wooden toothpick and a brush dipped in an opiate.

The Emperor was born, one might say, to be waited on by valets de chambre. While yet a general he had three, and he was served with as much luxury as when in the highest station; from that period he received all the attentions which I have just described, and which it was almost impossible for him to dispense with. Etiquette changed nothing in this respect; it augmented the number of his attendants, decorated them with new titles, but it could not surround him with more attentions. He very rarely submitted to the grand etiquette of royalty; never, for example, did the grand chamberlain put on his shirt for him; once only, at the repast which the city of Paris offered him at the time of his coronation, the grand marshal held the basin for him to wash his hands. I shall describe his toilet on the coronation day, and it will be seen that even then His Majesty the Emperor of the French required no other ceremonial than that to which General Bonaparte and the First Consul of the Republic had been accustomed.

The Emperor had no fixed hour for retiring; sometimes he went to bed at ten or eleven o'clock in the evening, but more frequently he sat up until two, three, or four in the morning. He was very quickly undressed, for it was his habit, on entering his chamber, to throw each piece of his apparel in every direction; his coat on the floor, his grand cordon on the carpet, his watch flying on the bed, his hat to a distance on a chair, and thus with all his garments, one after another. When he was in a good humor he called me in a loud voice with this sort of cry: "*Ohe! oh! oh!*" At other times, when he was dissatisfied, it was: "*Monsieur! Monsieur Constant!*" At all seasons it was necessary to warm his bed; he never dispensed with this except in the greatest heats. His habit of undressing himself in haste sometimes gave me nothing to do on coming in but to present him with his bandana; afterwards I lighted his night lamp, which was in silver-gilt, and shaded, so as to give less light. When he did not go to sleep at once, he had one of his secretaries called, or else the Empress Josephine, to read to him; no one could perform this office better than Her Majesty, and the Emperor preferred her to any other reader; she read with that especial charm which blended with all her actions. By the Emperor's orders, we burned in his chamber, in little silver-gilt vessels, either aloe-wood or else sugar or vinegar. It was necessary to have fire in all his apartments nearly all the year; he was habitually very sensitive to cold. When he was ready to sleep, I re-entered, took his light, and went up to my own room, which was directly above that of His Majesty. Roustan and a valet de chambre on duty slept in the little salon adjoining the Emperor's chamber. If he needed me in the night, a wardrobe boy, who slept close by, in the antechamber, came to look for me. Day and night water was kept hot for his bath; for often, at any hour of the day or night, he took a notion to have one. M. Ivan made his appearance every night and morning at the couchee and levee of His Majesty.

It is known that the Emperor often had his secretaries and even his ministers summoned during the night. During his stay in Warsaw, in 1806, Prince de Talleyrand once received a message after midnight; he came at once and talked for a long time with the Emperor; the work was prolonged far into the night, and His Majesty, fatigued, at last fell into a profound sleep. The Prince de Benevento, who feared that if he went out he would awaken the Emperor, and perhaps be called back to continue the conversation, looked around him and perceiving a convenient sofa, stretched himself upon it and went to sleep. M. de Menneval, His Majesty's secretary, was unwilling to go to bed until after M. de Talleyrand should have withdrawn, as the Emperor might need him after the minister's departure; hence he was very impatient at this long audience. Nor was I in a better humor; for it was impossible for me to go to bed until I had taken away His Majesty's light. M. de Menneval came to me ten times to ask whether Prince de Talleyrand was gone. "He is still there," said I, "I am sure of it, and yet I hear nothing." At last I begged him to stay in the room where I was, and on which the entrance door opened, while I would go and stand sentry in a private cabinet into which the Emperor's chamber had another exit; and it was agreed that whichever of the two should see the Prince go out, should notify the other. Two o'clock struck, then three, then four; no one appeared; not the slightest movement in the chamber of His Majesty. Losing patience at last, I pushed the door ajar as softly as possible; but the Emperor, who was always a light sleeper, awoke with a start and loudly demanded: "Who is there? who goes there? who is it?" I replied that, thinking that the Prince de Benevento had gone out, I had come to take the light. "Talleyrand! Talleyrand!" His Majesty exclaimed quickly; "where is he then?" and seeing him wake up: "Well, I believe he fell asleep! How, you rascal, you sleep in my house! ah! ah!" I went away without taking the light; they began talking again, and M. de Menneval and I waited the end of the tête-à-tête until five o'clock in the morning.

The Emperor had been accustomed to take coffee with cream, or else chocolate when working at night; but he had abandoned the habit, and under the Empire he no longer took anything, unless at times, but very rarely, either some punch almost as weak as lemonade, or an infusion of orange flowers or tea.

The Emperor, who endowed the majority of his generals so magnificently, who was so liberal to his armies, and to whom, on the other hand, France owes so many fine monuments, was not at all generous, but, if I must say it, a little miserly in his household. Perhaps he somewhat resembled those rich vain persons who economize very closely at home in order to shine more brilliantly abroad. He made very few, not to say no presents, to his attendants. Even New Year's day passed without unloosening his purse-strings. "Well, Monsieur Constant," said he to me, pinching my ear, "what are you going to give me for New Year's?" The first time he asked this question, I replied that I would give him whatever he liked, but I confess that I greatly hoped that on the next day it would not be I who would give presents. It seems that the idea never occurred to him; for no one was called on to thank him for his gifts, and never afterwards did he depart from this rule of domestic economy. Apropos of this ear-pinching to which I return so many times, because His Majesty himself returned to it so often, I must say while I think of it, and to be done with it, that it would be a great mistake to suppose that he contented himself with lightly touching the part exposed to his marks of favor; he squeezed very roughly, to the contrary, and I have remarked that he pinched hardest when he was in the best humor. Sometimes, as I was entering his room to dress him, he would rush at me like a madman, and while saluting me with his favorite greeting: "*Eh bien, monsieur le drôle?*" would pinch both ears at once in a way to make me cry out; it was not even rare for him to add to these soft caresses one or two slaps very well laid on; I was sure then of finding him in a charming humor all the rest of the day, and full of benevolence, as I have so often seen him. Roustan, and even Marshal Berthier, Prince de Neufchâtel, received their own good share of these imperial marks of affection; I have frequently seen them with their cheeks all red and their eyes almost weeping.

END OF VOLUME I

www.ingramcontent.com/pod-product-compliance
Lightning Source LLC
Chambersburg PA
CBHW032356230426
43672CB00007B/723